W9-AJR-807

Breakthrough

BREAKTHROUGH

THE MAKING OF AMERICA'S FIRST
WOMAN PRESIDENT

NANCY L. COHEN

COUNTERPOINT
BERKELEY

Library of Congress Cataloging-in-Publication Data

Names: Cohen, Nancy L., author.
Title: Breakthrough: the making of America's first woman president / Nancy L. Cohen.
Description: Berkeley, CA: Counterpoint Press, [2016] | Includes bibliographical references and index.
Identifiers: LCCN 2015037130 | ISBN 9781619026117
Subjects: LCSH: Women—Political activity—United States. | Women politicians—United States. | Women presidential candidates—United States. | Women presidents—United States.
Classification: LCC HQ1236.5.U6 C64 2016 | DDC 320.0820973—dc23
LC record available at http://lccn.loc.gov/2015037130

Interior design by Megan Jones Design

ISBN 978-1-61902-611-7

COUNTERPOINT
2560 Ninth Street, Suite 318
Berkeley, CA 94710
www.counterpointpress.com

Printed in the United States of America
Distributed by Publishers Group West

10 9 8 7 6 5 4 3 2 1

To my daughters, Helena and Camille,
and my stepdaughters, Morgan and Paloma

CONTENTS

PROLOGUE

Los Angeles, California. June 19, 2014. A line three people deep stretches out from the Barnes and Noble entrance, around the corner, and along Third Street for a quarter of a mile. It is early morning and about 3,000 men, women, and children are chatting on the sidewalk, cars whizzing past, waiting to meet Hillary Clinton.

"Well, I'm here because she is a trailblazer," Twyla Hodges says. "She has stood as a glass ceiling breaker and she is making history right now. I think that she is a great role model for women, for children, for the generations to come. It's great that she is coming out here and actually supporting and campaigning with her constituents—actually caring about us. Especially since she is going to become the next president. I have very strong faith in that."

In fact, Clinton won't officially declare she is running for president for another ten months. Her visit to Los Angeles is only a stop on her summer book tour.

"I'm hoping that Hillary breaks the glass ceiling this time out. I think it's long overdue," Tony Cowser, a slender, forty-three-year-old African American man, a few hundred people down the line, told me. "I like her integrity and I like what she represents. I think that she deserves to be the next president. I'll share with you a little story. I was in college and she was First Lady and I was driving to work one day. I remember this disc jockey said that Hillary Clinton was a briefcase-toting bitch. It was such strong lingo that I nearly had an accident. I felt that statement was so foul that I vowed that day that whatever she did, I was going to support her. So that's why I'm here."

Across the street at the Farmers Market people were milling about, carrying plastic bags with Clinton's new book, *Hard Choices*, showing through, grabbing breakfast before they got back in line for their moment with Clinton a few hours later. Joe Boccolucci, who had gotten into line at 4:00 AM, was seated at the counter of Phil's Deli and Diner. "I was going back and forth whether I should do it or not because I have a little son and I had to find somebody to watch him," he said. "I was a huge Hillary supporter in '08, so I was excited to have her book come out and support her in 2016—hopefully, if she runs." When I asked him what he liked about Clinton, he said, "The whole Democratic platform. She's about immigration reform, equal rights for everybody, women's rights."

"—He's a gay dad—gay rights," Boccolucci's twenty-eight-year-old sister Katelyn Rydzewski interjected.

"—Millionaires paying their fair share when it comes to taxes and stuff like that, and Clinton's all about that," Boccolucci continued.

"I think she needs to run, I think it would be stupid if she didn't," Rydzewski said. "I think she just has everything that we need, and I think it's time for a woman to be president. I would love to see that myself."

"She's the right woman, too. She's smart," her brother said. "It's the right time."

The new America was thrilled Hillary was there to meet them face-to-face. There was something uncynical, even old-fashioned, in the way they described Hillary—"my hero," "inspired," and "icon." Many people spoke of their hopes to elect the first woman president and be part of history in the making.

Wherever Clinton traveled for book signings in the summer of 2014, large crowds of fans appeared—more than 1,000 in St. Paul and Philadelphia, 1,200 in Seattle, thousands in Saratoga Springs. At Common Good Books in St. Paul, one woman told the *St. Paul Pioneer Press*, "I just look up to her so much. I think she's a great role model for young women." (Her nine-year-old daughter dreamed of being a congresswoman when she grew up.) One man had come straight to the bookstore from church with his two sons. "Clinton will be an excellent candidate if she decides to run," he said. "It would be good for a woman to be president."

GERMANS, BRAZILIANS, AND Brits have done it. Catholics, Muslims, and Hindus have too.

The citizens of more than fifty nations have elected women to lead them. But not us. Two and a quarter centuries after George Washington became the first POTUS, nearly 100 years after women won the right to vote, Americans have still not elected a woman president. Meanwhile democracies that are no more than ten, twenty, or thirty years old have chosen women to lead them. Indeed, the United States, birthplace of modern democracy, ranks a mediocre 72nd on the 2015 World Economic Forum index of women's political empowerment.

It is a national embarrassment.

Yet 2016 could change all that. America is at a historical inflection point. The old barriers that once blocked a woman's ascent to the Oval Office have crumbled, more so than we realize.

Like many political junkies, I started thinking about the 2016 presidential election just weeks after the 2012 votes were counted. I love a good political horse race as much as the next guy. But this coming election calls out for more than just the "she's up–he's down" daily punditry. We stand on the cusp of a historic milestone, and that's a story that needs to be told.

Granted, there are those who would say that we went directly from resistance to a woman president to apathy about it—in effect leapfrogging over the zeal-to-make-history stage. Several political consultants I interviewed insisted that only a tiny minority of voters would be motivated by the idea of electing a woman. When I mentioned this to Jennifer Granholm, Michigan's first woman governor and a Democratic Party leader, to get her opinion, she shot back, "What?!"—as if she didn't hear me right.

"I totally disagree with that, I totally disagree with that!" Granholm said. "Any woman who has run for office will tell you that you go down these parade routes and you see two things. You see women who are in their eighties or nineties who say, 'I want to vote for you because it hasn't happened before.' Or you can't get away from parents pushing their daughters forward and saying, 'Look, there's our governor, see? That's her!' The implicit message is, 'That could be you one day.' It is not about me. It is about what is possible for their daughters.

"People understand the symbolic significance and the real significance of putting somebody into office who has broken through a barrier," Granholm continued. "They did so with President Obama, and we saw that huge flood of excitement. I think a similar type of excitement will be there for Hillary Clinton. Hopefully this becomes a nonstory by 2020, that a woman has won the presidency. But it still is a huge moment in history because it has not happened yet."

THIS BOOK IS about the making of America's first woman president.

Of course, Hillary Clinton, the Democratic Party front-runner, is a central figure in this story. And yet this book is not only about her—because there is a bigger story to be told. Clinton's achievements—for instance, as a United States senator, as secretary of state—are inconceivable without the foundation laid by many others, past and present. Consider this: Just thirty short years ago, no Republican woman had ever served as governor and no Democratic woman had ever been elected to the Senate in her own right.

Moreover, Clinton is not the only woman who is capable of making a credible run for the presidency, and Republicans also look forward to a woman president—granted at this moment with more reservations. In the lead-up to 2016, close observers of U.S. politics widely agreed there were many women on the short list of potential presidential contenders. All of them, such as Democrats Elizabeth

Warren, Kirsten Gillibrand, and Amy Klobuchar and Republicans Susana Martinez, Nikki Haley, and Kelly Ayotte, were governors or United States senators. Although most major nonpartisan outfits found a large partisan gap between Republicans and Democrats in the desire to elect a woman president, that was largely because no Republican woman who could win entered the primary. (The only one who ran was Carly Fiorina, the former CEO of Hewlett-Packard. Fiorina had never served in elected office, and as we'll see, that pretty much disqualified her from any serious consideration by voters in a general election.) As Kay Bailey Hutchison, Texas's first woman U.S. senator and a Republican, who had in the past seriously considered running for president herself, put it, "I'm always going to vote for the best candidate, because I think America should have the right leadership for the respect in the world. I would want a woman who would represent my view of America and what I think is right for America. But I'd love for it to be a woman. I don't think it's in any way a negative anymore. I think it's a positive now."

This book is an effort to answer the fundamental questions raised by the prospect of a woman president: Why has America never elevated a woman to the Oval Office? Can a woman win? If so, how did it become possible and what obstacles might she face by virtue of her gender? Do women political leaders bring different styles or perspectives or priorities to their jobs? Finally, why does it matter and why should we care?

In the spring of 2013, I set out to answer these questions and I began talking to women leaders and experts on women's political leadership. In the years since then, I have interviewed senators and governors and ambassadors; Democrats and Republicans; men and women; political operatives and political scientists; girls and women from the age of nine to ninety-two; fathers of tweens, a mother of triplets, and a surprising number of parents with twins; men who are passionate about electing women and women who could not care less; single men, gay married couples, and women who are childless by choice; children of migrant farmworkers, recently naturalized immigrants, and the great-granddaughter of a president. The book is also based on scores of scholarly articles in the social sciences about American elections, women's leadership, and gender, as well as my own research and teaching over twenty years as a working historian.

What I've found may not be what we would expect.

Today, the S word—*sexism*—will not get us very far in understanding the current landscape for women in politics. True, America's history of gender discrimination in law, politics, and culture rendered it impossible for a woman to be president for much of our nation's life and then tilted the playing field against women for decades. How much the double standard still holds women back is a central issue and one that we'll look at closely. Yet America is long past the date when sexism itself explained the absence of an American woman president. Likewise, you will find here no misty-eyed affirmation of the superior virtue of the double X's. Instead, we have to look unflinchingly at some of the less heroic episodes of women's history. Consider this: One of American women's first major contributions to public policy was Prohibition. Or take recent women-on-women battles, such as the ones provoked by Sheryl Sandberg's effort to help women win an equal share of corporate power or by Beyoncé's ambiguous representations of feminism in performances of "Flawless." As we'll see, women themselves have not always been the most effective advocates for their own political power.

If you bring up the subject of a woman president, you will often hear some variant on the theme "not just any woman." The concern is pervasive. For instance, when I asked U.S. senator Benjamin Cardin his views on a woman president, he said, "It is critically important that we have a woman as president. It is. Now, we only have one president and it's got to be the very best person. In Hillary Clinton, we have a candidate who is eminently qualified to be president of the United States."

Cardin, it seemed to me, was trying to strike a balance, one that became familiar to me as I talked to men and women about their feelings about a potential woman president. How can you simultaneously express different values of equal importance, especially in our current media environment when words are ripped from their context to provide the most tantalizing or damaging sound bite?

So, before we dive in, let's acknowledge these considerations one by one:

First and foremost, any presidential candidate must be prepared for the most difficult job in the world, and anyone who isn't is out of consideration.

And yet, *at the same time*, America's history of gender discrimination has betrayed our highest democratic ideals.

Therefore, electing a woman president is a threshold the nation must cross. And better sooner than later.

As Cardin continued, he said, "My point, though, is that we haven't had a woman president. It's important to reach that milestone in this country. I am proud that we have had an African American as president of the United States. To me, that was a huge moment for America. The best person won, but we had to reach that point, and the same thing is true on gender. It has clearly been a difficult track for a woman to ascend to the presidency of the United States. That's not fair and I hope that we overcome that by electing a woman president in my lifetime."

When it comes to the presidency, Americans vote only for candidates who share their values, their ideals, and their dreams. In every case in our history, Americans have only elected men who possessed the right experience and qualifications. We can be confident that any woman who makes a credible run at the presidency won't be just any woman. There are plenty of women in the current pool of viable contenders, and their numbers grow—albeit slowly—every election.

Likewise, women—who make up the majority of American voters—are not looking for a figurehead. That should go without saying, but unfortunately, it has to be said. The all-too-common notion that women are motivated by identity politics when they express enthusiasm for women candidates is a myth. Many elections have disproved this patronizing charge, most dramatically the 2008 presidential election. Only 43 percent of American women voted for the McCain-Palin ticket, despite the campaign's well-documented play for women voters in the choice of Sarah Palin as John McCain's running mate. When Hutchison said she would insist on a woman who represented her view of America, she underscored an important truth universally confirmed by political scientists: When Americans are making up their minds about whom to vote for, partisanship and ideology trump gender. (As they also trump race, ethnicity, and any other particular identity—but that's another book.)

Finally, on the subject of political parties, it is helpful to enter here with an open mind. The 2016 election, like nearly all presidential elections, will be close, and there is no guarantee Clinton will prevail. The next time up, the woman with the best shot at the presidency could be a Republican. It is not hard to imagine a scenario in which Americans had already elected a woman president and she had been a Republican. For fifty years after women won the right to vote, politically active women—many of them self-identified feminists—found a congenial home and political power within the GOP. The first woman on the Supreme Court and the first credible woman presidential candidate were both Republicans: Justice Sandra Day O'Connor and Senator Margaret Chase Smith, respectively. Although Republicans have of late alienated women voters—and many men too—with their positions on equal pay, gay marriage, abortion, and women's health, it's important to keep in mind that the partisan landscape often shapeshifts quickly and dramatically.

"I DON'T THINK women are better than men, but I do think that women have experiences, we have perspectives, we have talents that really should have an impact on public policy," Melanne Verveer,

head of the Georgetown Institute for Women, Peace, and Security
and former ambassador for Global Women's Issues under Secretary
of State Clinton, said. "Public policy is being made for me, even if
there aren't many people like me making that public policy. Why
haven't we had any progress on child care in this country? Why are
we still struggling with equal pay for equal work? I think that if
we had larger numbers of women—Democrats and Republicans—
we would have made more progress on these issues. They impact
women, yes, but they impact fathers as much. They impact families.
But these issues are not put to the forefront as critical ones as much
by men in positions of power as women put them there."

On many measures, women lag behind men in the United States.
Although women make up six out of ten college graduates, at every
educational level and in almost every field of work, women are paid
less than men for the same work. In nearly every professional field,
there are far fewer women than men at the top. Even among CEOs,
women are paid less—an average of $1.6 million less—than men.
At our current rate of electing women to Congress, we will not
reach parity until 2121.

Nor are we doing as well as women in many other countries.
On broad measures of gender equality, the United States ranks only
28th in the world, behind Germany, Rwanda, and every Nordic
nation. Our gender wage gap is worse than that of seventy-four
other nations. Even though women make up more than half of all
Americans employed in professional and technical jobs, the U.S.
ranks only 50th in the percentage of women in top management
positions.

Such shortfalls on women's leadership and economic opportunity are not just bad for women and girls. They also place a tremendous burden on men and boys. They constitute a rich vein of untapped national potential. So expanding opportunities for women and girls would clearly be in the national interest.

And yet, the significance of a woman president for women shouldn't be discounted. As we'll see, the academic research is unequivocal that when women participate fully in political leadership, the lives of women and families improve.

Bringing women and girls into full participation in every sphere of our national life is one of the big items of unfinished business in the 21st century. To accomplish it will take visionary leadership and political will.

A woman president is more likely to keep her eyes on this prize.

Chapter 1

Outside In

"Don't think of this as some League of Women Voters type of thing to do. It's brutal. It's tough. You are going for power. It's never been just given away. As long as you understand that and are ready to take a punch square in the face, then you'll love it."

—Nancy Pelosi
Speaker, U.S. House of Representatives

"There's a special place in hell for women who don't help each other," America's first woman secretary of state Madeleine Albright has famously said, only partly in jest.

In today's political world, behind every great woman are women. There are women who can win the presidency in the world we actually live in, and behind them stand hard-nosed, pragmatic women leaders who have forged the relationships and built the institutions to make it happen.

The global pioneers in women's political leadership—the best-known "firsts" like British prime minister Margaret Thatcher and Israeli prime minister Golda Meir—won power by playing a man's game in a man's world. Had America elected a woman president way back in the 20th century, it is very possible she would have followed Thatcher's path. But that narrow way is now only one of many possible alternatives. After all, scores of women have by this point been elected to the top post in their nations.

When Americans finally elect a woman president, it will be thanks to the women—and a few good men—who piece by piece built an alternative to the old boys' club and rewrote the playbook for how women play the political game.

THIRTY YEARS AGO, exactly one woman served in the 100-member United States Senate. In 2016, women made up one out of every five U.S. senators. Today, when gridlock and dysfunction seem to be the default state of our federal government, you often hear praise lavished on the women senators for working across party lines to get things done for the greater good of the nation. The woman at the hub of this three-decades-long transformation in women's presence and influence in high office is Maryland Democratic senator Barbara Mikulski.

I met Mikulski in her office in the Hart Senate Office Building. In a large conference room hung a framed glass case of the signed Lilly Ledbetter Fair Pay Act, with handwritten notes from her Senate colleagues, and the pen with which President Barack Obama signed the bill into law. Mikulski was the sponsor of the landmark equal pay for women law and it is one of her proudest achievements. After she found herself in possession of the pen, curators at the National Archives called to make sure she was taking good care of it—it is the first pen used by America's first African American president to sign his first bill into law. Hanging next to the Lilly Ledbetter case is an image of Supernova Mikulski, 7 billion light years from earth, captured by the Hubble Space Telescope. Discovered in 2012, NASA scientists had named it in honor of Mikulski for her success in sparing the Hubble from Congress's budget axe.

Mikulski, the longest-serving woman in the Senate, is venerated as the dean of the Senate women. It is an unlikely position for a Polish Catholic grocer's daughter, who started her career as a social worker and community organizer. Mikulski made her first mark politically in 1968 as an activist fighting a sixteen-lane highway slated to cut smack through the middle of her Baltimore neighborhood. One day at a rally she had climbed on top of a table—she is only four feet eleven—and in front of news cameras shouted, "The British couldn't take Fells Point, the termites couldn't take Fells Point, and, goddamn, the State Roads Commission can't take Fells Point." A few years later, she won election to the city council, then a few years after that, to the U.S. House, where she served five terms before winning a tough race to become the first Democratic woman ever elected to the U.S. Senate in her own right. Mikulski grew up across the street from her father's small grocery store, and in her thirty years in the Senate, she continued to make her home in her childhood neighborhood, just a forty-one-mile drive from her office. When anyone joins Mikulski's staff in DC, they're driven up to Baltimore and given the "roots tour," with visits to Mikulski's dad's grocery, her old high school, and her first home. Roughly four out of five U.S. senators are millionaires, a few more than 100 times over. Mikulski is not one of them.

In the winter of 1987, a few weeks after Mikulski took her Senate seat, a Republican colleague exploited the novelty of her presence for a cheap punch line. "I'm blessed with the talent of whipping the electorate to a frenzy," he said. "Women often throw their panties at me when I speak. It happened again just yesterday. I just don't know what got into Senator Mikulski."

Mikulski was not amused by New Mexico Republican senator Pete Domenici's boasts. "I think it's outrageous and I find it insulting. I have other responses, but that's the one for public dissemination," Mikulski said, after a reporter relayed the incident to her the next day. She of course did not know about the remark, because Domenici had delivered it at the all-male Alfalfa Club annual banquet, and unlike all the men in the Senate and on the Supreme Court, she had not been invited.

But what was she to do? After victory in a hard-fought primary and general election, was she going to launch her Senate career by sidelining herself in a purely symbolic fight? So behind the scenes she accepted Domenici's apology, and then she helped draft his public apology. "She understands it's still an all-boys club, and she's going to be a player," Domenici said. "She already is."

More important, Mikulski knew where the levers of power were located and she immediately maneuvered to win appointment to the powerful Appropriations Committee, the place where key budgeting decisions were made. "There are plenty of reasons for taking on the establishment in Washington, but what would she have changed? If she had been a bomb-thrower in Washington, her appointment to the Appropriations Committee would not have happened," Benjamin Cardin, who would win Maryland's other U.S. Senate seat in 2006, said at the time. "She changed the U.S. Senate—not by taking it on, but by working her way into it."

But Mikulski also had to find her way into the culture of the Senate. Run a Lexis search on Mikulski in the 1980s and you'll get a sense of what she faced. "The Abrasive Lady from Baltimore Polishes Her Act," in the *Washington Post*, is typical. So she signed up for the senators' fishing trip to Alaska. "It was a pretty rough-and-tumble bunch of old senators. We said, 'What in the devil are we going to do with her on the trip?'" one senator told a reporter. "But she donned hip waders that went over her head and caught her fair share of fish. By the end of the trip, everybody was toasting her."

While the fishing trip seems to have softened her colleagues' hearts, Mikulski may have thought that was no way to integrate a new member into the most august legislative body in the world. She needed reinforcements to put an end to the boys-will-be-boys culture of the United States Senate. (To take one example, according to glass ceiling–breaking veteran reporter and broadcaster Andrea Mitchell, back in the '80s and early '90s, it wasn't safe to let your female interns get on the elevator with certain senators notorious for their wandering hands.)

So Mikulski urged California congresswoman Barbara Boxer to give up her safe House seat for a long-shot run for the Senate in 1992. That year Mikulski found herself in the company of the largest class of freshmen women senators ever in American history, when Democrats Boxer, Dianne Feinstein, Patty Murray, and Carol Moseley Braun won seats in the historic Year of the Woman. In

June of the next year, Republican Kay Bailey Hutchison won a special election in Texas and joined them. With the lone senator who predated Mikulski, Kansas Republican Nancy Kassebaum, there were now seven women.

The Senate's old boys' club had been 200 years in the making, replenished generation by generation via a pipeline running through men's fraternities, men's colleges, and secret societies like the Freemasons (fourteen presidents) and Yale's Skull and Bones (at least three presidents). Mikulski would have to make do with a crash course on Senate procedure and customs for her new colleagues. Boxer recalled in a 2015 op ed, "Just days after I won that first Senate race, Mikulski sent all the new Senate women a guidebook she wrote, 'Getting Started in the Senate,' and invited us to her office for lessons on Senate procedure, committee assignments, and setting up our offices." Patty Murray attested at the time, "She told us how to get a bill through, how to make the process work. Believe me, nobody else gave us that kind of help."

It was a contentious time in Washington. Democratic president Bill Clinton had taken office that January, putting an end to the Reagan Revolution and twelve years of Republican control of the White House. Democrats controlled both the Senate and the House, and Republicans in Congress had assumed a "just say no" stance toward every initiative Clinton put forward. The political oxygen was being consumed by Clinton's health care reform bill, led by First Lady Hillary Clinton. Both parties were digging in.

But not the women. Mikulski recalled, "Just when we had more women coming to the Senate, including more Republican women,

Senator Kay Bailey Hutchison reached out to me on a bill. Quite frankly, both of our staffs encouraged us not to work with the other. I heard, 'Oh she's a Republican, why do you want to help her?' And Kay heard—Senator Hutchison heard, 'Why do you want to work with Barb Mikulski? She's a Democrat.'"

But Mikulski disregarded her staff's advice. Hutchison's idea appealed to her, because it was aimed at eliminating a tax provision that patently discriminated against women. In the law governing individual retirement accounts (IRAs), individuals could make contributions from present earnings and defer taxes to save for retirement. But homemakers—mostly women, of course—were limited in what they could put into their accounts.

When I asked Hutchison about her bill, she told me that the idea for it came out of her own experience taking time out of the workforce. "I started an IRA when I was single, and then several years later I got married. I was going to contribute to my IRA and I was told I could contribute only $500 instead of $2,500—the difference was substantial," Hutchison said. "And I said, 'Wait a minute. This is terrible.' Women are the ones that may be out of the workforce for ten years or so to raise their children, and then they go back and they've missed that compound interest. It was so wrong. So I said if I ever can do something about this, I will."

But in 1993 when Hutchison joined the Senate, she was the most junior member of the minority party. There was little chance any bill of hers would go anywhere. Hutchison was already an experienced lawmaker—at age twenty-nine in 1972, she had become the first woman ever elected to the Texas state legislature—so she knew she had to seek out more powerful partners. She reached out to Mikulski. "I went to her and I said, 'Barbara, I want you to carry this, and I'll be your cosponsor,'" she recalled. "Democrats were in control of both the House and Senate, and I said, 'I really want to pass it. So I know it's going to be better if your name is on the front.' She said to me, 'Absolutely not. I wouldn't hear of it! This is your bill and I'm going to be *your* cosponsor.' That's the kind of person she is. I just almost hugged her. Well—I did hug her," she laughed. "Barbara Mikulski is just the most wonderful person and she's a great legislator."

Mikulski liked the idea. "I agreed with Kay. I thought the policy initiative was just terrific, because it went to economic empowerment, particularly for the homemaker who paid a mom penalty. I found we really could work together," Mikulski said. Hutchison and Mikulski introduced the bill in February 1994, and it passed a few years later.

But there was another significant result from their work, one that arguably has had a more far-reaching impact. "While we were working on the initiative, we went out to dinner together just to hash things over," Mikulski told me. "We had such a good time. We laughed and enjoyed each other, and we said, 'This is so great. Why don't we invite the other women?'"

Take just about any account of America's women senators, and you are bound to read about the private bipartisan dinners that have taken place for the past twenty years, and the role they've played in forging the women into a formidable, decisive force in Congress. When I asked Mikulski about the dinners' origins, she told me the story of her work on the IRA bill with Hutchison and their friendship, and then said, "I started it because of the prickly nature of politics that had been initiated in the House by Newt Gingrich, and brought to the Senate by others of that generation. They were creating a toxic environment. We felt that there should be a zone of civility, and why shouldn't it start with us? We had different views on everything from the budget to choice, but we would be a force and we would look at where we could work together. One of the things that we felt would be our biggest contribution is this zone of civility. That when we duked it out, when the day was over, the day would be over."

In other words, the conditions were ripe for new ways of doing business. Partisan rancor was extinguishing the gentlemanly customs of the institution, and those most adept at the old ways were not necessarily going to be the most nimble players in the new environment. Enter the outsiders.

"We had three rules, no staff, no memos, no leaks. That has now been established for over twenty years," Mikulski said. For many of those years the Senate women met monthly. Occasionally they would include the women Supreme Court justices—Hutchison recalled that one time Ruth Bader Ginsburg's husband cooked for them. "And of course," Mikulski continued, "this is where some of our women's health initiatives have come from—our whole effort on mammogram standards, just a list of things."

The Senate women themselves have become more ideologically polarized, for instance with the elections of Elizabeth Warren on the left and Joni Ernst on the right. Regardless, Mikulski said,

"Everybody still looks forward to the dinners. As they say, it's one of the few places where you can be bipartisan, relax, and be yourself. We talk about the same topics that women everywhere talk about. It's not like we all bring memos and CBO scoring, et cetera, and act like we're on Hannity versus Maddow."

Mikulski acknowledged there are conflicts between Democrats and Republicans over policy at times. "When we were working on Lilly Ledbetter, I had a bill, and my good friend Kay had a different means for achieving pay equity. She offered nine amendments. We debated. We duked it out. There we were and, at the end of the day, we came up with great bipartisan legislation that passed," she said. "And we had a glass of wine and another crab cake at the Monocle."

All the Republican women in the Senate voted for the Lilly Ledbetter Fair Pay Act. They were the only Republicans to do so.

Necessity is the mother of invention. To be sure, the bipartisan dinners grew organically out of the friendship Mikulski and Hutchison developed while working together on a pro-woman law. And yet in one fell swoop, the dinners countered the old problem of the clubby old boys and the new problem of hyperpartisanship.

AS PARTISAN POLARIZATION has paralyzed the federal government in recent years, in case after case, women senators have broken the deadlock between the parties and passed major legislation. Maine Republican senator Susan Collins crafted the plan and organized the coalition of senators that ultimately ended the 2013 federal government shutdown. Michigan Democratic senator Debbie

Stabenow engineered a major agricultural reform bill in 2014—one of the few pieces of major legislation accomplished by the 113th Congress. That American government would function much more smoothly if there were more women in power in Congress became a common refrain. For instance, *Time* magazine headlined a piece on the shutdown by Jay Newton-Small, WOMEN ARE THE ONLY ADULTS LEFT IN WASHINGTON. Many women politicians are happy to fan those flattering notions.

"The women have had a history of working well together and trusting each other. We actually get to know each other. We know who each other's kids are, we know what our lives are like," Minnesota Democratic senator Amy Klobuchar told me. "And that's just not always true with the men. I think that helps to build trust, and trust is what you need in a time of crisis."

"There are a lot of great men, obviously, who are pragmatic problem solvers as well," Michigan Democratic governor Jennifer Granholm said. "But, at least in this moment in our culture, women are the ones who are willing to do the hard work, be pragmatic, and work together. There is a shortage among male politicians of a willingness to do this." Men see politics as "a zero sum game" while women work together, Granholm's Republican counterpart New Jersey governor Christine Todd Whitman said. "Women approach issues in a different way. They're less intent on having it their own way."

"I trust the female style of management much more than I do the classic male form of management, which is way too structured and macho," Wilma Goldstein, a retired Republican pollster and behind-the-scenes party leader, said. "In an interesting way, men are a lot less flexible than women. Well, you saw it in that stupid dinner that I guess took place on the night of Obama's first inaugural, when the GOP swore, 'We will not support anything Obama does,' and they can't get off it." She continued, "Women realize that they have a lot in common, without having as much access to power as they should. Does every woman I have ever met in politics operate that way? No. Does every man operate in ways that I don't like? No. But the style of operation that is now affecting American politics certainly comes from a style that is more male than female." Jeffrey Slavin, a Maryland Democratic Party leader, mayor of a suburban DC town, and longtime backer of women political leaders, told me, "I'm usually the only man on this stuff. Why am I so attracted to women candidates? Women run to solve the problem, men run because they think they're great."

Granted, not everyone thinks women's leadership style is qualitatively different from men's. "I agree that women bring an important perspective to the process and it's important to have women in a representative number in the process," Senator Benjamin Cardin told me. "I don't know if I would agree that women act more cooperatively. I have forty-seven years in legislatures, so I've dealt with a lot of legislators. I can tell you I've had run-ins with women legislators that haven't been pretty. We've had some great bridge builders in both sexes." Cardin underscored that women make substantive contributions to governance. "Particularly in a country in transition, in a developing country, women are better investors than men," he said. "They're much more interested in families, education, and health care. Men are more interested in buying the best guns in the world."

Still, it has become an accepted truth in American politics, well aired in the media, that women legislate in a more collaborative and bipartisan fashion. A substantial amount of academic research supports this view. Political scientists have shown that women in Congress are in fact more apt to work across party lines. Studies of state legislatures have found that women lawmakers cooperate and collaborate more than men do. Other studies conclude that women legislators encourage inclusive participation in debate, whereas men try to limit participation and exert their own control. Women senators cosponsor bills with women of the other party at a significantly higher level than men do, and compared to men, women senators gather a greater number of cosponsors for the bills they introduce, according to a 2015 data analysis by Quorum. According to a McKinsey consulting survey, global business executives believe that women engage in "participatory decision-making" more than men do. Now some scholars, interestingly, speculate that women might be acting more collaboratively in order to maneuver around the sexism of powerful men. As political scientist Maryann Barakso suggests, it could be that "in mixed-sex workplaces, legislatures, and other organizations, women opt for more participatory leadership styles because they are expected to behave in this way, not necessarily because they prefer to do so."

Why are women virtuosos of collaboration? Does estrogen make us more compassionate? Are we nurtured to be agreeable? Are the observed behavioral differences between men and women hardwired into our brains or programmed into our genes, or are they the product of how boys and girls are raised? The Mars-versus-Venus question is an old one. Clearly we have to step into the debate with extreme caution. Since the beginning of time, men have spun self-serving tales of the differences between the sexes, and rarely have women come out well.

On the one hand, some new research on the human brain has identified subtle differences, on average, between men and women. In brain imaging, men show more neuronal connectivity within the hemispheres, while women show greater connectivity between the hemispheres, perhaps explaining women's better memories, social adeptness, and ability to multitask. On the other hand, scientists caution against reading too much into these results, and even if further research confirms these differences, the debate won't be resolved by pictures of our brains. That is because contemporary neuroscience has also proved beyond doubt that our brains change throughout life; hormones, lived experience, and the social and physical environment all shape this continuous development.

An intriguing recent study suggests that the advance of gender equality itself improves brain functioning in women and reduces the typically observed cognitive differences—such as in mathematical ability—between the sexes. Daniela Weber and her team at Vienna's International Institute for Applied Systems Analysis tested 31,000 men and women in thirteen European nations on areas of cognitive ability in which sex differences have typically shown up. They found that the more developed a nation or region was on measures such as education, employment, health, and family size, the more women's cognitive abilities increased. For example, women in developed regions and nations had partially closed the math gap with men. On tests of episodic memory, which is linked to emotion and on which women tend to outperform men, in some cases women's lead over men increased. In the last analysis, the big questions—if and why men and women are different today and whether any differences will persist in the future—are unanswerable until we are a couple of generations into a culture of equal opportunity and participation for all genders. America has moved far along this path, but we are not yet at its end.

In any event, our national history provides a perfectly adequate explanation for why women politicians today, on average, are better team players than men.

Think of it as an adaptive response. Women entered political office as outsiders. It wasn't until 1993 that more than a handful of women served in the Senate; only in 2001 were there enough women senators to sit on every committee. For any individual woman to succeed, she had to recruit allies outside the usual circles of power. And in many cases those other individuals were women. In situations where those with established power—that is, men—are dug in, outsiders gain a competitive advantage.

"The reason why I'm such a big booster of women running for office is that once they get there, they are the most effective, and it gets back to that notion that we're pragmatic," Granholm said. "When I was governor, if I had a really difficult policy that I wanted to get through, legislation that was complex, that was going to generate a lot of controversy, there were two women that I would ask to carry it. One was a Republican in the Senate. One was a Democrat in the House. They made this unstoppable team. They took the time. They were willing to bring everybody in and listen, to make the difficult decisions, and do all of the work behind the scenes that caused the pieces of legislation to go through."

Klobuchar agreed. "When a lot of us came into politics, we couldn't just walk around on a flight deck in a flight suit and look strong. We had to look strong by getting results."

To get results in the 100-member Senate and the 435-member House, you have to be able to work well with others.

And voters have noticed. According to Democratic pollster Lisa Grove, polling shows voters look for what she called the three C's. "Women are able to collaborate, compromise, and cooperate," she said. "Years ago, people would be like, 'Eww, that sounds like negotiation and we want them to be tough and make things happen. That's what leaders do.' Increasingly, they're looking at this dysfunctional Congress and saying, 'I want someone in there who knows how to work with others to get something done.' And the default is women."

On reflection, it isn't surprising that women have mastered the fundamental skills demanded of political leaders in large, diverse, and complex democracies: more dialogue, less posturing. Or as Granholm put it, "It's hard to know whether it's gender or pragmatism that makes women more collaborative. I do think it is probably borne out in social science that women don't want to just thump our chests, we want to get things done."

I asked Mikulski if she thought there were differences between men and women in how they exercised power. "I think for the women, number one, they do want to get things done. One of the methods is to concentrate on knowing the individuals and the people in your committee, particularly your ranking member, even traveling to their states and just listening to their side of the story," she answered. At the time she was chair of the Appropriations Committee and another budget crisis loomed. She then added, "I think we exercise power by not having to prove that we have power."

By 2016, WOMEN had come a long way. Recall, just thirty years ago, Senator Mikulski and Senator Kassebaum were not invited to one of the most important gatherings of DC's powerbrokers simply because they were women.

Twenty women senators serve in the 114th Congress—twenty times the number who served in 1986. The progress of America's women politicians from absence to influence, from social exclusion to toast of the town, could not have happened without help from another group of women, working behind the scenes to mobilize voters and resources, send reinforcements, and change the very way Americans viewed women in politics.

Chapter 2

THE NEW GUARD

I N THE SPRING of 2013, I met Stephanie Schriock, the president of EMILY's List, the powerful political action committee that elects pro-choice Democratic women, the week before EMILY's List launched its first salvo in the 2016 campaign. Schriock is tall, with an athletic physique, a blond bob, a wide smile, and the easygoing manner of a native of the Mountain West. Like many of the young-ish women at the forefront of the new push for women's political leadership, Schriock did not come up through the feminist move-ment. Rather, she attributes her passion for politics to her family's progressive values and the community where she grew up, the labor union, copper-mining town of Butte, Montana, where Democrats were strong and visible in the community. By junior high she was a political junkie. After running for student body president and los-ing several times, she figured out how to organize an untapped pool of voters. "I realized that I could just focus my entire campaign on the freshman and sophomores, because the entire school voted. Then I got the younger sister of one of my opponents to endorse me—she was a freshman, she was great! And I won."

Over the years, Schriock has finely honed that youthful intuition into strategic brilliance about how to win elections for other people. Before turning thirty-five, Schriock had managed and won two long-shot Senate campaigns, one for a comedian and one for a guy who described himself as a dirt farmer. (Respectively, Minnesota senator Al Franken and Montana senator Jon Tester.) A senior Clinton campaign veteran once described her as "spectacular, one of the best campaign managers I've ever worked with"—a view several Washington insiders expressed to me unprompted. Coming off huge success in the 2012 election, at forty years old Schriock had already appeared on many lists of America's most influential women in politics. As 2016 heated up, she was rumored to be on the short list to lead Clinton's presidential campaign.

Before Schriock took over at EMILY's List in 2010, she had been cycling back and forth between campaign management and her job as Senator Tester's chief of staff. A senator's chief of staff is one of the most powerful positions in American government, just short of serving in high office itself. Leaving that influential perch to run a women's organization is not on its face a power move.

When I asked Schriock why she gave it up to come to EMILY's List, she recalled a few experiences at the top level of campaigns where she had been struck by the absence of women. "I really felt, and still do, that as a woman I can do anything I want to do. My folks made it clear that I could, and they gave me a set of values to use as a compass—which is why I'm a strong Democrat, I can thank my parents for that," she said. "I felt like I was growing up in an era, not so different from how the millennial generation feels now, where everything was going to be equalized. It wasn't until I got a little bit older that I realized that there are still fights to be won and a lot of glass ceilings that need to be crashed through."

Undoubtedly Schriock was chagrined to observe how few women were seated at the table of power. But a full answer to why she came to EMILY's List would likely include the fact that the group, from its founding in a basement by twenty-five second-wave feminists, had grown into one of the powerhouses of the Democratic Party.

THE YEAR WAS 1982. Ronald Reagan was president. In June, the Equal Rights Amendment to the U.S. Constitution, the single most important goal of political feminists, went down to defeat. That same month, when Argentina invaded the British-controlled Falkland Islands—a sparsely populated, desolate, oil-rich island chain 300 miles off Argentina's coast—Margaret Thatcher, Britain's first woman prime minister, ordered British warships to the scene. After more than 1,000 casualties on both sides, Argentina retreated. Since a hostile Soviet journalist had called Thatcher the "Iron Lady," the prime minister had relished the moniker; the Falklands War proved to the world it was no mere talking point.

At the time, nine out of ten members of Congress were white men. One woman, Nancy Kassebaum, was a United States senator—her father had been the GOP's 1936 presidential nominee against Franklin D. Roosevelt. In late fall, on the eve of the midterm elections, polls in the Missouri U.S. Senate race showed Democratic state senator Harriett Woods in striking distance of defeating the incumbent Republican. But Woods had nearly run out of campaign funds.

"So Harriet Woods came to Washington, DC, looking for $50,000 for a week of television in Missouri," Schriock said. "She went to the typical places you would go in the early '80s—the labor unions, the party caucuses, the party leaders. And they all said no. They basically said, 'Women can't win.' And they let her run out of money." Woods narrowly lost. "There was a group of women here led by Ellen Malcolm who were just livid at what happened. But they realized that they didn't have a network to help fill that hole either."

In 1983, Malcolm gathered some of her friends together to strategize about how to bust through the Senate's glass ceiling. They faced a Catch-22: Money was the measure of a candidate's viability, but campaign donations flowed only to those who looked like winners. Malcolm had been press secretary for the National Women's Political Caucus, and she had a lot of contacts in the feminist movement. There were plenty of women who were giving money to feminist causes, but they were not contributing to women candidates. The group agreed that women needed funds early in their campaigns to, in Malcolm's words, "convince these old boys that they could win." They experimented informally for the 1984 cycle, and then in 1985, Malcolm realized that if they wanted to elect more women, they needed to get serious about building a fund-raising machine.

Every good tale includes an origin story, and the story of EMILY's List begins one night in 1985 in Malcolm's basement.

Malcolm invited twenty-five friends from the women's movement to her house in Washington and told them to bring their Rolodexes. That night they sent 450 women a letter with two requests: join EMILY's List and donate $100 directly to two women candidates of their choice. In effect, they were bundling money to candidates. Campaign donations did not pass through their hands, but their handiwork was there for all—the candidates, the party, the operatives—to see. Barbara Mikulski's 1986 election to the Senate was their first big win—EMILY's List gave her critical support in the Democratic primary. They got themselves on the national map a few years later with Ann Richards's successful 1990 bid for Texas governor. In 1991, when Supreme Court nominee Clarence Thomas was accused of sexual harassment by law professor Anita Hill, and televised hearings showed the all-male Senate Judiciary Committee, chaired by Joe Biden, impugning Hill in a way all too familiar to many women, EMILY's List was there to harvest the groundswell of political will.

From the beginning, EMILY's List set out to change these well-worn habits and decided that the fear tactics typical of movement organizing wasn't the best way to do that. "It wasn't one of these 'The world is coming to an end so you should give.' It was 'Here's what happens in a campaign. Here's what candidates do with the money,'" Malcolm recalled. "We went through years of building a trust relationship with women donors. The early money strategy worked. It gave women tremendous credibility in the political world. Over the years, all those Democratic Party people—all those know-it-all employees of PACs who would decide who should get the contributions—came to believe more and more that women were credible contenders."

Money is key, but there are many other components to a successful electoral campaign, and in the mid-1990s, EMILY's List expanded their portfolio. They started campaign-training programs and kept people on their own staff to advise women candidates on everything from communications to strategy. Malcolm continued, "We then decided that women voters were key, not only for women but also for Democrats. We spent tens of millions of dollars on understanding what is important to women, what groups need extra motivation to get to the polls, what groups we can persuade to vote for our candidates. It has really put us at the table with the party in a very different way."

Three decades after Harriett Woods could not raise $50,000 to run television ads, EMILY's List is a huge operation that provokes envy in Republican women and not a small amount of pique among some progressive women's groups. When I asked Malcolm how she felt about accusations that EMILY's List threw its weight around by choosing winners and losers, she shot back, "I hope so!" She continued, "I think you need to be smart and strategic in where you put your resources. You can't look at what EMILY's List was doing in 1986 and where we are now and not realize that we've changed dramatically in our ability to find and help women become credible candidates. In the old days, we used to look for credible candidates. Now we make them credible."

In 2010, after twenty-five years as EMILY's List president, Malcolm passed the torch to Schriock. The organization was ready for a generational change, to keep up with the new nature of campaigns in an age of social media and data mining, as well as to expand its membership beyond the second-wave feminists who had remained the group's stalwart supporters. In the 2012 election, under Schriock's leadership, EMILY's List elected a record number of women to the Senate and was rated one of the top five most effective political action committees by the nonpartisan Sunlight Foundation. As EMILY's List marked its 30th anniversary in 2015, it could take credit for electing 600 Democratic women, including ten governors, nineteen senators, and more than 100 U.S. representatives. In her five years at its head Schriock had tripled the membership once, and then again, to more than 3 million.

Clearly, electing a woman president was the next frontier. And given the news cycle and the voraciousness of the political press, that challenge began the day Barack Obama began his second and last term in office. "Everyone in the press decided they should start talking about the 2016 presidential election immediately after the 2012 election," Schriock recalled, in an amused yet exasperated tone. "We were seeing all of these stories being written—of course about Secretary Clinton—but then a long list of Democratic men. We at EMILY's List said, 'Wait a second, if you're going to give us a list of folks that includes Governor Martin O'Malley and Governor Andrew Cuomo, we're going to give you a list that includes Senator Kirsten Gillibrand and Secretary Kathleen Sebelius and Secretary Janet Napolitano and Senator Amy Klobuchar.'" (Elizabeth Warren, whom Schriock had encouraged to run for the Senate, had only just taken office and was not much on anyone's radar yet.)

There was really no real news to feed the outsized demand. Clinton had zero incentive to announce her candidacy so early. Any woman who might have considered a presidential run was waiting on Clinton's decision. (And in case anyone was loath to wait, Senator Barbara Boxer organized a private letter to Clinton from all the Democratic women senators expressing their heartfelt support for her to be the first woman president and their party's 2016 standard-bearer. Unsurprisingly, the letter quickly leaked to the press.

But if you're not on top of the message, the message gets on top of you. So EMILY's List conducted polling about women's leadership, signed up respected spokeswomen like Senator Claire McCaskill and Governor Jennifer Granholm, made a cute video of young girls talking about their hopes for a woman president, and invited the media to cover their new "Madam President" campaign. Eighteen months later, Schriock was justifiably pleased with how they had changed the conversation. "We succeeded in awakening the press, and thus the country, to the great pipeline of women who should be considered." She added, "When we think about potential Democratic women candidates for the presidency, Hillary Clinton stands above everyone. Period. Forget gender. She stands alone. But when we think about this, we don't just think about the first woman president. We see a pipeline for the second, third, and fourth."

"IN MY MIND, EMILY's List is, if you will, the shadow campaign for the Democrat Party," Maria Cino, deputy chairwoman of the Republican National Committee (RNC) during the 2004 presidential election, told me. In 2011, Cino had been a top contender for chair of the RNC; after seven rounds of balloting, she came in third to Reince Priebus, the current RNC chairman.

"EMILY's List has done a terrific job. It will be the gold standard for many, many decades to come," Cino continued. "They have put their money where their mouth is and they have built almost a separate party organization. If you look, they do all the things that a party does—recruiting candidates, helping them staff up, fund-raising. They've established a very, very strong financial network to be able to be very competitive. It's as strong, I think, as the Democratic Party."

And the cornerstone of that infrastructure is money. To state the obvious, political campaigns in America are astronomically expensive, especially after the Supreme Court's *Citizens United* decision.

Candace Straight, a pioneering woman in investment banking and a self-described mainstream Republican, is something of an evangelist for women to step up on the money side of politics. "I don't mind asking for money. I never had a problem with it," she told me. "Because if you care about politics, that's what you've gotta do. You've gotta raise money for candidates if you believe in them. It comes easy if you do."

Straight comes to political activism naturally. "I believe in public service. That was my grandmother—she believed in public service. To her, running for town council was serving the public. I believe women want to serve the public. I think men see it as a career move and an opportunity for power. My investments in politics have always been in candidates I've believed in." She has been a big champion of several New Jersey Republicans, such as former governor Christine Todd Whitman and current governor Chris Christie, and in 2008 she was a bundler for John McCain. (Federal election law limits the amount an individual can contribute to a candidate. A bundler is someone who solicits donations from others and yet is typically given credit by the candidate for bringing in that total haul. The Center for Responsive Politics' database, OpenSecrets.org, lists bundlers for all federal candidates.)

As EMILY's List started to rise on the Democratic side, Straight and others decided Republicans needed their own vehicle to raise money from women for women. "I am pro-choice. I would never ever make that decision for another woman—that's the reason I'm pro-choice. But it's not a litmus test for me per se on whether I will vote or support a candidate," Straight explained, as she recalled how they went about creating their own PAC. "I asked some people in Washington if we should be a group that had no litmus test on anything but being a Republican. I remember Linda DiVall [a leading Republican pollster] said to me, 'Well, how can you raise more money?' And I said, 'In New York, I'm confident I can raise more money with a litmus test than without a litmus test.' So she said, 'Go for raising more money.'"

In 1992, Straight and others founded the WISH List, a PAC that supported Republican women candidates who met their pro-choice litmus test. (Straight emphasized that, personally, she also supports pro-life Republicans.) Among their early successes were New Jersey governor Christine Todd Whitman (1993), Maine senator Olympia Snowe (1994), and Maine senator Susan Collins (1996).

Straight, like many women candidates and donors I talked to, observed that women are less acculturated to donating money and, when they do give, have different motives than men. "Primarily as a fund-raiser in the Republican Party, you're asking men more than women. I think women are more cause-oriented. They'll give because somebody is really good on the environment. Or they'll give to them because they're pro-choice or pro-life—I mean, depending on their position. I think men are still more power-oriented. They give more because they're in the business of political giving and they see it as part of their business life. Women, I don't think, see it quite that way. Now, I'm not saying that about women CEOs—if I was a CEO of a high-tech company in Silicon Valley and I want change as it relates to immigration and things like that, I'm sure I'm going to be seeing it that way. But your average American woman I don't think sees politics as something that they want to give money to."

This is not a Republican problem. It is a woman problem. Women simply do not donate to political candidates at anywhere near the level men do. Bettina Duval, a Democrat, a major donor, and the founder of the CaliforniaLIST (modeled on EMILY's List), characterized women's relationship to money and politics in almost exactly the same terms as Straight. "Men understand the relationship. They just get it: 'You give money, I give money. You give to my candidate and I'll support yours, within reason.' Most of my social friends don't even contemplate giving political money, at all," she said. "In my world, early money is always small donors. One hundred to two hundred dollars, up to one thousand. But what happens now more than ever is that independent expenditure groups come in. That's where the money is. Progressives do have an argument that this is really ugly. But at the same time, this is the way the game is now played. It is what it is. If you want to win, you've got to play the game. Period. You just have to raise money."

AND YET THE Republican Party does have a woman problem. A minority of American women identify as Republicans; a minority of women nationally vote for Republican candidates in federal elections; a minority of women-elected officials at the local, state, and federal level are Republicans. By every measure, as those who follow American politics closely know, the Republican Party is behind with women.

One of the Republicans who has been most committed to changing that is Wilma Goldstein, retired now from a five-decade-long career as a Republican operative, pollster, and RNC official. Goldstein got her start in Republican politics in the 1960s in Flint, Michigan, fighting to protect black civil rights against the right-wing John Birchers—many of them women—who were vying for control over the state party. (The "Birchettes" wouldn't talk to her even years later. "I thought it was wonderfully amusing and I don't like the Tea Party wackos any better today," Goldstein told me.) Goldstein was one of the women, with veteran Republican pollster Linda DiVall, who tried to impress on Reagan-era Republicans that they should pay attention to the gender gap. Snowe told me that when she first came to DC looking for party support for her first national run in the late 1970s, Goldstein helped introduce her to party leaders. "Everybody told me she was a person I had to know," Snowe said. "Wilma was a great guide and mentor. She knew everybody in the Republican Party establishment."

Like many of the women behind the scenes inside the Beltway, Goldstein's social circle is bipartisan. That has given her an opportunity to observe the different ways Democrats and Republicans have brought women into the inner circles of party leadership. One evening many years ago, when a group of Democratic and Republican operatives were hanging out at her house, Goldstein recalled, "One Democrat observed that they had these titles like, 'woman's consultant on political issues to Senator Kennedy or Senator Harkin,' or something similar. There was always some qualifying 'woman' thing in their title. We didn't have those. I was director of survey research. My friend was director of the field office. Any guy could have filled those positions. The Democrats noticed that and said, 'We give the information, but then we don't sit in the room when the decisions are made. So we don't really know what's going on. Are you telling us that you do?' One of my friends jokingly said, 'Well, you might be interested in knowing that Wilma and Nancy and I are going to leave here, and we're going to my house where three of the field office guys are cooking our dinner!'" In other words, Goldstein concluded, "They pointed out that they had titles but we had power."

Cino, like every Republican woman I spoke to about the subject, hoped to see more Republican women in elected office. And like many other political operatives and academics alike, she believed the main reason for women's underrepresentation was that not enough women ran. She thought that an entity where you could target more money for women, like EMILY's List did for Democrats, would be good for her party. But her caveats about women running for office were both sensible and revealing. "Where I might be different—maybe because I'm a party person—is that we shouldn't push every woman. I don't care whether it's a Democrat or Republican, just like we shouldn't push every man," she said, laughing. "There has to be viability. The person has to be a good fit."

And when considering potential women candidates, she preferred people who had prior experience working behind the scenes in politics. "They come a little bit more qualified. They're not all bright-eyed and bushy-tailed. It's great to get the job. But what happens when the dog catches the car?"

Goldstein's story illustrates a broader paradox. In some ways, individual women rose faster and higher in the GOP. The first woman elected to the Senate, the first woman appointed to the Supreme Court, the first woman to make a serious presidential bid, and the first woman to lead the White House speech-writing office were all Republicans. In today's GOP, many women hold powerful positions, and there are many Republican women in elected office.

And yet Republican women have not formed a cohesive and influential pressure group—either inside the party or outside the government. Among GOP women, as we'll see in chapter 6, there is significant ambivalence about women acting collectively to achieve the goal of gender parity in politics. The key to understanding why that might be the case, I am convinced, is to acknowledge that many of them would view Albright's dictum—"There's a special place in hell for women who don't help each other"—as utter nonsense.

"POLITICAL POWER IN DC has a formula. There are groups that can elect people, that can cause political pain when they're in office, and that can un-elect people. Things get done because people make them happen," Tara McGuinness, a senior executive at the Center for American Progress (CAP), said. (Shortly after we spoke McGuinness went to work in the Obama White House on implementing the Affordable Care Act.) McGuinness believed that women had mastered some of the plays in the political playbook, such as becoming successful candidates, but that they fell short on others. "I don't think you could find a member of Congress who says, 'I'm worried when I don't vote for an update of Family and Medical Leave Act. No one's going to cut off my money or run an ad attacking me for being anti-family.' There are some missing pieces of the political architecture on the issues that matter to women."

Soon after his election to the presidency, in the midst of the Great Depression, Franklin D. Roosevelt legendarily told a group of advocates lobbying him for their cause, "I agree with you. I want to do it. Now make me do it." Every democratic advance in America, from the end of slavery to the end of child labor to the end of Jim Crow, from women's suffrage to the Americans with Disabilities Act, happened because ordinary men and women made politicians act. The American ship of state does not shift course unless pushed. The founding fathers designed the system to make change difficult. Change happens only when people outside the government, acting together through social movements or interest groups or political parties, apply strategic pressure.

McGuinness saw signs that women were learning the formula and crafting the missing pieces. "I think some of the smartest strategists really see that change is not made in a one-size solution. You need women champions in Congress and you need some edgy, activist organizations. You need rank and file boots on the ground and you need traditional organizations working with a common set of goals. And there are really a lot of the pieces in place now." The emergence of a new generation of women leaders gave McGuinness hope. "There are just so many great young women leaders right now who are taking the helm of organizations and anchoring some new big ideas," she continued. "You've gone from John Podesta to Neera Tanden at CAP, from Malcolm to Schriock at EMILY's List, from Nancy Keenan to Ilyse Hogue at NARAL. You have the first woman president of a major union, with Mary Kay Henry at SEIU. I don't want to sound Pollyannaish about it, but it feels different and exciting to watch and be a part of."

NARAL Pro-Choice America, founded in 1969, is the nation's oldest abortion rights organization and was a leader in the early campaigns to win the legal right to abortion. I met Ilyse Hogue, the organization's new president, at her corner office a couple of months before the 2014 midterm elections. Hogue, in her midforties with auburn hair, a mischievous glint in her eyes, and a confident stride, describes herself as a proud Texan and a total extrovert. The whiteboard in her office is covered in scribblings and there are randomly placed stacks of paper and books. But you get the impression Hogue is oblivious to the nondescript '90s decor of her office. There are just too many fires to put out and too many opportunities to mine.

"I never thought I would end up sitting here," Hogue told me. That was in part because, like her colleague and friend Schriock, Hogue was not part of the feminist movement during most of her career. She attributes her present circumstance, leading a woman's organization, to a series of epiphanies. "My degree is in ecology. I'm an advocate at heart. The first part of my career was all international work, where environmental integrity met human rights, and I loved it. I loved it," Hogue said. Her job took her to Papua New Guinea and Latin America, among other places. "One of the things I found was that anywhere we were facilitating negotiations between corporations and communities, where women were empowered the negotiations went better and tended to stick more. So I thought, that's really interesting."

After the 2004 election, Hogue went to work for MoveOn, the online organizing community that was pivotal in revitalizing the progressive wing of the Democratic Party. "One of the things we found at MoveOn," she continued, "was that disproportionately our best volunteers, our most dedicated members were women. People say, 'Oh, that's because they have time.' No, that was not true. They were working women who had a deep investment in making a difference. Again, that was interesting for me." She was at MoveOn, essentially working as the group's top congressional liaison, during the passage of the Affordable Care Act. "The health care fight was a real eye-opener about how the progressive community had not fully integrated an understanding of what was required to bring women to full equality in the bill," she continued. And then in the 2012 election, women and women's access to contraception and abortion took center stage.

"There was all this awareness that women voters made the difference, and yet I could foresee that it was not going to result right away in substantial policy change," Hogue said. So when NARAL approached Hogue, when they were looking for a new leader to engage millennials after Nancy Keenan decided to retire, Hogue was surprised. But, she thought, let me see what they think about my ideas. She stepped into the post in 2013.

Not only was Hogue concerned that women weren't going to capitalize on their electoral clout, but she was also convinced that the reproductive rights movement had ceded too much ground to their opponents. She wanted to go at the issue more directly. Hogue explained, "If we lean into our values and say what we mean—specifically, say what we mean around abortion access— we can win more races than we're winning right now. When we win by talking about our issues, then we have more clout to follow through on the policy components of it."

And to make real progress, they would have to flex some political muscle.

IN 2013, PRESIDENT Obama nominated Georgia state judge Michael P. Boggs to a lifetime appointment on the federal bench, a position that requires Senate confirmation. When Boggs was a state legislator, he had voted to maintain the Confederate flag as part of the Georgia state flag and to ban same-sex marriage. Not only was he pro-life, he had also voted to post on the Internet the home addresses of doctors and nurses who provided abortions.

Hogue decided NARAL was going to block his confirmation. "It was lonely. A lot of people did not want to jump on this campaign," she said. If you haven't heard of Boggs, you aren't alone. Few people pay attention to judicial appointments below the Supreme Court level, and that was exactly the problem. Hogue continued, "We looked and couldn't find a time when we had won something like this. Because the president didn't have a movement at his back, he was going to do what any good negotiator would do, and say, 'I'll take four good judges for your two bad ones.'"

Civil rights and women's groups thought Boggs would be terrible, but they did not want to pick a public fight with Obama over a cause they viewed as unwinnable. Hogue had no confidence that the typical business-as-usual below-the-radar lobbying would work. "We couldn't put millions of women's fates in his hands," she said. "But it was also time to draw a line in the sand. The other side was running a real campaign to say abortion can't be a litmus test. We went along with it for decades and this is what got us the judicial system we have."

So NARAL publicly called on the Senate to reject Boggs's confirmation and spearheaded a public opposition campaign by a diverse array of forty-two organizations, including the NAACP, the AFL-CIO, and other women's health groups like Planned Parenthood. They used all the tools in the advocate's arsenal. They reached out to local activists and the press in Georgia and then spread the news about Boggs's views nationally. They organized a social media campaign, as well as face-to-face voter delegations to senators. Forty thousand NARAL members contacted members of Congress to express their opposition. The coalition sent a letter to the president and Senate Judiciary Committee members, which they also released to the news media. "We made sure that the story was being told through the political press that covers the judiciary, not just through the reproductive rights press," Hogue explained. "That was critically important."

As the Senate committee hearings commenced, NARAL kept a running tally on what each senator said and how it looked like they would vote. "There was a point when Sheldon Whitehouse said he might vote for Boggs. He heard from a lot of people in his state and reversed himself within twenty-four hours," Hogue recalled. She was impressed to see Democratic senators asking Boggs hard questions and actually using the word *abortion*. "They were emboldened by the fact that they had heard from people all over the country and from us." The 113th Senate adjourned without voting to confirm Boggs, and Obama declined to renominate him.

It was a textbook case of how the real decisions in American politics get made.

"We've absorbed this idea that if we don't talk about abortion, the other side will shut up and go away. We've seen how that has played out," Hogue continued. Since 2010, states had enacted almost 300 measures restricting access to birth control and abortion. "If we're afraid to be the ones who say we are here to protect and expand access to abortion because it is fundamental to women's human rights, who do we expect to say that? Now I would like to change people's hearts and minds and I work every day to do that. But I'm also a political pragmatist. So my short-term goal is to convince people that it is bad political strategy to buy into the opposition's narrative."

"WHEN I BECAME president of Center for American Progress, I realized that at a point in my career when it mattered the most about whether I was going to move up, I just happened to win the boss lottery," Neera Tanden said laughing. "I was very lucky. But the problem with American policy for families, and particularly for women, is that's like all we have—you better win the boss lottery or you're screwed."

The boss Tanden was talking about was Hillary Clinton. Before becoming the first woman president of the nation's leading progressive think tank, the Center for American Progress (CAP), Tanden had served as Clinton's top domestic policy aide. When she was twenty-seven, Tanden was hired right out of law school to work on policy in President Bill Clinton's administration, and she had been assigned to the First Lady's office. From there Tanden joined Clinton's 2000 Senate campaign, then became her Senate legislative director and rose to become policy director on the 2008 presidential campaign. (Tanden was one of the few people from the Clinton '08 team who moved into a top position in the Obama '08 campaign.) Tanden took the helm at CAP in 2013, after CAP's founder and Bill Clinton's former chief of staff John Podesta stepped down. Dark-haired and just clearing five feet in heels, Tanden is quick-witted and intense. Speaking in a rapid clip and dropping mild obscenities here and there, she is blunt and self-revealing in one-on-one conversation. And much like her former boss, she is more calibrated in public.

We had been discussing CAP's new focus under her watch on women's participation and leadership when the conversation turned to her own experience juggling work and family. "We're just asking too much of families to actually achieve our goal of true equality. We have fewer women leaders of business and politics because they're not moving up in the same way, because a million times a day they make a choice, where they have to offset their career aspiration to be a good parent," Tanden said. "I remember when I was pregnant with my daughter, my first child, and I was kind of freaked out because, what am I going to do? I wasn't working for Hillary at the time, but she found out I was pregnant and called me. She said, 'People do this. It's going to be okay.' My husband is an artist, and she was like, 'Ben's an artist, he can be more flexible. Just make him understand that he can be more flexible.'"

Tanden and her husband managed, and she was soon back in Clinton's Senate office as the legislative director. Clinton gave her flexibility to leave the office to have dinner with her kids, put them to bed, and then finish her work. By the time the 2008 presidential campaign rolled around, Tanden had a toddler and a preschooler. Still, like any working mother, Tanden faced stark choices, moments when being a good parent clashed with the demands of what she described as an intense and stressful job. She recalled the time a debate prep session was scheduled for the same morning as her daughter's pre-K graduation. Tanden was in charge but she decided that her deputy would handle the session with Clinton.

"Did I have a fear about my career prospects having handed it over? I did. It was the beginning of the campaign when you're still proving yourself to your colleagues. I mean, I knew Hillary really well, so I wasn't super freaked out," she told me. Hillary found out about the graduation and rescheduled the session so Tanden could lead it. "She's fantastic. But it's also, from an economic perspective, she had invested in my human capital. Hillary knew that I knew her policy choices, so it made more sense for her. But I've worked in male situations and, I'll just say, no one is ever accommodating. They just don't think that way!"

In 1997 when Tanden had been assigned to the First Lady's policy office in the West Wing, she was inducted into a close-knit group, mostly made up of women. Prior to Clinton, First Ladies had always worked out of the East Wing of the White House, from where they attended to social and ceremonial duties. (POTUS is the head of government *and* the head of state and in the latter capacity has duties similar to those performed by kings and queens in other nations.) Hillary Clinton was the first to have a West Wing office. And it was out of this office that Clinton, her chiefs of staff Maggie Williams and Melanne Verveer, and a staff of wonkish, workaholic women launched a series of policy initiatives. True, there was the failed health care reform effort, but also, once the dust settled, there was the successful push to provide health insurance to poor children, the State Children's Health Insurance Program (SCHIP), and, as we'll see later, Clinton's global campaign on behalf of women's rights.

One day Clinton overheard her scheduler answer the phone, "Hillaryland." She loved it, and the moniker stuck. "We were our own little subculture within the White House," Clinton wrote in her memoir *Living History*. Karen Finney, who worked for Bill Clinton and then moved into Hillary's office, described the atmosphere to me. "I was twenty-five years old. It was 1993. Here the First Lady of the United States says, 'I believe that you can do this job.' In terms of being empowered, that was like, Whoa! I think people forget that it wasn't so common for women at that time," Finney said. "To me it wasn't unique—my parents are divorced and my mom has always worked—but it was still a struggle for women. It was so different to be in an environment where you were working with mostly women on Hillary's team. Nowhere was it like that." She laughed, "We joked about some of the token men, right?!"

At a time when American work culture was still quite buttoned up—remember, not only had Google, Facebook, and the iPhone not been invented yet, but the Internet had just opened to public access—Hillaryland was famous for throwing birthday parties and for the camaraderie and intimacy of its members. As *Washington Post* reporter Lois Romano described it in a 2007 profile, "Among her own staff, Clinton has cultivated a nurturing culture of collegiality and loyalty, a leadership style based in teamwork, and often favored by women, that values consensus over hierarchy. The Clinton women have a personal connection virtually nonexistent among male colleagues." In an interview with *Glamour* last year, Clinton was asked how she identifies women she wants to mentor, and Clinton said, "I look for people who have raw intelligence and a great work ethic and loyalty, and I can quickly identify people who have the right ingredients."

More often than not, however, the media treats Hillaryland in feverish tones, as some kind of nefarious, secret conspiracy of yes-women, at once all-powerful and inept. In January 2014, the *New York Times Magazine* cover pictured Hillary's face—grotesquely distorted, superimposed onto a bald, giant planet—with tiny faces of her friends and aides orbiting the image, as if they had been sucked into her gravitational field. Reporters Jonathan Allen and Amie Parnes, authors of a largely flattering book about Clinton's tenure as secretary of state, reached back to the shopworn insults of the Cold War era—"troika," "cult of personality"—to make their case that Clinton "still relied on an intensely insular inner circle that prized loyalty to Hillary above all else." Do a Lexis search on "Hillaryland" and your feed will be chockfull of sophomoric, unhinged pieces by *New York Times* columnist Maureen Dowd. The way the press portrays Hillary Clinton's closest staff and advisers, the women and men who have remained with her from the White House to the Senate to the State Department, you would think that no man ever had gotten an assist from his fraternity brothers, his golfing buddies, or his law firm partners.

Many Hillaryland veterans are back on Clinton's 2016 presidential campaign, determined to elect America's first woman president. Finney, for instance, is a senior spokesperson and strategic communications adviser. Others, like Tanden, are remaining outside the presidential campaign. But they're making sure Clinton's concern for women's opportunity is part of the core mission of the institutions they lead. Tanden has beefed up CAP's focus on women and families, especially regarding policies to boost women's earnings and participation in the paid workforce. "The truth is, when I became president at CAP, I realized that there was a significant gap in policy making," Tanden told me. Paid leave for new parents is at the top of the to-do list—the United States is one of only three nations in the world that do not guarantee paid maternity leave. The others are Papua New Guinea and Suriname.

To accomplish that, Tanden knows that she has work to do to inspire voters. "I went through Hillary Clinton's campaign in '08, and she had a state-based paid parental leave program. She had that program because she believed in it. It wasn't like there was a large swath of voters demanding it from her. It wasn't like, 'Oh my God, these people are on our ass and we have to do something!' Which was exemplified by the fact that Senator Obama didn't talk about it in the general election, and he didn't do anything on it for several years, right?" Tanden recalled. "So, I thought, we need more public pressure. The president's talking about it a lot more now. We pushed the White House to have the Working Families Summit. They were like, 'Okay, we'll do it if you do it with us.' We do take a little bit of credit for moving the debate in Washington. Our goal for the next couple years is to create that public demand for positive change, in the presidential cycle as well." In short, she intended to forge the hammer that women have lacked in the political arena.

I spoke with Tanden a few months before Clinton declared her candidacy, and I asked her how she anticipated Clinton might handle the issues around family and work should she become president.

"Well, I don't speak for her, I am a separate person," Tanden stipulated. "Hillary hasn't just talked the talk, she has walked the walk. I'm not saying you have to be a woman to care about them. I'm a big fan of a lot of the men who have been president. There are definitely progressive men who are better then conservative women on these policies. But I think the priority you place on them, how you treat your own staff, it matters in a myriad number of ways. You can have very well-meaning people, but unless you live this experience of being a woman—" Tanden trailed off and collected her thoughts about the idea of Hillary Clinton as America's first woman president. "I mean, I honestly think it is going to be trans-formative to the kind of topics we discuss. I just honestly believe, the more I've been in politics and policy, the more in an almost scary way it really matters who is making the decisions."

OVER THE LAST three decades, a new guard has been at work inside government and behind the scenes to bring women into full and equal participation in American politics.

You get a sense of how much work was required and how far women have come when you talk to Eleanor Smeal, the influen-tial second-wave feminist leader, former president of the National Organization for Women (NOW), and founder and head of the Feminist Majority Foundation.

"In the 1960s, you were taught that women didn't care as much about politics as men did. Politics was a male arena," Smeal recounted. "In fact, the leading book of the time was called *Political Man*, written by Seymour Martin Lipset, who essentially had as his major hypothesis that it was men who mattered in politics. He interviewed no women—that was acceptable at the time. Women were not supposed to be interested in politics. They said women didn't vote as much. When more women voted, they said they didn't vote at the same percentage. When women voted at the same percentage, they said they only voted their husband's pocketbook. That was the theory. Now, there was no data at all to substantiate these assertions."

Smeal was in graduate school when Lipset's theory reigned supreme. Later, when she was NOW's president, Smeal looked at the polls and discovered that wherever she could disaggregate the data by gender, men and women expressed sharply different views on the issues. "You could see the difference—about a 20-point difference on sending troops abroad. On Social Security, Medicaid, and Medicare, there was about a 15-point difference." She became convinced men and women had different opinions on candidates as well.

"How I proved that there was gender gap on candidates is that I went to Lou Harris, who was the dean of American pollsters, and said to him, 'It's my assumption that there's a gender difference in attitudes toward Reagan.' And he said, 'Oh yeah, there is.' So I said, 'Well, would you start reporting it by gender?' We needed a short, pithy name to report the data. We called it the *gender gap* and that stuck." And that is how the gender gap was born. "We leveraged the hell out of the gender gap," Kathy Spillar, who succeeded Smeal as the head of the Feminist Majority Foundation, told me.

"They made nothing but fun of us at first," Smeal said. "When Reagan won, they said, 'See, it doesn't matter anyway!'" But Smeal, with NOW communications head Kathy Bonk and political director Molly Yard, pushed back. "We knew we had a tiger by the tail. I must have done a couple thousand interviews between 1980 and 1982 trying to sell the idea. In 1982, the gender gap elects governors. By 1992, when women's votes elect Clinton, then everyone can see it. In reality, it's there the whole time."

A woman's journey to the Oval Office had its tentative start in Eleanor Smeal's press office, in Barbara Mikulski's Senate briefings, in Ellen Malcolm's basement, in Candy Straight's Rolodex. It gained momentum in the private "no staff–no memos–no leaks" bipartisan women senators' dinners, in the K Street offices of EMILY's List and NARAL, and others like them, in the policy shop at CAP and the First Lady's West Wing office. Fund-raising? Check. Lobbying? Check. Policy analysis and lawmaking? Check and check. All the tools in the kit had been sharpened and the networks wired.

Women had built a machine to elect a woman president. But would voters go along?

Chapter 3

LEADING WHILE FEMALE

W HAT DOES IT take to win the presidency, and do women have an equal shot at the prize?

America has never elected a woman president, of course, and why we have not is a part of the bigger puzzle of our nation's gaping gender gap in political representation. The United States ranks 81st on the World Economic Forum's measure of women elected to national congresses, below Germany, Canada, and Mexico, and just a notch above Morocco. Currently, more than 80 percent of America's governors and members of Congress are men. In the entire span of American history, 11,872 men have served in the U.S. House and Senate, compared to 308 women.

Why does the United States lag so far behind on women's political leadership? Is it that we believe men are the norm and women are the exception when it comes to electing our democratic leaders?

"The requirement to be the first woman president, you have to be better, faster, stronger, smarter, kinder, better looking—all of these things to be the first woman anything, to replace a seat that's always been held by men," Democratic strategist Tara McGuinness said. "The threshold for viability for the first woman president will be higher than the threshold has been for men for eternity. That's been the case for the House and Senate and Fortune 500 companies. The margin of error for women in leadership is much smaller than the margin of error for men. I would love to be proven wrong! I hope to be!"

McGuinness's view that a double standard puts obstacles in the way of a women's path to elected office is widely shared—especially by women. According to polling by the Pew Research Center in 2014, for example, almost half of all women said that women were held to higher standards, and that was the reason there were not more women in high political leadership. (Only about a quarter of men agreed.) In the same survey, four in ten women said many Americans were not ready to elect a woman to higher office.

At its most fundamental, the double standard holds that male is the default mode for a political leader, that the qualities voters prefer in candidates are stereotypically masculine ones. Men face voters holding the benefit of the doubt that they have the right qualities for the job. Women, on the other hand, are judged by a measuring stick calibrated to the masculine persona.

To put it more starkly: Sexism is the principal cause of our missing political women. Without question, acts of everyday sexism against women who dare to run for office are still committed by some reporters, pundits, politicians, and voters. And let's be clear, in the not-so-recent past, biased views on women's leadership were prevalent. In 1977, 50 percent of Americans said women were not "suited for politics," according to the General Social Survey, the gold standard of public opinion research.

So as we consider whether America is ready for a woman president, we need to determine whether sexism remains a major obstacle to a woman's chance of election. Do Americans today enter the voting booth primed to hold women candidates to higher or different standards? If the double standard is in fact the cause of our missing political women, how then does it work its mischief?

LET'S LOOK FIRST at the media, frequently accused by politicians, political commentators, and feminist advocates of treating women candidates by different standards. Ask just about any woman in politics about this, and she will have a story about unfair gender-based treatment by the press. Polling after the 2008 election found that women were far more likely than men to observe media bias in the coverage of both Hillary Clinton and Sarah Palin. National surveys by the political scientists Jennifer Lawless and Richard Fox, authors of landmark studies on women's political ambition, found that a majority of women believed that Clinton and Palin faced sexist media coverage.

But as surprising as it may seem, a new picture has emerged that suggests that the media does not in fact cover women politicians in a biased way. In an analysis of 2006 Senate election press coverage, American University political scientist Danny Hayes found no evidence of "direct gender stereotyping" by the media and "minimal evidence that news coverage promoted gender stereotyping." In another study published in 2015, Hayes and American University political scientist Jennifer Lawless reviewed more than 4,000 articles about 350 U.S. House races in the 2010 midterm elections.

Women and men were equally likely to have their looks and family life mentioned; women and men were equally likely to be described as being empathetic, a conventionally feminine trait, and displaying leadership, a conventionally masculine trait; women and men were equally likely to have their policies discussed. In conclusion, they found no significant difference in how men and women were covered or the amount of coverage they received.

In short, once you compare how the media currently treats men and women, you find that on balance they receive the same treatment. Men and women both receive negative and positive coverage. Men and women both attract comments about their clothes, their looks, their experience, and their behavior. Men and women both are evaluated on the typical traits voters seek in political leaders, such as compassion and leadership. Most importantly, no study has ever directly linked sexist media treatment to voter attitudes. Take all these findings together and you have an explanation for the seeming paradox. Unfair treatment is in the eye of the beholder, and often the gaze doesn't take in the full picture.

If the media isn't imposing a double standard on women candidates, then perhaps gender bias against women candidates is being cued by attacks by their opponents. The academic research tells us, however, that negative commercials, a common tactic in American elections, have less effect against women candidates than they do against men. In other words, the gender difference helps women rather than hurts them. Moreover, negative advertising might not pack much of a punch—at least in high-profile races in our current electoral landscape. In an important book on the 2012 presidential election, *The Gamble*, political scientists Lynn Vavreck and John Sides concluded that negative advertising had only fleeting and marginal influence over presidential vote choice.

If it's not the media, and it's not their opponents, could it be how women behave on the campaign trail that is triggering latent assumptions about political leadership that disadvantage women?

Consider crying, to some the telltale sign of membership in the weaker and more emotional sex. Nothing, absolutely nothing, is so catastrophic to a woman's political career—at least that is what you could conclude from the thousands of words journalists have penned on the exceedingly rare cases of women crying on the campaign trail. To test the assumption that women candidates are hurt more than men by emotional displays, Dartmouth political scientist Deborah Jordan Brooks decided to compare how voters respond to emotional outbursts by candidates of both sexes. In a large experimental survey, she gave participants several identical scenarios, describing candidates who cried or expressed anger, changing only the name of the hypothetical politician, to determine if they responded differently to men and women. Crying did pose some risk to candidates; their strength ratings fell somewhat. But the crying candidates on balance gained more than they lost, because the survey respondents perceived a candidate who cried, whether a man or a woman, to be more honest and more empathetic. Expressions of anger, on the other hand, were unequivocally damaging to candidates of both sexes. Together these scenarios demonstrated that people did not judge men and women differently on emotionality. "Men and women are similarly penalized for both crying and anger," Brooks wrote. Even more surprising were the potential implications of her conclusions. The absence of a difference in the evaluations suggested that people held different ideas about gender than was commonly assumed, she surmised. If stereotypes about women's emotionality "do not exist in the current era," then when a female candidate cries, "there is nothing to activate." In short, Brooks wrote, "we should not be too quick to conclude that the public holds double standards for female candidates."

Perhaps the double standard operates on a more basic level. Could it be simply that substantial numbers of voters do not see women as leaders and prefer to elect men? If so, it doesn't require a journalist or an opposing candidate or a slip by a woman candidate to raise doubts about women's leadership abilities. Instead, without any external prompting or direction, voters judge women candidates through gendered stereotypes that disadvantage women. In other words, on some very deep level, voters are sexist.

Again, the recent scholarship points in the opposite direction. Kathleen Dolan, a leading scholar on women in politics, in a study on congressional candidates, found that party, not gender, was the main driver of how people viewed candidates. In other words, the operative stereotypes were those about what Democrats and Republicans were like. Hayes, in the article on the 2006 Senate elections we saw earlier, examined public opinion survey data about candidates, in addition to conducting a media analysis. He tested for two of the principal gender stereotypes that have long been thought to shape women's electoral chances: compassion and strength. Voters weren't free from bias, but just as Dolan found, partisan stereotypes rather than gender stereotypes shaped voters' views of candidates; voters assumed Republicans were stronger leaders and Democrats were more compassionate. "Despite the literature showing that people perceive women as more compassionate and empathetic than men, and men as stronger leaders than women," Hayes concluded, "I did not find this to be true in assessments of political candidates." Hayes and Lawless's analysis of the 2010 House elections likewise confirmed that the assessments people made of candidates were influenced by partisanship, ideology, and incumbency, not by sex. To our point, the key findings of these studies were that voters were not sexist. They did not hold women congressional candidates up to a masculine ideal of a political leader and find them lacking.

Brooks, in her 2013 award-winning book *He Runs, She Runs*, went even further in debunking commonly held beliefs about the power of the double standard. She created a series of hypothetical scenarios to comprehensively test whether voters held gendered attitudes that hurt women's chances of election. (Her study about crying and anger was one of these tests and is included in the book.) Women did not have to be smarter or more experienced in order to perform as well as men in elections; men and women of similar qualifications were rated equally qualified to hold elective office. Women were not punished for displaying conventionally feminine traits, as Brooks's crying and anger study demonstrated. Granted, women were judged harshly if they appeared to lack empathy, but so too were men. "People heavily penalized candidates, male or female, for acting in an uncaring manner," Brooks wrote.

But if women candidates aren't hurt when they fulfill expectations of how a woman should behave, are they hurt when they violate expectations of how a woman should behave? Governor Jennifer Granholm put the dilemma vividly. "If you had a woman governor who behaved like Governor Chris Christie, who would have his staff follow him around to catch the moments when he confronted somebody by yelling at them, or by shaking an ice cream cone at them, she would be labeled as a bitch and unlikable. So, yes, women absolutely have to be careful about seeming to be shrill, seeming to be bitchy, and yet being tough and strong. That fine line is one that every woman who runs for office has to navigate," she said.

We are in the territory of the B-word. Women leaders face an impossible choice, a double bind. If they are warm, they risk being perceived as weak. If they are strong, they risk being perceived as pushy, cold, and unlikable.

This particular variety of sexism has recently gained much attention, thanks to Facebook executive Sheryl Sandberg's advice from her rare perch at the top of corporate America. (Among Fortune 500 companies, women make up only 5 percent of CEOs and only 15 percent of all C-suite executives.) In her global bestseller *Lean In*, Sandberg cites research that finds that "success and likability are negatively correlated." For example, women who negotiate their salaries are viewed as demanding, and both men and women prefer to work for a woman who did not negotiate rather than one who did. If it is this treacherous for one woman to ask for a raise from one supervisor, think how much more daunting it must be for a woman to ask thousands or even millions of men and women for their vote.

Essentially, the settled opinion about the double bind says that when women play the man's game the way men play it, they lose. But like many of the other myths about the double standard, this one does not appear to be true, at least not for politicians and not anymore.

Brooks found "no evidence of a backlash" against candidates who acted tough. They were not perceived to be uncaring, unfeminine, or unlikable. "My results show that women can be tough in a highly 'unfeminine' dominant and forceful manner and not get penalized for it by the public," Brooks wrote. Indeed, acting outside the bounds of conventional femininity gave women candidates a boost. Women's favorability ratings went up, not down, when they projected toughness, and tough-acting women were viewed as more likely to be effective presidents. Taking these findings on toughness with those of the crying study, which showed no penalty for acting in conventionally feminine ways, Brooks concluded, "the conventional wisdom about a double bind for female candidates is wrong."

America is not, of course, a postgender nation. Some subtle gender distinctions persisted, Brooks found, but they had no significant impact on women's electoral chances. Overall the public evaluated women candidates as "politicians," not as "ladies," Brooks explained, and held them to the "standards of good leadership rather than to the standards of good femininity." The double standard and sexist stereotypes, Brooks concluded, did not "hold back female candidates on the campaign trail."

Although everyone agrees that the double standard has abated over time, some experts think it lingers in a more subtle guise and don't share Brooks's optimism. Some have demonstrated that women incumbents draw more primary challengers, which, they conclude, suggests that women are perceived to be easier to beat. Others have found that women candidates tend to be objectively more qualified than men, leading them to posit that women have to be objectively superior candidates—for example, smarter or more experienced— to achieve similar rates of success. These results don't necessarily tell us anything about how voters judge women candidates. How potential women candidates view themselves, how they perceive the double standard and assess their odds of victory, could instead be the cause of the phenomenon of the superwoman candidates. In other words, if women assume they face a higher hurdle, they will run only if they think they can clear it. As retired Republican senator Olympia Snowe told me, "Women in general think that they don't know enough about the issues yet, that they have to be more well versed before they run for office. I say to them, 'Do you think that your male colleagues give that a second thought? No, they don't.'"

But for all the disagreement about the nuances of the double standard, one fact stands out. When women run, they win at similar rates to men. "Winning elections has nothing to do with the sex of the candidate," three political scientists concluded twenty-five years ago in a widely cited study. Almost every scholar since has reached similar conclusions. As Dolan wrote more than a decade ago, "Levels of bias are low enough to no longer provide significant impediments to women's chances of election."

So far, we see that many of the myths about the double standard are just that—myths. Then where are the women? Why are women vastly underrepresented among America's political leaders?

Our history explains a large part of the gap, as we'll see. Only in the last quarter century have women been able to compete with men on anything close to a level playing field. In the contemporary era, experts currently have settled on two likely reasons for America's unusually large gender gap in women's officeholding.

One, fewer women than men run for office, making it difficult to make progress toward parity. Influential research by Lawless and Fox on the "gender gap in political ambition" demonstrates that, compared to men, women express significantly less interest in running for office than men do, hold themselves to higher standards in judging their own qualifications, and rate their chances of victory lower. This suggests, as Lawless, Brooks, and others have noted, that the conventional wisdom about the sexism women politicians face may itself be the source of women's more critical self-evaluation. In other words, women assume they have to be better, stronger, and smarter to win elections because they think that voters will judge them more harshly than they judge men.

Two, the rules of the game—the structure of our electoral system—puts up obstacles to *any* new person or group. From our exceedingly high rates of incumbent reelection, to weak political parties, to winner-take-all elections, to America's resistance to quotas (adopted in more than sixty nations to increase women's representation), America's political institutions block the rise of women. One of the strongest findings in the global scholarship on elections is that, in political scientist Lisa Baldez's words, "electoral rules play a critical role in determining who gets elected." Perhaps less hand-wringing about the American woman's psyche—about her confidence gap, her ambition gap, or the need to lean in—and more attention to the structural impediments to women reaching gender parity in leadership might be in order.

Still, the heart of the matter is this: At least in any of the ways we have commonly assumed that the double standard undermines a woman's chance of election, the evidence overwhelmingly indicates that it does not. Campaigning while female is not a walk on a tightrope or a sprint over higher, pink-hued hurdles. Ginger Rogers had to dance backward in heels, but walk into any gathering of the Washington elite and you will see plenty of powerful women in pantsuits, sensible flats, and glasses. In the final analysis, being a woman is not a liability. And as we'll see later, many consultants in both political parties have come to think it might even be an advantage.

"FIRST, I WOULD try to disabuse any woman that there are certain attributes or qualities you have to have to be successful. Certainly if my mother were here, that would be her advice," Cecile Richards told me. Richards is the daughter of the late Ann Richards, the legendary Texas governor, and she has followed in her mother's political footsteps. Beginning her career in the 1980s as a labor organizer, over the years Cecile has held a number of high-level political posts, including deputy chief of staff to Democratic House leader Nancy Pelosi. In 2006, she became president of Planned Parenthood.

"Mom had none of the classic attributes you'd say are required to be a successful woman in politics. By the time she ran for governor, she was a recovering alcoholic—publicly. She was a divorcée—as they said back in the day. She was a liberal. She had an undergraduate degree from Baylor University, which is a fine institution, but she wasn't a lawyer and she had no other professional degrees and skills. And she was single. All of those in Texas would almost immediately disqualify her from being a candidate for much of anything. But certainly for being a candidate for governor."

In other words, if ever the double standard was an insuperable obstacle to a woman candidate, it should have stopped Ann Richards. But it didn't. As Cecile Richards recalled of her mother's campaign, "She went through fire and came out the other side. When she ran for governor, that was totally gloves off. There was no 'We're going to tone this down a little bit because we're running against a woman.'" I assumed she was referring to the negative campaign Karl Rove managed for George W. Bush's successful run to unseat Ann Richards in 1994, but she was in fact talking about attacks by fellow Democrats. "Oh my God! The Democratic primary the first time around, that was the worst thing I've ever been through. Everything was fair game and I think she felt it was tough. She's a human being too. It was her friends and her family that kept her going. She went through the fire and came out the other side."

In 1990, Ann Richards became the first woman elected governor in a Deep South state and only the sixth woman ever elected governor in the nation. Her story points to a potential alternative obstacle to women's rise into political leadership: insider politics.

Political scientists agree that throughout the advanced democracies, political parties dominated by men have historically acted as "gatekeepers" blocking women's access to office. To be sure, personal self-interest exerts a powerful force here. Most politicians are men, so from their perspective, any seat picked up by a woman is one men have lost. But far more important is the long-term interest of the group. Particularly in ideologically polarized democracies, party leaders have one overriding concern: Can their party's nominee beat the opposing party's nominee in the general election? And how insiders and large donors assess electability dramatically influences who they support in party primaries. Take Richards's case. As Cecile described it, her mother seemed categorically unelectable.

It's a familiar predicament for women politicians.

"I've been less discriminated against because of my ethnicity and probably more discriminated against because of my gender," California state controller Betty Yee, a first-generation Chinese American, said during a campaign stop, answering a college student who asked her about running for office. "Discrimination doesn't necessarily come from men. I've been a little astounded— oftentimes it's the sisterhood that is lacking." As Yee elaborated, gender bias manifested in a very specific context: campaign fundraising. "I've asked people multiple times for donations before being taken seriously—especially new donors who I know give to men," she told me.

In her 2014 primary, Yee was up against California's second most powerful Democratic officeholder. "I was running against the speaker of the assembly, and the attitude was, 'How can you possibly beat him? He will out-raise you.'" In her experience, she found that women were judged differently than men about whether they could win, women were sometimes harder on women than men were, and women donors were especially risk-averse. "The obstacles are more about perceptions about women being viable candidates," she said. "Can they raise money? Can they do the rough-and-tumble? Can they deal with being judged?"

Yee was out-spent by a three-to-one margin, but her low-budget, grassroots campaign, in which she drove up and down the state of California for over a year to meet with any group who would have her, overcame that disadvantage. Ultimately, she won her primary in a recount by just a few hundred votes and then went on to defeat a Republican woman by a large margin in the general election.

What with the demands of fund-raising, the rigors of the campaign trail, and the personal attacks, you often hear that the nasty and brutish nature of American elections turns women off from politics. Democratic consultant Mary Hughes and Republican consultant Katie Packer Gage both cited the nature of campaigns as a barrier that deters women from running and thus depresses the number of women serving in office. "I think politics is very off-putting to a lot of women," Gage told me, "because there is a sense on both sides that it's a bit of an old boys' club, and that it's very dirty and dog-eat-dog and not really an environment that women want to partake in. I think the challenge is to educate women and convey that we're not going to change things unless we have a seat at the table."

But women political leaders take the sharp-elbowed competition in stride. "I mean, it's challenging, of course. But if you want to make change, you just have to know that's part of it," Richards said. "Anything you're going to do that's going to be taking on big institutions and social mores, that makes a big difference in the world, is going to come with its share of attacks. So why not do something really worthwhile? Honestly, it doesn't bother me too much. Maybe it's just that the benefits outweigh whatever the rest of it is." The tall, muscled, stone-faced man sitting at the reception desk at Planned Parenthood headquarters indicated that the attacks on Richards and her staff go far beyond run-of-the-mill partisan sniping. "I never really think about the negative side of the money or the campaigning," EMILY's List president Stephanie Schriock said. "Because when you're in it, you find the most amazing passionate people, who care desperately about the future. When I walk in the doors and see this staff of dedicated, mostly young women, who are absolutely here to change the world, I am energized. I want to be part of it." New York Democratic senator Kirsten Gillibrand recalled, in her book *Off the Sidelines*, how she felt about attacks by her Republican opponent in her first race: "My attitude was 'Fuck 'em.' One of the lessons I'd learned from my grandmother was to ignore negative press. Politics, she taught me, is a sport, just like football. You put on your protective gear, get out on the field, and hit your opponent as hard as you can. You should expect your opponent to do the same."

In other words, you have to be tough to compete in the major leagues, attacks come with the job, and it's all worth it. And like any competitor, sometimes you lose. "Everyone goes through loss—you don't get that job you wanted. But not everyone in the world sees it on the front page of the *LA Times*," Wendy Greuel, who was defeated in the 2013 Los Angeles mayoral election, told me.

"What's interesting is that afterward, there are a lot of people who kind of look at you as though there was a death in the family, as though, 'Wow, what's going to happen to you now that you lost this race?'" She suspected that people did not treat men who lost in the same way, but no matter. It wasn't in her DNA, she continued, to be deterred. "I remember President Clinton called afterward, to say, 'Good job. You did your best. Now onto the next.'" And that was her attitude.

"You can't go into a race thinking—if you are a woman or a man—'If I lose, it's the end of the world.' You have to be willing to do what it takes to win, to be part of the rough-and-tumble. You've got to be competitive. You have to give it your all."

"I KNOW THERE is a lot of research out there on the barriers to a woman as president," Democratic consultant Rose Kapolczynski, who ran several of Barbara Boxer's winning U.S. Senate campaigns, told me. "I do think that when you get into life-and-death decisions, voters aren't sure if women are tough enough to make those decisions. Can a women deal with foreign governments and war and the decision to place our armed forces in harm's way? That is a little bit more troubling for voters. Women are still seen as weaker and more emotional, perhaps more cautious. So there is a different standard. On the other hand, some of those issues have changed as Americans have changed."

Call it the double standard, limited edition. On the one hand, Americans have become acclimated to women serving in Congress, state legislatures, and city councils, and as we've seen, gender bias isn't hurting women legislative candidates at the polls. But it has long been thought that voters doubt that women are tough enough for the top executive offices, such as governor and president, and in that way sexism places greater obstacles in the path of women who run for the top leadership posts. "Running for governor is harder than running for Congress if you're a woman," Democratic consultant Lisa Grove said. "You look at the kinds of women who've run successfully for governor, and they're often attorney general types." Grove gave the example of Janet Napolitano, the Arizona governor who went on to become secretary of Homeland Security for Obama. "Napolitano was kind of badass as attorney general. She cracked down on Wall Street and scammers who preyed on the elderly." In other words, in order to overcome the bias that women aren't executive-caliber material, women have to overcompensate.

Is it true that the tired old gender stereotypes flare up when people choose governors and presidents? Does executive office present a higher hurdle for women to clear? In determining whether America is ready to elect a woman president, this is a central question.

"The research shows" was a common refrain from consultants, pollsters, and operatives in both parties about how women face unique challenges when they campaign for executive office. But when I followed the trail back into the research, the peer-reviewed academic scholarship, I found that this settled opinion is based on old studies and questionable assumptions. For example, in one of the most frequently cited studies, political scientists Leonie Huddy and Nayda Terkildsen gave 297 undergraduates a questionnaire and concluded from it that people preferred candidates for executive office who displayed "masculine personality traits," and that this finding implied "a bias against candidates who lack[ed] masculine traits." Because of this bias, they concluded, women were in fact at a disadvantage when they ran for the plum executive offices. But women candidates shouldn't despair, the two political scientists suggested, as they dispensed advice about how women should present themselves to voters in these types of races. Women could still win, they wrote, "if they convince voters that they possess masculine traits and are competent on 'male' policy issues."

And it turns out that many political consultants followed the advice that women candidates for executive office should present themselves as experienced, qualified, and tough *like a man*. If you have ever wondered why a woman candidate says again and again that she is the best-qualified candidate, or why she is introduced by a man touting her experience—even when her résumé makes her qualifications abundantly clear—you have this study and its hidden influence over consultants to blame. When Hillary Clinton said in the 2008 campaign, "I am not running as a woman. I am running because I believe I am the best-qualified and experienced person," she was following this script. I've come to think of this as the Lady-Doth-Protest-Too-Much syndrome. Tell someone not to think of an elephant and they can't help but think of an elephant. (Try it.) That is how our brains work, according to neurolinguistics.

Several recent studies call into question the assumption that America has elected comparatively few women governors because the public thinks women don't have what it takes. Brooks, in *He Runs, She Runs*, found that people did not think that women lacked toughness or other leadership qualities, traits that are "typically seen as being especially critical at the executive level." Likewise, her data showed that people did not judge executive office candidates differently than they judged legislative candidates. Scholars have started to examine other potential reasons for the executive-level gender gap, especially paying more attention to the political and social environment shaping how women fare in gubernatorial campaigns. Valerie O'Regan and Stephen Stambough have found the political parties are nominating women with very different chances of victory. Democrats were more likely to nominate women who had a strong chance of winning, while Republicans were more likely to nominate women as "sacrificial lambs" in contests in which the Republican had little chance of winning. In a separate paper, the two scholars found that the more experience women gubernatorial nominees had in prior elected office, the more likely they were to win. That is hardly a surprising result. Nevertheless, it suggests that the double standard is not the sole or even the primary cause of America's missing women governors. Political scientist Jason Windett, in a 2011 article, turned the focus to distinct state political environments—the "cultural history and views on gender equality" in each state. Analyzing every case of a woman entering a primary for governor between 1978 and 2008, he found that women were significantly more likely to win a primary or the general election in those states with a history of progressive views on women's roles and a history of greater gender equity in education, political representation, and workforce participation. This is powerful evidence that changes in gender ideology and women's representation work together in a positive feedback loop, more egalitarianism leads to more women in office, and vice versa. It is also powerful evidence against the assumption that old views of femininity survive to penalize women candidates in places where gender equity is valued.

Nor does a specific bias against women in executive office show up in public opinion. For example, in a comprehensive survey on women and leadership by the Pew Research Center in 2014, when people were asked if women were better at legislative or executive jobs, more than eight out of ten saw no difference between the two levels of office for women. And by the same margin, they saw no difference between the two levels of office for men.

In short, although there is as yet no consensus in the scholarship, there is plenty of cause to doubt the conventional wisdom that the double standard is to blame for the low numbers of women in elected executive office.

Still, even if Americans ten or twenty years ago believed women were less fit than men to be governor or mayor or president, we can't simply assume that they continue to believe so now. In 1990, when Huddy and Terkildsen collected data for their study, only five women had ever been elected governor in their own right. As of 2015, twenty-seven states had been led by a woman governor.

There is, however, a bigger problem here that should make us skeptical of any claim that voters prefer candidates with "masculine traits" for executive office. The research is based on personality assessments created in the early 1970s, in which traditional gender stereotypes were baked into the questions themselves.

Here's how the two most common assessments work. Participants are asked to place themselves on a five-point scale about how well certain adjectives or statements describe themselves, for example, "independent," "very submissive–very dominant," or "sensitive to others' needs." Each question was coded masculine or feminine, and the total score determined whether you had a "masculine" and "instrumental" personality, or a "feminine" and "expressive-nurturing" personality.

Consider some of the "masculine" traits: strong leader, assertive, competitive, confident, rational, tough, intelligent, power hungry, uncaring.

Now consider some of the "feminine" traits: warm, compassionate, kind, gentle, sensitive, trustworthy, cautious, emotional, weak, incompetent, unintelligent.

Whatever validity these notions might have once had—which is hard to tease out given the circular reasoning in the assessments—it defies common sense to think they are accurate descriptions of how Americans view men and women today. It simply defies common sense to assume that a typical American considers trustworthiness a distinctly feminine trait or rationality a distinctly masculine one, for example.

Ideas about gender have changed rapidly and dramatically, to say the least. Just two presidential elections ago, few could have predicted that the Supreme Court would rule that same-sex marriage is a constitutional right and that the U.S. military would adopt a non-discrimination policy to protect transgendered service members.

To be sure, we're not in a postgender age. The central problem here is that too much of the gender scholarship still relies on notions of femininity and masculinity, of "male" leadership and "male" policy areas, that prevailed before the sexual revolution, feminism, and the gay civil rights movement changed America. It's like using an abacus to calculate string theory. It is time for a new paradigm for analyzing how we think about gender, in general, and women's leadership, in particular.

Fortunately, in the real world of electoral politics, the old fears and tropes have largely been retired. A new paradigm is being forged in the crucible of political campaigns. "It used to be you had to be tough, and it was almost impossible to be tough as a woman and still be likable. Now you just have to be strong, and you can show strength in a variety of ways," Democratic consultant Celinda Lake said.

"I get pissed off when I see an ad for one of our candidates, and she's behind a desk with an American flag, and it's late at night, and she's got the office light on. That is just an old model," Jonathan Parker, former political director at EMILY's List, said. "Ten years back, I think women felt like they needed to be the business-suited, behind-the-desk type of candidate. They'd portray themselves that way in ads, almost as a way to make them look like leaders. Voters don't want to see that. They want to see women candidates with groups, talking to people, being regular Joes." While Parker thought some voters still judged women running for executive office more harshly, he believed it was less the case now. "I have no doubt that Hillary Clinton's run for president—showing that a woman could be a totally strong, qualified, and capable executive—helped women running for other executive offices. Republicans and Democrats. I don't think it was a partisan thing."

NEARLY EVERY POLITICIAN and operative has a story to tell about the annoyances of leading while female. But if you parse their comments carefully, you get the impression from them that they are eager to move on. Recalling incidents of everyday sexism—the reporter who commented unflatteringly on a dress, the voter who asked about her children—is like kissing babies or posing for selfies on the campaign trail. It comes with the job. Some politicians don't mind it, some enjoy it, and some tolerate it. (From all appearances and reports, Hillary Clinton genuinely enjoys kissing babies, Jeb Bush genuinely enjoys posing for selfies, and Barack Obama reportedly dislikes the flesh-pressing part of retail politics.) Just as a candidate has nothing to gain by saying no when a voter holds up her phone and asks for a photo, she also has nothing to gain by telling a voter who is convinced that women face a double standard that it just isn't so.

Consider how Granholm, the first woman governor of Michigan, chose to frame the discussion about women in politics. At the beginning of my interview with her, she said, "Well, as a warning to you about my perspective about women running, I'm often asked, how was it as the first woman attorney general and the first woman governor, and I don't have a response other than

I've never been anything else. So, it's hard for me to know what it would be like otherwise. And I don't like to look at things in a victim's frame. I mean, there's a lot of negativity about politicians in general. But my frame is not the negative side."

Granholm was not saying that gender was irrelevant to her campaign, but rather that it was not the essential factor; she is deeply involved in several efforts to boost women's political leadership, because she believes women bring an important and unique perspective to governing. Granholm prevailed in an extremely competitive Democratic primary in 2002, won the general election that year, and was reelected in 2006. (She was termed out in 2010.) "It was a great and momentous race for historic reasons," she acknowledged. "But it also represented a significant change more than that related to gender or to policy change. It was change in the way of doing business. The previous guy was a very conservative Republican who, they said, 'ruled with an iron fist.' He was very closed to outside input. I ran on specific values as a candidate. I said I'm going to be somebody who has five specific values: inclusive, integrity, excellence, creativity, and teamwork. From each of those values flowed certain policies that I would highlight. Obviously, my agenda was different, but I also think that I embodied a fresh perspective on government, a fresh way of serving people."

"The biggest barrier to electing women really has nothing to do with gender," EMILY's List founder Ellen Malcolm said. "The biggest barrier to electing women is the power of incumbency and how difficult it is to put newcomers into office."

In short, sexism in politics is a paper tiger—showy but toothless.

Still, the presidency could be different.

"When we were rolling out EMILY's List's Madam President campaign," consultant Lisa Grove recalled, "I was backstage at the National Press Club with Stephanie Schriock. Here we were having a press conference to say that America is ready for a woman president. I said to her, 'I'm trying to figure out what a win is. Is a win today that no one shows up? Because it could be. Seriously, do we really have to have a press conference and roll out data to prove this? Wouldn't it be a win if no one showed up because it wasn't news?' We laughed about it."

The room was packed, standing room only.

"We were like, 'Okay, we still have to prove that!' There's a part of me that felt we had blown past that."

"People say it's no big deal. Well, this country has never ever elected a woman president," EMILY's List president Stephanie Schriock told me. "It is a huge deal. It's not a huge deal in what we are going to campaign on, but we are going to do something that has never happened. It is just like electing Barack Obama. We elected an African American president, and that was a huge deal to every young African American in this country. I don't think we understand what it is going to mean to women and girls around the world to have a woman president of the United States of America."

Chapter 4

GOLDILOCKS NATION

I N THE ENTIRE sweep of American history, very few women have made a serious attempt to run for president: a grand total of eight. The two major parties have nominated only two women, Geraldine Ferraro and Sarah Palin, for vice president. Hillary Clinton remains the only woman who has won a single state primary—she won many, of course—and the only woman to have stayed in her party's contest until the end. To put this in perspective, more than twice as many men ran for president in the Republican Party in 2016—that is, in just one party and one year—as all of the women presidential aspirants in our nation's history.

On its face, these figures suggest an open-and-shut case for the power of the double standard at the presidential level. To be sure, discrimination against women was historically the main cause of women's political exclusion, as we'll see in more detail later. But in recent times, why America has never elected a woman president has a lot to do with whether qualified women run. After all, since the mid-1990s, dozens of women have served as governors and senators, the conventional presidential stepping-stones.

One of those qualified women who seriously thought about running for president is retired Texas Republican senator Kay Bailey Hutchison.

"If George Bush hadn't run for a second term, I think I would have. The timing would have been right. But after he did, then I felt like . . . Well, first of all, I had children by then," Hutchison told me. She was driving in Dallas after a long day at work, and the thrum of her teenagers could be heard in the background as she recalled her considerations about running for president. "Secondly, I think there was Texas fatigue. I just couldn't even imagine somebody from Texas winning or making a serious run for president after eight years of a Texan."

Indeed, she had also weighed running in 2000. Hutchison entered the Senate in 1993, just as women were attaining critical mass there, and to her the fact that they had proven themselves equal with the men allowed her to see herself as a viable and competitive presidential candidate. "After I had been in the Senate for maybe one term, that would have been the right time for me, but then George W. Bush was rising. He certainly got out there. Because his father had been president, people were used to a Bush, and he had broad support from Bush supporters and friends from the past. He had a ready-made operation. That was realistically going to be very powerful." Hutchison added, "I would never have considered running against him, because we're friends and I like him. But certainly, when Bush made the decision to run, that affected me greatly."

In short, "timing was everything," as she said. In each of the three cycles Hutchison might have been able to mount a successful campaign, she was boxed out by another politician from her own party and her own state. But Hutchison was convinced that had she run, she would not have faced a higher hurdle because she was a woman. "I think if I had run for president, people would have judged me on my policies, and I thought I would be right for America, because my policies would have been right for leading America."

Americans set a supremely high bar for choosing a president—for good reason, given we're electing the single most powerful individual on the planet. Every president in the last sixty-five years either held an advanced degree or served in the military; each had deep experience in public service and other professional fields. Still, as many political scientists remind us, when we enter the voting booth, our emotions—not our minds—are in control. Consider that since 1960, according to the American National Election Studies, the candidate rated the highest on personal qualities became president.

America, we are a nation of Goldilocks. We prefer our presidents not too young and not too old, not too cool and not too hot-tempered. We thrill to charisma, and then we mock those who possess the gift. We complain about the superficial tenor of the presidential race, yet voraciously consume news about faux scandals and gaffes. We swoon over the new face and then suffer buyer's remorse.

In other words, we size up candidates by a host of subjective evaluations about the men and women running for president—about their personality, character, temperament, family life, and style.

Americans say we are ready for a woman president. But can any woman meet our extravagant and paradoxical demands?

SINCE BARACK OBAMA catapulted from the Illinois Senate to the Oval Office in just five short years, pundits and party operatives have been scouting the political farm teams in hopes of finding the next superstar. But history suggests the career paths to the American presidency are narrow. Exactly zero mayors and zero state attorneys general have become president of the United States. Since 1900 only two men who never held prior elected office have become president. One, Herbert Hoover, served in the cabinet, and the other, Dwight D. Eisenhower, a five-star general and bona fide war hero, led the Allies to victory over Hitler in World War II. A college degree is not a formal requirement for the presidency, but only two presidents in the last 130 years lacked one. The last time Americans elected a sitting member of the House of Representatives to be president, the streets of Washington, DC, were still lit by gas lamps.

In reality, presidential elections before 1900 give little guidance about what is possible for 21st-century would-be candidates. The presidency as we know it is a relatively new phenomenon. "Most 19th-century presidents were rather weak," Columbia University historian Eric Foner told me. "You had Andrew Jackson who saw the latent power of the office to mobilize popular opinion over and above Congress. You had Lincoln, but he was a war president—war always exalts the power of the office. Politics was more state-oriented, except in wartime, like the Civil War. Politics was more controlled by the political parties, and the president was the creature of the party. There were no primary campaigns like we have today—it saved a lot of money that way. You didn't have this media focus on the one person."

The modern presidency, with its candidate-centered politics, bully pulpit, and expanded power, was largely an invention of Theodore Roosevelt. Born into a wealthy New York political dynasty, Theodore was a sickly child and a restless young man who nursed grandiose ambitions. Before he became president in 1901, he had won fame as a cowboy and hero of the Spanish-American War, a big game hunter and a conservationist, an author and explorer. He had held prestigious positions as New York City police commissioner, New York governor, assistant secretary of the navy, and vice president.

What elevated TR to the presidency, however, was not this impressive list of accomplishments. It was an assassin's bullet. In 1901, President William McKinley was assassinated, like Presidents Lincoln and Garfield before him. TR's career path reveals an underappreciated fact: American presidents have an alarming propensity to vacate the office in the midst of their term. Since 1900, two presidents have been assassinated, two have died in office, and one—Richard Nixon—resigned to avoid indictment. Thanks to political violence and the grim reaper—and in one case, corruption—the vice presidency offers one of the most common paths into the Oval Office.

On the other hand, sitting vice presidents have fared poorly when they have stood for election on their own account. Since 1900, exactly one sitting vice president has won a presidential election in his own right: George H. W. Bush. Three of the four recent vice presidents who tried were defeated: Al Gore in 2000, Hubert Humphrey in 1968, and Nixon in 1960.

That leaves the two main launching pads for winning presidential campaigns: the Senate and the governor's office of any one of the fifty states. Since 1900, three sitting senators have run for president and won: Warren G. Harding, John F. Kennedy, and Barack Obama. Six governors have won the presidency in this time, including four of our six most recent presidents: Jimmy Carter, Ronald Reagan, Bill Clinton, and George W. Bush.

One job that has been a dead-end on the path to the White House is CEO. In recent times, business titans who have never held elected office have run for president, promising they could rescue America from professional politicians. In 2016, real estate mogul Donald Trump and former Hewlett-Packard CEO Carly Fiorina, the first woman to lead a Fortune 20 company, entered the GOP primary with essentially the same rationale as past hopefuls Ross Perot and Steve Forbes had offered. As Fiorina put it in her campaign tagline, "Our Founders never imagined a government led by career politicians. It's time to put a citizen leader in the White House." So far, Americans have not bought the CEO's pitch, and despite Trump's and Fiorina's strong performances in early polls of Republican 2016 voters, that is unlikely to change in the near future.

Keeping in mind this robust historical pattern, at any given time there are only roughly 200 people in the nation with the credentials to mount a credible presidential run: current and recent senators, governors, and cabinet members.

To be sure, women are vastly outnumbered among this elite group. Nevertheless, there are currently plenty of women with the right qualifications and experience to compete at the exalted presidential level. In 2016, twenty women serve in the Senate, and dozens more are current or recent governors or cabinet officers. Nearly every election cycle, women's numbers in these high offices increase—albeit not as rapidly as many would hope.

In short, women make up a sufficient proportion of the presidential pool. But when every competitive presidential contender has more or less the same qualifications and experience, it takes more than the right résumé to win. It takes the right stuff.

"THERE IS AN intangible in campaigns," Democratic consultant Rose Kapolczynski said. "Voting is an emotional decision, so people are voting for a person who they like, who they trust, who they think shares their values and will fight for them. I'm very research- and data-driven, but I also believe that grassroots excitement around a campaign can influence that emotional decision. Is it the only way people make decisions? No, but it can help."

"The 'it factor' matters more and more as politics becomes more about the ten-second sound bite," Bettina Duval said. Duval is a major donor to pro-choice, progressive Democratic women. When we spoke, U.S. senator Barbara Boxer had just announced her retirement, and California attorney general Kamala Harris had already announced she would run for Boxer's seat. Duval recalled that when she first met Harris, Harris was an obscure San Francisco district attorney, running for attorney general, and polling at 2 percent. Harris ultimately defeated the Republican frontrunner in the race, becoming California's first woman, African American, and Indian American attorney general. "When I first met Kamala, she just had it. What is that 'it'? I knew she was going to be a winner," Duval said. "I went to her swearing in and it was an electric room. Why is that? She was an attractive woman, she spoke very well, with passion—a little bit too long but nobody cared." I asked her how much she thought charisma—the "intangibles," to use Kapolczynski's word—mattered for candidates. "I think people want to reach out and touch a candidate. It matters that you are warm and make people comfortable. You have to have a sense of humor. You don't have to be an amazing beauty to run for office. I don't think it matters if you're fat or thin or what color your hair is, you just have to look like you are pulled together. You have to be able to articulate why you are running, and truly believe in what your issues are. So, the charisma component is important, but it is the whole package that matters."

The view of Kapolczynski and Duval, who are in the business of getting candidates elected, is supported by a significant body of scholarly research. "The data from political science are crystal-clear: People vote for the candidate who elicits the right feelings, not the candidate who presents the best arguments," Drew Westen, an Emory University psychology professor, wrote in his influential 2007 book, *The Political Brain: The Role of Emotion in Deciding the Fate of the Nation.* "The political brain is an emotional brain. It is not a dispassionate calculating machine, objectively searching for the right facts, figures, and policies to make a reasoned decision." Westen elaborated, "We are not moved by leaders with whom we do not feel an emotional resonance. We do not find policies worth debating if they don't touch on the emotional implications for ourselves, our families, or things we hold dear. From the standpoint of research in neuroscience, the more purely 'rational' an appeal, the less it is likely to activate the emotion circuits that regulate voting behavior."

Not all experts agree, however, that voters' feelings about presidential candidates influence the outcome of elections. Princeton political scientist Larry Bartels analyzed public opinion data on the six presidential elections that took place between 1980 and 2000 and concluded that assessments of personality traits rarely influenced presidential election outcomes, even though there were modest effects on the vote share. In five of the six cases, how positively voters assessed the candidates' character and personality did not affect the outcome of the election.

The conclusion of this study, however, would likely strike panic into anyone with skin in the electoral game, given the one election when personality did matter. In 2000, George W. Bush registered a half-point advantage over Al Gore in voters' estimation of the two candidates' personal traits and character. Bartels conceded that in such a close election the slightly more positive feelings voters held about Bush were "quite probably, large enough to be decisive." Another way of looking at this is to note that in one out of six elections, voters' assessment of the character and personality of the two major party candidates determined who would become president of the United States.

"Al Gore changed the whole world because the poor guy was stiff," Eleanor Smeal, who has spent decades working on campaigns, scoffed. "Politics is a retail business. Personality matters.

You've got to be good on television. You have to have a warm personality. If you don't, go be the campaign manager or something."

WHEN PEOPLE THINK about the intangibles that factor into voters' judgments and how women seem to face different standards, it's common to rail against the media and its obsession with women's looks, appearance, and dress. Former governor Jennifer Granholm, who reporters have called "gorgeous" and "charismatic," agreed that women receive more attention about their hair, their clothes, and their makeup, but it didn't faze her. "That just is, that's our world. Every TV show you see reinforces that, so why wouldn't you apply that to women in politics?" And because politicians were in the public eye more often, they faced it more than women in other professions did. "When you're out there and the wind is blowing your hair straight up, and you have to make sure your skirt isn't blowing up, and your opponents take that picture and make a commercial out of it saying, 'Look! The Wicked Witch of the West!' But they would be doing that with a man too. Unflattering photos are unflattering photos no matter what," she said with a laugh.

Granholm made an important point, one that people who cry sexism whenever a woman's appearance is mentioned almost always neglect. The public spotlight shines harshly on men too. Jeb Bush's Paleo diet earned its own *New York Times* story. Kentucky Republican Senate leader Mitch McConnell was routinely likened to a turtle by comedian Jon Stewart on the popular the *Daily Show*. Vice president Joe Biden's cosmetic enhancements were dramatic enough that a *New Yorker* fact-checker let the following passage by reporter Evan Osnos stand: "When [Biden] was thirty years old, he became one of the youngest senators in history, and he has parted with youth begrudgingly. . . . At seventy-one, with his hairline reforested and his forehead looking becalmed, Biden projects the glow of a grandfather just back from the gym, which is often the case." And then, of course, there was Donald Trump's hair.

Men with designs on the presidency have long known that vigor and physical attractiveness are part of what they had to sell. FDR, a tall and striking man before he was nearly paralyzed by polio, would not allow himself to be photographed sitting in his wheelchair. JFK, a handsome philanderer who revolutionized men's fashion, deliberately lied about his health. Given access to hitherto private papers, historian Robert Dallek wrote, "The lifelong health problems of John F. Kennedy constitute one of the best-kept secrets of recent U.S. history—no surprise, because if the extent of those problems had been revealed while he was alive, his presidential ambitions would likely have been dashed." Ronald Reagan was an actual Hollywood leading man. Mitt Romney, the 2012 Republican nominee, was once named to *People* magazine's list of the "Fifty Most Beautiful People."

So if we want to know if women face a double standard regarding their physical appearance, we need to look at the whole landscape. What we then see is that men too are under the media's gaze, and as we've seen, on average equally so. It also becomes apparent that men who run for office are highly conscious of their physical appearance.

But the real question is, do looks matter to voters?

"The best available evidence says that politicians don't get elected because of their good looks," Harvard political scientist Ryan Enos wrote in the *Washington Post* during the 2012 presidential election, when the media was chattering about how handsome Romney was. (On a candidate attractiveness rating system that Enos and his colleagues Matthew Atkinson and Seth Hill developed, Romney scored in the 99th percentile.) By comparison, Joe Biden scored in the 62nd percentile, and Sarah Palin in the 95th. An analysis by the three scholars on every Senate election between 1990 and 2006 found that good looks never tipped a Senate election. It wasn't for lack of trying by parties and candidates. In competitive races, the out-party tended to run an above-average looking challenger to the incumbent, but that factor did not influence who won or lost. What about the much-touted studies that showed a relationship? Enos and his colleagues argued that those famous studies had left out important variables related to the particular election context and had erroneously found a cause-and-effect relationship where none existed. (Or to put it in statistical lingo, the correlation between looks and election outcome was probably spurious.) Enos wrote, "This isn't surprising: Politics and voting are greatly affected by factors such as partisanship, the economy, campaigning, and even policy—all of which leave little room for voters to cast votes based on politicians' looks." When it comes to the ultimate test—winning or losing—appearance does not matter.

Could it be instead that expectations about a woman's role, rather than how a woman should look, is the hurdle that knocks would-be women presidents off the ladder to the Oval Office?

EVEN IF AMERICANS see women in general as equally qualified as men to hold executive-level office, as we have seen, do we nevertheless hold candidates who are mothers to a different standard than candidates who are fathers?

There is no question that we used to. Amusing evidence of this double standard regarding mothers and fathers can be found in Theodore White's classic book about the presidential race, *The Making of the President 1960*. The fact that John F. Kennedy would be parenting a two-month-old on the day he moved into the White House merited just five words in White's 382-page book. "JFK was tense, it seemed, as he voted, thronged and jostled by [reporters]," White wrote, "only now his wife was with him in the press, and he was uncomfortable at how the pushing might affect her, she being eight months pregnant."

In our own lives, Americans have strayed far from the traditional family model of husband, wife, and children. Half of all marriages end in divorce; 41 percent of children are born to unmarried mothers; a record percentage of American adults are single. Nevertheless we demand that POTUS and FLOTUS stage the old-time show. Every president but one in American history was married. (The perpetual bachelor was James Buchanan who, for sixteen years, shared a Washington DC home with the also unmarried Alabama senator William Rufus Devane King.) Ronald Reagan broke the divorce barrier but was in a devoted second marriage. Even as late as 2015, GOP presidential candidate Senator Lindsey Graham found himself having to defend his status as a single man. One fellow Republican senator was caught on a hot mic referring to Graham as "a bro with no ho." Graham, facing days of unflattering headlines, protested that he was not "defective" because he was not married. "I don't think there's anything in the Constitution that says single people need not apply for president. And if it bothers some people, then they won't vote for me. I offer what I offer." In the last 100 years, every president has had children, many of whom were raised in the White House.

Given the fact that women still perform the lion's share of parenting, does a qualified woman who is also a mother of school-aged children have a chance to be president? Given cultural biases about proper gender roles, could a woman who was single or childless by choice win the affection of voters in a presidential contest?

"People would ask me, 'How can you do this as a mother of three?'" Granholm told me. "They never would have asked my predecessor, who had young triplets at home, because of course they knew that his wife was going to be doing that."

For Granholm, the key to putting those questions to rest began with the conscious choice she and her husband had made about how to share parenting responsibilities. After asking themselves which of them would be a better primary parent, Granholm said, he won hands down. "He is somebody who could spend hours staring at a baby. He plays music. He takes his time. He smells the roses. I make the lists. I'm like, 'Come on, come on, come on. Let's go, let's go, let's go.' If you looked at our personality traits on paper, you would pick him to be the one to stay at home, for sure." Granholm continued, "I certainly would never have run for office without that support, without my husband being willing to be the primary caregiver at home. There's no way I would have run. But once people knew that we had taken care of our arrangements at home, there was not a question. Ever."

In the 1990s, Granholm and her husband's division of parenting labor was uncommon, but it is less so now. Currently, women are the primary or sole breadwinner in 40 percent of American households. Fathers spend triple the amount of time on child care now than they did in the 1960s and they make up 16 percent of stay-at-home parents. Two data points particularly underscore the shifts in thinking and values accompanying these day-to-day changes in behavior. Among fathers in dual-earner households, six in ten report feeling a work-family conflict, a 71 percent increase since 1977. In a large survey of millennials, the Public Religion Research Institute found that two-thirds of millennials did not think that family life suffered if women worked full-time. More of a problem, in their view, were men who concentrated too much on work.

In short, a host of old assumptions about women, work, motherhood, and the breadwinner husband have fallen. New ideals of involved fatherhood and a saner balance of family and work for men and women both has taken root, especially among couples in their twenties and thirties.

Increasingly, women leaders across the political spectrum are seamlessly incorporating motherhood into their public personas. Republican Representative Cathy McMorris Rodgers, the highest-ranking woman in the GOP House leadership, proudly claims in her official congressional biography that she is "the only Member of Congress in history to give birth three times while in office." Democratic senator Kirsten Gillibrand has written about how she spent the day she went into labor in an hours-long Senate Armed Services Committee meeting. Gillibrand's husband works in New York City, while the family's main home is in DC, and Gillibrand is essentially the lead parent during her workweek. In contrast, Republican senator Kelly Ayotte, a mother of two, commutes back and forth to work in DC, while her husband stays with the children at the family's New Hampshire home during the workweek.

While I heard from some older Republican women leaders a more conventional expectation that women were naturally the primary parent, it soon became apparent that to the extent that there is any divide on this question, it is generational, not partisan or ideological. NARAL president Ilyse Hogue, a progressive and a Democrat, was six months pregnant with twins when we spoke. "There is no presumption in my marriage that I am going to be the one to stay home. If anything, this experience has made my husband way more outraged about the lack of paternity leave," she said. Margaret Hoover, a conservative and a Republican, concurred. "My husband's way more involved with our eighteen-month-old than my dad was ever involved. But we're also a split partisan household. Maybe because I didn't marry a Republican I have a more involved husband, I don't know," she laughed. "But I do think it's generational. I think there's far more cooperation and collaboration in all areas of family than previously."

On both ends of the electoral equation—candidates and voters—old concerns about women balancing political office and motherhood appear to have waned. Political scientists Richard Fox and Jennifer Lawless found, contrary to their anticipated result, that the challenge of balancing family and work is not deterring women from running for office, because American women in all fields have so fully integrated the expectation of balancing work and motherhood. (It's worth a reminder that the United States is the only advanced nation without guaranteed paid maternity leave.) Although some politicians and consultants report that voters question women candidates about who is taking care of their children, I found no academic study that suggests mothers are penalized at the polls. It seems that like many other examples of everyday sexism, these are isolated events that have no systematic effect on women's chances of election.

Likewise, many political professionals believe that voters have become less judgmental about the family choices women politicians make. "People are more respectful of people's private decisions about how to manage their personal affairs," Granholm said. "It used to be you had to hide your family, but now you can run with your family in a more 360-degree candidacy," Democratic pollster Celinda Lake said. "People still worry if you have young kids, but it's a lot easier than it was." Others think even that has changed. "If I was advising someone, I wouldn't be worried about young children," Eleanor Smeal said. "It used to be harmful, but it's not anymore. Pat Schroeder, who had a baby while she was in the House, told me that once you're in there and you do the job, you're no longer hypothetical, you're a person. All politics is personal. Once you're in, people forget that other stuff and see you as a person."

That issue would not be raised in 2016, as no woman running for president had children at home. Instead, another assumption about how the double standard hurt women would be put to the test.

In a piece titled "Clinton Is Too Old to Run," Republican syndicated columnist Linda Chavez wrote, "Clinton will be sixty-nine in 2016—the same age as Ronald Reagan was in 1980 when he ran and won. But age was kinder to Reagan, as it often is to men." (Chavez had worked in Reagan's White House and had run for Senate and lost to Democrat Barbara Mikulski in 1986.) "Reagan managed to convey energy and vigor by riding horseback and chopping wood in his leisure time and engaging with voters and debating on the campaign trail. Clinton doesn't seem to have that same gift. Sure, it's not fair that women are judged more harshly on age—but it probably matters in an election, even if few people are willing to say so."

Was she right that age hurt a woman more than it did a man? On one hand, the three most recent American presidents were an average age of forty-nine at the time of their election. So any presidential candidate, man or woman, who was significantly older than this average could reasonably worry about falling victim to age-based judgments. It was an issue John McCain's 2008 campaign confronted—and arguably mishandled. On the other hand, calling attention to a woman's age is such a well-worn trope of crude sexism that to do so could easily backfire. Early in the 2016 campaign, GOP operatives warned Republicans to avoid talking about Clinton's age. When GOP candidate Rand Paul said, "It's a rigorous physical ordeal, I think, to be able to campaign for the presidency," and McConnell, age seventy-three, said Hillary seemed like a cast member of *Golden Girls* (a syndicated sitcom about four older women), they were roundly denounced for sexism.

However, in Clinton's case, the subtext of these sorts of remarks was more politically significant. Clinton's age wasn't really the main issue. Rather, McConnell, Paul, and others were reminding voters that she had spent two decades in the national spotlight. And for a younger opponent, like the boyish-looking, fifty-two-year-old, one-term senator Rand Paul, activating negative associations about age could establish a useful contrast, one that not incidentally recast his own deficits—a lack of experience and seasoning—as strengths. Think of it in Westen's terms of activating the neuronal pathways to trigger a thought that you might not want to state explicitly. Seen from this angle, Republicans were saying that Clinton wasn't so much old as old news. She was the status quo, not the future—a theme Jeb Bush, son of a president, a two-term governor, and a whopping six years younger than Clinton, hammered home in his presidential campaign announcement speech.

Still, Clinton's apparent predicament was enough to make a second-wave feminist's head spin. For years it had been said that America had never elected a woman president because no woman had the experience to be a serious contender. And now the potential first woman president had too much experience to be president? Journalists and pundits often speculated that Clinton's lack of freshness should make Democrats panic about their odds of holding the White House.

Would Clinton falter in the race because her vast experience had made her too familiar to voters? "People yin and yang, they alternate between change and experience, experience and change," Democratic consultant Celinda Lake told me. "They've also concluded, rightly or wrongly, that Barack Obama didn't have enough seasoning and that he's had trouble getting things done, and that maybe it is time for someone who is more seasoned and knows how to get things done. In 2008, the mood was the opposite of Hillary Clinton. I think in 2016 the mood will be exactly in her direction." Only time would tell if Lake's prediction about the mood of the country in 2016 was right. Nonetheless, she was onto something. Talk of Clinton's biological age was a proxy for the quadrennial choice between change and experience, not a case of gender-based bias. Clinton's age probably didn't matter, and it certainly mattered no more for her than it would for a man.

Not to mention that 69 percent of millennials, according to a Pew survey earlier that year, thought Hillary was in her fifties or younger.

IN THE FALL of 2007, Hillary Clinton led every one of the many talented men in the Democratic primary on almost every measure related to leadership and competence. She had the qualifications and experience to match any major party candidate in recent history. She had topped Gallup's ranking of the Most Admired Woman in the world in nine of the prior ten years. But she fell short on one measure: Voters rated her less inspiring than Obama.

That 2007 poll validated a feeling many women harbor, that a woman faces a natural disadvantage on the exalted stage of a presidential election. Most voters never meet a presidential candidate in person, and their impressions of the candidates are formed largely through mediated experiences, especially the big speech to an audience of thousands or tens of thousands. And what makes the impression is not just ideas, it's how candidates present themselves, and those ineffable qualities are something that can't be measured and quantified. When men quite literally speak in a more commanding voice, can women hope to compete?

"When I taught speech writing at Harvard and American University, one of the segments that I always did was about women candidates. And I always used Hillary as an example," Chriss Winston, President George H. W. Bush's lead speech writer and the first woman ever to lead the White House speech writing office, told me. "Are women different from men, style-wise or rhetorically? There are differences between men and women. Some are physiological differences and that is just reality. There are exceptions. There was Barbara Jordan, who was a powerful, amazing woman speaker. There have been other women who have that ability to really deliver. I think Elizabeth Warren is pretty good. I happen to think she is just one of the absolute worst ideologues ever, but looking at it just as someone who can deliver a message in a way that people respond to I think she's pretty good. But there are differences. I do think women have some disadvantages that men don't have. The timbre of our voices is physically different. It doesn't project as well. It sounds thin if you really try and push the emotion or power." Winston herself has a lovely, sonorous voice.

"There's a difference between projecting your voice and raising your voice, where you can really sound harsh and very atonal. Hillary Clinton I think is an example of someone who has struggled with this." (When Winston and I spoke, Clinton had not yet launched her 2016 campaign, and her evaluation was based on the 2008 bid.) Although Clinton delivered formal speeches well, Winston continued, "You can look at some of the clips of Hillary. She does what a lot of women speakers do when they're in a situation like a political rally, when they're going out to rally the troops. As women try to pack more power and emotion into their words, their voices tend to rise. There are some men who do this too, but it is more so I think with women, and Hillary is an absolutely prime example. As Clinton would get revved up, her voice would go up and by the time she was done it was like a half scream. It was not good TV. It was not good sound. I noticed that by the end of the 2008 campaign, she was much, much better than she was at the beginning. I think she had some speech coaching. The voice rising and so on is something as a woman you have to be aware of." Still, she emphasized, every woman's voice was different, and some men also tended to shout and scream when they got worked up. Moreover, some speeches were poorly written and no one could do much with a "colorless speech." Ultimately, she concluded, it wasn't a huge factor in a campaign. "It is just that you have to be aware of it."

While there were physiological gender differences, Winston believed they only went so far in explaining why some candidates were so good and some weren't. "Some people simply are not good at communicating their emotions," she said. "Mitt Romney wasn't great at it. Ronald Reagan was great. Some people are just like Bill Clinton, the guy is awesome. He can deliver a speech like nobody's business. He has you in the palm of his hand. He's amazing. George W. Bush? Sometimes yes, sometimes no. His father? Same thing. George H. W. Bush could deliver a good speech, but most of the time, he just didn't pay attention to it," Winston laughed. "That's the truth. When he decided it really was an important speech, he could deliver it fine. He just never spent the time he needed to on most speeches to really deliver them well."

In other words, no one could spin gold from the dross of a badly written speech, practice was essential to competent delivery, but what captivated people was something ineffable in the delivery. Unlike national GDP and the unemployment rate, you can't quantify the 'it' factor. But maybe you can break it down into its key ingredients. I asked John Neffinger, communications strategist and author of *Compelling People*, a book about communications and leadership, what was it that impressed audiences or left them unmoved.

"There is actual science that shows that when me meet someone, we size them up quickly. We have a giant occipital lobe in the back of our head," he said, touching the nape of his neck. "We take in visual signals through it, and our visual neurons are wired to process facial expression, posture, all of these kinds of nonverbal cues." Human beings process nonverbal information in milliseconds. Most of that judgment—80 percent, according to a scientist who measured it—was based on two dimensions, Neffinger explained. "The science suggests we are looking for two signals: first warmth and second strength. There is a little bit of warmth primacy as we size up people."

Effective and charismatic leaders, Neffinger and his coauthor Matthew Kohut argue in their book, embody an exquisite balance between strength and warmth. If strength is an irreducible component of leadership, and nonverbals are the key signals of strength people use to assess a person's leadership, at a physiological level, is it simply more difficult for women to clear the bar? "Remember, John Kerry lost even though he was taller than almost everyone. So it's not an ironclad rule," he answered, explaining that people perceive physiological characteristics in a relational, not an absolute way. A tall man who slouches, such as Kerry, is perceived to be lacking in strength. On the other hand, a woman of just average height can be perceived to be strong, as long as her voice registered in the midrange proportional to her height. "What people are trying to suss out is how you feel on the inside. If you feel assertive and confident and determined, that is going to show in your voice just by where in your range you are speaking."

This theory of the Goldilocks zone allows us to drill down on Winston's criticism of women's tendency to go high, thin, and shouty. Those qualities simply don't project confidence, resolve, determination, and assertiveness—traits any person with vast power in their hands must possess. Recent research confirms our intuitive understanding of the effect certain voices have on people, as well as Winston and Neffinger's complementary takes on public speaking. In an article titled appropriately "The Sound of Power," three psychologists found that people who speak in a voice that is steadier in pitch yet varied in volume are perceived to hold more authority and a higher rank than those whose voices waver and sound strained. They also found, as did Harvard psychologist Amy Cuddy (with whom Neffinger has worked), that imagining oneself to be powerful or striking a power pose—"faking it," as Cuddy put it in her immensely popular TED Talk—can enhance our feelings of our own power and change how powerful others perceive us to be.

But are women damned if they do and damned if they don't? My conversation with Neffinger took place a few weeks before Clinton announced her candidacy, and Neffinger assessed Clinton somewhat differently than Winston had. "Hillary projects tons of strength. Her posture is great. There is something she does that is more subtle, but it is an incredibly strong nonverbal cue. The lay term for it is poise. She is one of the leading examples of this in public life. It demonstrates control of your body in space and it projects a lot of strength," he said. But at the same time, he cautioned, such composure can feel intimidating. Strength and warmth tend to work like a seesaw: when one goes up, the other goes down, and rarely do they stay balanced. Nonverbal strength displays can create the impression that a person lacks warmth, particularly if that person was a woman, Neffinger believes. So Clinton's poise and composure, a personal strength and a display of strength, were sending mixed messages. Neffinger felt that men were given more latitude than women to stretch beyond old gender stereotypes—that a man suffered less of a hit if he showed warmth than a woman did if she showed a lot of strength. In other words, unlike Brooks who concluded that voters judge women politicians as "leaders, not ladies," Neffinger thought women still faced something of a double bind. Although, he observed, "It is all changing, and mostly by example. The stereotypes suggest certain ways, and you're comfortable with them. You're not comfortable when you see them mixed and matched. As you see mixing and matching happen successfully, it will rewire the stereotypes. The culture is changing in a way that makes it possible for us to envision a woman president."

We'll see that Clinton's projection of strength was as much a campaign strategy as it was a reflection of her authentic self. But she is not unique on this score. All candidates craft a public persona, and it is the performance of a "self," not necessarily the true "self," that touches us as voters. Consider the case of President Ronald Reagan, known in his day as the "Great Communicator." In 1937, Warner Bros. signed Reagan, an aspiring actor, to a film contract specifically because of his appealing baritone voice, Reagan's biographer Edmund Morris wrote in a *New Yorker* profile. Fans loved it so much they wrote letters saying, "You have the most wonderful voice in pictures." Reagan was a natural actor, in appearance and presence. "Reagan never required makeup, even when he was a movie actor. He didn't sweat under hot lights: he basked in them." But according to Morris, Reagan felt little connection to anyone but his wife Nancy, even to his own children. "Reagan's scrupulously kept presidential diary is remarkable for a near-total lack of interest in people as individuals. In all its half million or so words, I did not find any affectionate remark about his children."

Again, it's worth emphasizing, little of this is playing out at a conscious level. Not only are we making nonrational snap judgments based on nonverbal cues about a speaker's character as shown by certain traits, but all it takes to thrill us, move us, and touch us is a good performance of heartfelt feeling.

Still, our expectations for the big presidential speech have been calibrated to the masculine persona, which is not surprising, given that historically men have been the only ones on stage. In this one area, women on average do appear to start from a biologically sex-based disadvantage. But it is far from an insuperable obstacle to victory. Rare talents like Obama or Reagan or Bill Clinton, to be sure, will always have an edge on the presidential campaign trail, but only a handful of individuals of this caliber have emerged in American politics in the last forty years. Most presidential candidates—both men and women—are distinctly average public speakers, and practice and training can go a long way to improving performance for any candidate. More importantly, the stump speech to a large crowd is simply becoming less important. Technological advances in social media and changes in how Americans consume culture and news have created new platforms for candidates to show off their "it factor" and cultivate an intimate bond with voters. And in this virtual world, height, voice, and the gendered body itself are immaterial.

That doesn't mean that warmth, strength, likability, and all those other ineffable qualities become irrelevant. As Neffinger and I talked more about how people's perceptions of candidates' character might influence their vote choice, Neffinger offered, "I have this notion of the lifestyle voter who tunes in every four years. Yeah, maybe they care about policy, but it's hard to connect a vote to a policy outcome. What is easier to connect is that one of these two characters is going to be on my television every day for at least the next four years. I'm going to have to talk to my friends about them. I'm going to have to talk to my kids about them. And that's going to be a more or less pleasant experience depending on how they present themselves. That is part of the deal, part of the assessment. We are looking for leadership characteristics and we're judging on character."

Or as Westen put it, winning politicians "understand what the philosopher David Hume recognized three centuries ago: that reason is a slave to emotion, not the other way around."

BY 2016, WAS America ready to elect a woman president?

"In the same way that President Obama always had a slice of the electorate who just couldn't bring themselves to vote for a black president, Clinton will have a slice of the electorate who cannot bring themselves to vote for a woman president," Granholm said. But, she underscored, the numbers of those holdouts were shrinking quickly. "I think it will be to her advantage and not to her detriment."

Women candidates at all levels remain targets of the occasional gender-based attack, to be sure, but the best evidence tells us that sexism has no power to influence the outcome of elections.

Women who can compete at this exalted level believe that the double standard has minimal impact on their chances. Hutchison, who said she ultimately decided not to run for president because the Bush factor, Texas fatigue, and family obligations all made it untenable to do so when the time was ripe for her, felt confident that being a woman would not have been an obstacle. "After I had a term in the Senate and virtually no opposition running for reelection, I felt like people did not think of me as a woman senator anymore. People thought of me as a senator representing Texas. I didn't ever feel again like I had to prove myself in a different way."

Hutchison, the first woman ever elected to the Texas state legislature and a U.S. senator for more than two decades, believed that voters would have judged her on her policies. Realistically, they also would have viewed her through their partisan sympathies and antipathies, their ideological views, and a host of ineffable qualities as well. But Hutchison's point stood. Voters apply those same judgments to all presidential candidates, regardless of their gender.

Before casting votes on the second Tuesday of November every four years, American men and women have already sized up the Republican and Democratic nominees by standards that are partisan, contradictory, arbitrary, superficial, and finally, in many ways, tangential to the job requirements. Fortunately, the pool of potential candidates has been winnowed down through a challenging and merciless climb up the professional career ladder.

We feel, therefore we vote. When we step into the booth to mark our ballot, our lizard brain scampers out. To vote is as much an emotional act as it is a rational decision, particularly when we are choosing a president.

It is a touch deflating to contemplate that the most important decision in America's great democracy plays out like a nationwide election for homecoming king. But there is a silver lining to our shallowness. American voters subject the men and women who want to be president to the same absurd measures.

The double standard is dead.

Chapter 5

HILLARY

*"I know there are still some people who roll their eyes when I or
others say that women's issues are America's issues. But they're
just going to have to get used to it. I'm going to beat this drum
as long and as loud as it takes."*

—HILLARY CLINTON, MARCH 3, 2015

ON THE NIGHT of March 3, 2015, some 1,700 women and
men gathered in a Washington, DC, hotel ballroom to celebrate the 30th anniversary of EMILY's List. In the room was
nearly every Democratic woman senator and U.S. representative,
many Democratic congressmen, and hundreds of the party's powerbrokers, donors, influencers, writers, and operatives. The day
before, to many people's surprise, Senator Barbara Mikulski had
announced her retirement. Speaker after speaker feted Mikulski,
and she beamed with pleasure as she took the stage. *Saturday Night
Live* alum and Minnesota's U.S. senator Al Franken endorsed
Hillary Clinton for president and introduced EMILY's List president Stephanie Schriock. "If it were not for Schriock, I would not

be standing here as a U.S. senator," he said, giving testimony to Schriock's managerial skills and tactical brilliance. "When you win by 312 votes, believe me . . ." he deadpanned. Boston City Council member Ayanna Pressley, the recipient of the Gabrielle Giffords Rising Star award, brought down the house with her moving and charismatic delivery of her story of being raised by a struggling single mother, surviving a sexual assault in college, and stepping up to run for office.

Still, the fund-raiser's main draw was Hillary Clinton. Clinton had not yet announced her presidential run, and the crowd was in high anticipation for her speech. But Clinton remained coy about the elephant in the room, saying only at the very end of her thirty-minute speech, "Don't you want to see more women running for mayor and governor? Don't you want to see more women running for Congress? And I suppose it's only fair to say, don't you some-day want to see a woman president?"

In fact, the last time so many people who cared so much about electing a woman president had come together in one place was in June 2008 to hear Clinton concede to Barack Obama. No one doubted Clinton would run. The pressing political question for these champions of women's political leadership and for this politi-cal party was not so much whether America was ready to elect a woman president. Rather the question was, could this woman win?

"GOSH, SHE'S JUST got to run a better campaign than she did last time," retired Republican pollster Wilma Goldstein told me. "I wouldn't have any trouble voting for her, but that's the thing that might stop me. Because you don't always feel like you want to support a sinking ship! That wasn't a very good campaign for somebody who's as good as she is on policy and mission." Feminist Majority Foundation president Eleanor Smeal, similarly, accused Clinton's 2008 campaign consultants of "malpractice."

That view, that her campaign had been dysfunctional, was a common one, yet many conflicting opinions still circulated about why Clinton had lost and what that foretold for 2016. Some said the problem was Clinton herself or Clinton fatigue more generally. Some believed that 2008 was a once-in-a-lifetime moment, where the national mood for change and an unusually capable candidate converged. As Maryland Democratic Party vice chair and Hillary '08 supporter Jeffrey Slavin put it, "Obama was like Gandhi. 2008 was a crusade, it wasn't a political campaign." Others said that Clinton was too centrist or too polarizing—claims that are in essence self-canceling, showing yet again that Hillary Rodham Clinton functions as a kind of national Rorschach test.

Regardless, all agreed that at some level, campaigns matter.

As Clinton reentered the political fray in the spring of 2014 with the publication of her memoir, *Hard Choices*, she owned her own mistakes. She told *60 Minutes* host Diane Sawyer, "Honestly, I felt like I let people down, especially women and girls. Because I really didn't have a good strategy for my campaign. I have to earn your support."

So what had been Clinton's fatal error? For starters, her refusal to say her 2002 vote to authorize the use of force against Saddam Hussein was a mistake. Specifically, the price for that was a third-place finish in the Iowa caucus to Obama, the anti-war can-didate, and John Edwards, who had also voted to authorize force. But Edwards apologized for his vote.

Before Clinton declared her 2016 candidacy, she cleared away that old business on multiple channels. "Many Senators came to wish they had voted against the resolution. I was one of them," Clinton wrote in *Hard Choices*.

> While many were never going to look past my 2002 vote no matter what I did or said, I should have stated my regret sooner and in the plainest, most direct language possible. I'd gone most of the way there by saying I regretted the way President Bush used his authority and by saying that if we knew then what we later learned, there wouldn't have been a vote. But I held out against using the word *mistake*. It wasn't because of political expediency. After all, primary voters and the press were clamoring for me to say that word. When I voted to authorize force in 2002, I said that it was "probably the hardest decision I have ever had to make." I thought I had acted in good faith and made the best deci-sion I could with the information I had. And I wasn't alone it getting it wrong. But I still got it wrong. Plain and simple.

So if that's what she believed, why hadn't she cleared the air when it mattered, in 2007, when the Iraq War polled as the number one issue for Democratic primary voters?

"They ran a 1990s campaign in 2008," Ellen Malcolm, a Clinton '08 national co-chair said. Referring to Clinton's lead strategist, she continued, "I think Mark Penn underestimated the hunger for change, particularly on the Democratic side. He felt that the biggest problem that Hillary was going to have as a woman candidate was that people wouldn't think she was tough enough and smart enough to do the job. Traditionally that has been a big issue for women. But I think that credentialing Hillary after a very short term was sufficient, because I don't think there were many people in the world that thought that Hillary Clinton wasn't smart and effective and pretty tough. What they did not do was speak to what was in people's hearts, which was the need to make a change in the way politics work. Obama was superb at harnessing that energy. So, they ran the wrong campaign with the wrong message."

As Penn saw it, Clinton's biggest challenge was to reassure people that a woman was tough enough to be president.

In late December 2006, as Clinton readied her campaign, Penn wrote a strategy memo with his recommendation for how Clinton should position herself. Voters, Penn asserted, "see the president as the 'father' of the country," and in a dangerous world, they "do not want someone who would be the first mama." Yet, Penn continued, "there is a yearning for a kind of tough single parent—someone who can combine the toughness they are used to with the negotiating adeptness they believe a woman would bring to the office. They are open to the first father being a woman."

Take Margaret Thatcher as your beacon, he continued. "And the best role model proves the case. Margaret Thatcher was the longest serving Prime Minister in British history. She represents the most successful elected woman in this century—and the adjectives that were used about her (Iron Lady) were not of good humor or warmth, they were of smart, tough leadership. As we move forward it is important to understand who we are and who we are not. We are more Thatcher than anyone else." In other words, just follow the Iron Lady's battle plan and march into the Oval Office.

The single most important tactical decision that flowed from this strategy was that regarding Clinton's vote to authorize the Iraq War. To admit that her Senate vote had been wrong would make her look indecisive and weak—that is, lacking in the masculine traits voters presumably demanded from their president. Under Penn's direction, Clinton expertly pulled off a textbook case of a woman running for executive office—circa 1990. As we have seen, continuously hammering on the message that a woman is strong and experienced is poorly suited to the contemporary voter's hunger for authenticity in their political leaders.

Behind the tactic of projecting strength was a more fundamental strategy, which was also mismatched with Clinton's actual personal strengths and appeal. The target audience, to Penn, was men. Sure, Clinton had enormous support among women and many men too, but when push came to shove, it was more important to placate a particular kind of man than it was to inspire a groundswell among women.

Even when the evidence starkly pointed in another direction, Penn remained consumed with the votes of men. The key moment for Clinton in 2008, remember, was the week between the Iowa caucus and the New Hampshire primary. Having come in third in Iowa, pundits were already writing Clinton's political obituary—as they would have done with any frontrunner in any year who did so poorly in such a key contest. In New Hampshire, Clinton was down in all the polls in the days leading up to the vote. But a last-minute surge of women, following a widely covered emotional moment in a New Hampshire diner, clinched it for her. (Although the media widely reported Clinton "cried," in fact she had become a little emotional.) To many within Clinton's circle, it appeared that she could cut into Obama's momentum if she would simply allow more of her true personality to show.

Instead, Penn argued in an eight-page March 5 campaign memo, although the "personal moment" in New Hampshire was "a wake-up call to women," white men were the key voters once it was down to a two-candidate race. (Edwards dropped out after the South Carolina primary.) In New Hampshire and Virginia, Penn claimed, white men had "defected in droves," and although Clinton's personal moments were "loved by our supporters," they were "not the kind of thing beer-drinking men would warm up to, and as such that did not get us any new votes. Weakness has been our downfall," he continued, "so the idea that this can be won all on smiles, emotions, and empathy is simply wrong." Penn went on to mock Obama's supporters and Obama himself. "Their image of Obama Camelot is simply nothing but campaign pitter-patter," and he recommended that at least half of Clinton's ads be "negative or implied negative." This election "is not about change, not about experience, but about leadership." Proving Clinton could "keep us safe as commander in chief" remained paramount. Keep in mind Penn was assessing the Democratic primary, where the most enthusiastic participants were opposed to the Iraq War and hoped to scale back American military adventurism. It was as if Penn had spent the Bush administration in a hermetically sealed chamber at his corporate public relations firm.

Within Hillary's campaign, the conflict over how she should present herself to voters was ongoing. Among her friends and long-time staff, as we've seen, Clinton is known as warm, funny, and the one who's always there for you with a birthday cake or a hospital visit. But in the media, she was being portrayed as cold and inauthentic—as we will shortly see, a persistent theme in Clinton coverage. Many on Clinton's team tried to budge Penn off his one-dimensional caricature of a woman commander in chief, but he was immovable. According to reports in multiple media outlets, Penn conducted his own polls but shared only the results, not the raw data, with the rest of the campaign team. His numbers silenced their warnings. That is, until Clinton fired him in late March for other reasons. But it was too late.

The commander-in-chief positioning was intimately related to another point left relatively unspoken in 2008: that Clinton was poised to make history as America's first woman president. To be or not to be a historic figure, that was the question that nagged unresolved, even as Clinton sat down with her speech writers to compose her concession speech. Ultimately, Clinton famously said, "Although we weren't able to shatter that highest, hardest glass ceiling this time, thanks to you, it's got about 18 million cracks in it."

Still, Clinton had at first objected when one of her advisers wrote an "18 million cracks" line into the draft, Amie Parnes and Jonathan Allen reported in their book, *HRC*. Clinton told her speech writers that her campaign "wasn't about being a woman," and she relented only after an advisor persuaded her that many of her supporters did indeed care about electing a woman president. The metaphor of the highest glass ceiling was as much about their aspirations, he said, as it was about Clinton's unprecedented achievement.

To be fair, Clinton was in a paradoxical situation in 2008. Consider how history must have shaped the Clinton campaign's assessment of her odds of victory. All forty-three American presidents and every major party nominee since George Washington had been a man. No woman had ever won a presidential primary in any state. Few people questioned that women faced a double standard, particularly about their capacity for executive leadership. Only thirteen women were CEOs of Fortune 500 companies. On the other side of the ledger, however, Clinton looked inevitable. She was a sitting United States senator and one half of the era's most talented political partnership. With Republican president George W. Bush's low approval rating and a badly faltering economy, every political science model predicted a Democratic victory in the 2008 election.

So was a Hillary Clinton presidency in 2008 improbable or inevitable? Unfortunately, we cannot wind back the clock and reenact history to see what might have happened had the first viable woman presidential candidate acted as though voters already believed she was tough enough for the job. Still, we can reach a reasonable conclusion from the evidence.

Clinton sent the wrong message for the time, and the source of that fundamental error was Penn's stubborn belief that men applied a double standard to women candidates for high executive office.

Hillary Clinton lost her 2008 bid to become president in large part because she did not make the case for the historic significance of a woman president—until it was too late. Her actions since suggested that she would not make the same mistake twice. The main reason things could turn out better for Clinton in 2016 is because of her reboot at the State Department, where she acted without apology on her lifelong dedication to women's empowerment. It was almost as if Clinton's loss liberated her to return to her authentic self.

I MET MELANNE Verveer on a gray and icy morning in early March at her Georgetown University office, where she leads the Institute for Women, Peace, and Security. Arrayed around the Georgian townhouse that houses the institute were photos of Verveer with Madeleine Albright, Hillary Clinton, Laura Bush, Condoleezza Rice, and her own family and awards from global women's organizations. Verveer, who was First Lady Clinton's chief of staff, served as U.S. ambassador for Global Women's Issues when Clinton headed the State Department.

"Secretary Clinton put a lot of emphasis on economic statecraft, that being so vital both to governance and to people's prospects in their countries. As well, as you know, it's a contributing factor to conflict if there is not economic opportunity," she said. Verveer noticed during her prep for the 2009 meeting of the twenty-one-nation Asia-Pacific Economic Cooperation that there was nothing on the agenda about women in the economy. Around that time, she continued, "I had stumbled across a statistic from the UN that said that upwards of $90 billion was lost annually in GDP in the region because the potential of women wasn't being tapped. It's a staggering, staggering amount."

The oversight was symptomatic of the second-tier status of women and gender issues. Verveer set about trying to change attitudes—to see, in her words, if "maybe we can move this baby down the tracks." And they did. By the time of the 2010 APEC meeting, the United States had moved women's economic participation into the discussion of Asian economic growth. She recalled, "One of the first men who came up to me—it was almost all men in the room—said, 'My goodness, you talked about economic growth.' And I thought, what did he think I would talk about? Probably he expected me to talk about a feminist framework of some kind."

Those skeptical responses sometimes devolved into downright condescension, as Clinton described it in her memoir. "In one *Washington Post* article about our efforts with women in Afghanistan, an unnamed senior administration official sniffed, 'Gender issues are going to have to take a backseat to other priorities. . . . There's no way we can be successful if we maintain every special interest and pet project. All those pet rocks in our rucksack were taking us down.' I wasn't surprised the official was afraid to be named making a comment like that. Melanne and I started calling her shop the Pet Rock Office and kept on working."

So to address that kind of old-school myopia, Verveer and Clinton unleashed on their diplomatic counterparts and colleagues a barrage of facts. Using data from the World Bank and private sector producers of research and data, they showed that women's economic participation was vital to a nation's bottom line. "It was a rather forceful case. You couldn't just sit there and say, 'Well, it's nice hear-ing from you, but we're important people and we deal with the econ-omy and we want to make a lot of progress,'" Verveer continued. At the 2010 APEC meeting, the participating nations adopted the San Francisco Declaration, which committed them to take action to tap the full economic potential of women in their nations.

"I think one of the biggest contributions we made, and in many ways I think this is a paradigm shift, was to recognize that we had to make our case in a way that will always be rights-based, that is foundational, that is something none of us will ever give up," Verveer reflected. "But we had to add to it with the data to make the case that it was the smart and effective thing to do. Many times working with my own colleagues—mostly, not all, male— my stance was always to say to them, 'I want to make you more effective. I want to make us—the United States—more effective in what we're doing. Whether we're doing it in Africa or we're doing it in Asia, or we're working on human rights or we're working on the economic issues, or we're working on conflict and stability. How do we become more effective if we bring in the perspective of women and the participation of women?' That began to galvanize people. Obviously, Secretary Clinton was deeply committed, they got that. But they also understood themselves that we had to bring in the other half of the population. We don't have the luxury. It is not optional. It is necessary if we're going to do our jobs and try to create the kind of world we all want to see."

Clinton's predecessors, of course, had addressed women's issues. Albright was the first to insist that peacemaking failed when half the population wasn't at the table, and to integrate attention to women into our diplomacy. During George W. Bush's presidency, Colin Powell and Rice had both continued Albright's legacy. But Clinton elevated it to an entirely different level. No one had ever made it, in her frequently used expression, "a cornerstone of American foreign policy." No secretary of state had ever expended so much time and effort on women. As the pet rock story suggests, focusing on the less powerful half of the world's population wasn't the most obvious way to win respect and praise from the foreign policy establishment.

"I think the value that Secretary Clinton brought was that very explicit recognition that these were central issues," Liesl Gerntholtz, director of the women's rights division at Human Rights Watch, said. "Not just in the U.S., but globally, they've always been treated as an add-on. Clinton said, 'Women's rights, child marriage, sexual matters,' I'm going to ask about all of these things. She brought them to the big table. Because she was the secretary of state of the United States of America, if she said, 'I want to talk about this,' no one was going to say, 'No. Can we talk about the real stuff?' At the highest levels, she was forcing people to engage with it."

Gerntholtz continued, "Obviously, Melanne had a profile, because behind her was Hillary Clinton. I think Melanne understood the importance of building the relationship with civil society and how to manage it. It's a tricky relationship, because sometimes we are your allies, sometimes we are yelling at you, sometimes we are trying to hold you accountable to what you said you were going to do, et cetera. I think both Hillary and Melanne were very skilled at managing that relationship." Gerntholtz was less impressed by what happened in the State Department after Clinton left. "Kerry has been disappointing for us. He certainly has not leveraged the platform she created for women. Joe Biden has been a much stronger supporter than Kerry has."

In the foyer of Verveer's office hung a framed front-page *Washington Post* article headlined CLINTON PUTS SPOTLIGHT ON WOMEN'S ISSUES. Reporter Mary Beth Sheridan accompanied Clinton to Kenya, South Africa, and other nations, and she asked the secretary why she spent so much of her time meeting with groups of women citizens around the world. Clinton answered, "It feeds my heart."

"So where did this all come from in terms of her own life?" Verveer said. "Clearly she was a professional woman. She was the first professional to be First Lady. It's a position you only inherit by virtue of your marriage, and when you're a professional and you know you can give back and make a difference—you have to work all of that out. Clearly she spent time in this space as a governor's wife, as a lawyer, as someone who in Arkansas made her contribution to education, health care, and other issues. But I think in terms of this global approach, what really happened was a metamorphosis of sorts—sort of an evolution—while she was First Lady. There were several events. Probably the most galvanizing was Beijing." Clinton's trip to China in 1995 to speak at the United Nations Fourth World Conference on Women marked a turning point in the international debate about gender equality. Verveer continued,

"And here we are twenty years since, trying to understand how far we've come, what it represented, and where we're going."

Ironically, Clinton almost never got there.

IN 1995, DELEGATIONS from 189 nations were to gather in Beijing, China, for the United Nations Fourth World Conference on Women. Clinton was slated to participate in the U.S. delegation, headed by secretary of state Madeleine Albright.

"It was enormously difficult for her to get to Beijing because we had all of these forces, those who said, 'Why is she going? It costs money,'" Verveer said. "We had forces that said, 'Oh, they're going to propound five genders there. It will be a ridiculously absurd, ideological agenda.' Others in the human rights community said, 'Oh, she can't go to China, they're a human rights violator.' It was very, very tough to get there."

Clinton was determined, however. She wrote in her first memoir, *Living History*, that Albright asked her, what do you want to accomplish? She answered, "I want to push the envelope as far as I can on behalf of women and girls . . . to strike the right balance between seeing women as victims of discrimination and seeing women as agents of change."

In September 1995, Hillary Clinton delivered a twenty-one-minute speech in Beijing. "If there is one message that echoes forth from this conference, let it be that human rights are women's rights and women's rights are human rights, once and for all," she said, in a line that has become a rallying cry for women around the globe. As Clinton wrote, that idea was "obvious and undeniable but nonetheless too long unsaid on the world stage." In many ways, the themes of the speech prefigured what she would put into practice fifteen years later as secretary of state. "The advancement of women and the achievement of equality between women and men are a matter of human rights and a condition for social justice and should not be seen in isolation as a women's issue. They are the only way to build a sustainable, just, and developed society. Empowerment of women and equality between women and men are prerequisites for achieving political, social, economic, cultural, and environmental security among all peoples."

Veteran reporter Andrea Mitchell covered Beijing. During a 2014 public appearance with senator Kirsten Gillibrand, Mitchell recalled the atmosphere Clinton faced. "There was such pressure from the male foreign policy establishment, the White House, and State Department against the First Lady making news on a foreign trip—in Beijing no less. There was so much hostility against the delegation. It was a really difficult moment for her, but she just stood up and did it."

Clinton's Beijing speech was greeted with wild enthusiasm. The next day Clinton and the U.S. delegation drove forty miles to the small town where 26,000 members of nongovernmental organizations—the feminists, that is—had been shunted off to where they would make less trouble. As they drove up in a driving rain, thousands of people were already inside the hall where Clinton was slated to speak, and Chinese police were roughly treating the hundreds more outside who wanted to get in. Meanwhile, the agreement on measures to advance gender equity was nearly scuttled by the Vatican's opposition to birth control. Nevertheless, the participating nations agreed to an ambitious plan of action, which in many nations has resulted in measurable progress on women's rights.

Verveer recalled, "One of the most powerful people in the world—by virtue of being married to the most powerful person in the most powerful country—comes and says that these are violations of human rights, at a time when women's rights were still marginal to human rights, not chiseled in international law, and the reaction was deafening. I think that reaction certainly impacted me. Certainly, it had a profound impact on her. It really put her on a course to do as much as she could to take on these issues, use the time that she had in the position she was in to try to have greater impact, to put a spotlight—not in a negative way but in a positive way—on what's working, whether it's girls education, or microcredit, or the kinds of investments we were making. To constantly make that case about the difference it would make and basically educating, without seeming to be a schoolmarm, leaders who would listen to her."

It is not an exaggeration to say that in Beijing, HRC changed the global dialogue on women's rights.

As Clinton retired from Obama's cabinet, she had never in her life been more popular with ordinary Americans. She won praise from some for her visionary leadership. For instance, *New York Times* columnist and coauthor of *Half the Sky* Nicholas Kristof wrote, "Clinton understood that impact and leverage in 21st-century diplomacy often come by addressing poverty, the environment, education, and family planning. . . . She understood that educating girls isn't a frilly 'soft' issue, but a way to transform a country to make it less hospitable to extremists. No one argued more presciently that women's rights are security issues."

Yet some foreign policy hands mocked Clinton for her focus on women's empowerment—one called it "planetary humanism." Many pundits damned her with faint praise, saying she was competent but not one of the all-time greats. Beltway oddsmakers dismissed Secretary Clinton's pro-women initiatives as nothing more than campaign theatrics, dress rehearsals for her next performance on the campaign trail. Hillary and her team at State saw it differently. In *Hard Choices*, Clinton wrote, "It was no coincidence that the places where women's lives were most undervalued line up with the parts of the world most plagued by instability, conflict, extremism, and poverty. This was a point lost on many of the men working across Washington's foreign policy establishment, but over the years I came to view it as one of the most compelling arguments for why standing up for women and girls was not just the right thing to do but also smart and strategic."

"I think in the end she will be proven to have really made a difference," Verveer said. "Really, it's hard to understand in the 21st century, even with all of the horrors that are being perpetrated, how you can write off half the population of the world and expect to succeed. If you look at the Arab development report, for example, all the countries on the bottom of that list are there because women are not participating economically, politically, or are as educated as they need to be.

"Now, you've got forces today in the world—whether it's Boko Haram or it's ISIS—whose first desire seems to be to hold women back, and a girl with a book is a very dangerous weapon, obviously. But I think we are recognizing that this is a critical issue of our times, and we can no longer give it short shrift, put it on the margins, say, 'Oh, it's a women's issue. Let's tackle it after we do all the important things.' No. This belongs with the important things."

OUTSIDE ROYCE HALL at the University of California, Los Angeles, where Hillary Clinton was due to speak a couple of hours later, the line of students stretched around the neighboring buildings. Vanessa Perez and Crystal Boceta were ecstatic after just scoring tickets. Several weeks before Clinton's March 2014 speech, the university had announced it would give out hundreds of free tickets to students, but the demand had overwhelmed the supply. "The first time we lined up there was a stampede," Boceta told me.

"Yeah, people started lining up at 12:00 AM. They hadn't like even brushed their teeth," their friend Zach Rosa, a Bruin Democrat, said. He described how some students had tried to outfox security guards with fake signs and pilfered badges. By 5:00 AM, six unofficial lines snaked around the ticket office building. Some time around sunrise, upwards of 1,000 students rushed the office. "I got trampled," eighteen-year-old Natalie Kirsten told me. "It was like Times Square on New Year's Eve," UCLA College Republican William Gleason, wearing khakis, a striped tie, and a navy blazer to Clinton's speech, said. "I know, I've been there." Ultimately a lottery was held, but the students in line before the speech hadn't gotten lucky, and they were trying again. Clarice Chan said, "I would compare the lottery to the California education system. No matter how long you wait, how hard you work, it is totally random!"

Ultimately nearly 2,000 students got in to hear Clinton speak. Although Clinton would not formally enter the 2016 presidential race until a year later, she field-tested themes for her expected presidential run and charmingly dispensed advice to the rapturous students on how to change the world. Her keynote address for UCLA's annual Luskin award focused on what she called America's "youth unemployment crisis—because I think that's what it is" and gave signs that long before anyone imagined that Bernie Sanders might run for president as a Democrat, Clinton already intended to run as a progressive.

"A particular challenge here at home that is directly relevant to the students here—and to so many worried young people who are not in college—is this: How will we make sure that the young women and men of the millennial generation and those who follow after will find good jobs, with rising incomes, in an economy that produces inclusive prosperity here at home and increasingly across the world? A whole generation is being deprived not only of the right, but also the opportunity that frankly those of us in prior generations took for granted," Clinton said. Underscoring that she wasn't just talking about college students, their debt, and their job prospects, but more broadly about their generation, she continued, "But let's not kid ourselves. Not far from here are people who feel despair. They attend schools that are not preparing them. Young people, not too different from the students here, for whom a 21st-century economy seems like a distant, unreachable abstraction. They want to participate. They want to learn and work and contribute. But they need a fighting chance."

After the speech I spoke with more students, and the verdict was virtually unanimous: Clinton's words resonated with them. "It was amazing to see a women of that stature, of that power, care about youth employment, with all she deals with," Liliana Kroll, a UCLA senior, who had volunteered for Obama in 2012, said. "It made me feel recognized and acknowledged. I know that seems petty compared to what's happening in Ukraine, but it's virtually impossible to find a job." Asseret Frausteo described Clinton as "my biggest role model" and signed up with Ready for Hillary organizers who had been canvassing the waiting lines. I caught up with Perez and Boceta. Boceta found Clinton inspiring and was impressed that she had not given a cliché answer when she was asked about student debt. "We're all worried about it," she said. Perez agreed, "Income inequality is a huge issue. Just look at what is happening a couple miles away from here."

A few weeks after Clinton's UCLA speech, protests erupted throughout the state over a nearly 25 percent tuition hike proposed by University of California chancellor Janet Napolitano.

THE UCLA SPEECH was Clinton's first public event in months. That morning a story had come out that at a private Democratic Party fund-raiser the previous night, Clinton had likened Russian leader Vladimir Putin to Hitler, and the political press was chewing on the morsel of the day. Dozens of reporters, photographers, and

TV crews were staked out in Royce Hall. When Clinton took the stage, the former secretary of state put aside her prepared speech to comment first on Russia's recent intervention in Crimea. In a wide-ranging, policy-heavy disquisition on the Ukraine-Russian conflict, its history, and the role of the international community, she underscored her support for the Obama administration's "very careful" multilateral diplomatic efforts.

And she called Russian president Vladimir Putin "a tough guy with a thin skin." In the flurry of postspeech coverage, hardly a story mentioned that Clinton had talked about youth employment. No one thought the student's enthusiasm for Clinton merited notice. Nazis and thin-skinned autocrats were all too delicious for reporters to resist.

A year later in spring 2015, the media still had other things on its mind. Clinton was giving speech after speech on women's empowerment, but you would have been hard-pressed to know that. On the 20th anniversary of the Beijing conference, Clinton spoke at the United Nations in New York. "It has never been a better time in history to be born female. But you know there would be a *but*. We're not there yet," she said. "The United States has a responsibility to make our own country a beacon for what is possible, whether that is equal pay for equal work, or encouraging more women to pursue careers in STEM fields, or defending a woman's right to make her own reproductive decisions."

Certainly, one role of the press is to act as a public watchdog. But the media's stance toward Clinton seemed to be invested with a surfeit of emotion. "Can Twitter Solve Hillary Clinton's

Relatability Problem?" the *Atlantic* asked. The *Daily Beast* pronounced, "Hillary's Got a Millennial Problem." (As we'll see later, the polls of millennials contradict that assertion.) Renowned columnist Frank Rich wrote about Hillary, "What is worse than being depicted as a bloodthirsty power-monger with a filthy mouth? Depicting yourself so blandly that no one cares." At the EMILY's List 30th anniversary event, as Clinton accepted her award from the group by starting with the obligatory thanks, one reporter gestured dramatically, twisting her arms and shoulders wide in disbelief to catch the attention of other reporters, so they could share in her outrage. Granted, it was the same day the *New York Times* broke the story about Clinton's exclusive use of a private email that would dog her for the next many months. But during the long parade of famous politicians who spoke before Clinton, the reporters covering the event had rarely looked up from their computer screens or interacted with each other. Was it surprising that Hillary was delivering a stump-like speech from a teleprompter? Truly, it was impossible to figure out what Clinton's offense was.

A week later, the *New York Times* strongly insinuated that the press would just have to anoint itself Clinton's challenger, since it did not look as though she would have a serious opponent in the Democratic primary. (Martin O'Malley wasn't gaining traction, independent Bernie Sanders hadn't yet announced his candidacy, and Joe Biden hadn't yet made up his mind about what he would do.) Reporter Patrick Healy wrote, "How she and her emerging campaign organization react to critical articles and unwelcome surprises from the news media, as well as to questions posed by journalists in Democratic primary debates, will reveal her strengths and weaknesses as a candidate in some of the same ways that running against Mr. Obama did in 2007 and 2008."

The media's self-coronation reached its apogee in *New York* magazine just days before Clinton formally announced her candidacy in April. "The danger to the Clinton campaign, at this early stage, is not that she might slip in a debate or never quite muster an adequate explanation for deleting emails as secretary of state. It's that she might not have the ability to break through the cynicism and noise of our political circus and deliver a striking, clear message. In other words, she might never figure out how to get journalists to stop writing articles like this one," Jason Zengerle wrote. "Journalists love badass Hillary—the one who checks her BlackBerry with her sunglasses on. But as much as they (and she) might wish otherwise, that Clinton is a rare sight. And covering the regular Clinton is often a drag. She's been around too long, and reporters know her story too well, to get much of a thrill from it." The article was headlined IS HILLARY CLINTON ANY GOOD AT RUNNING FOR PRESIDENT?

As Zengerle noted, the dysfunctional relationship between Clinton and the media had a long history, and it was particularly fraught in New York, the nation's media capital as well as the state that Clinton had represented during her eight years in the Senate. Karen Finney was Clinton's traveling press secretary in her first Senate race. "When we were in upstate New York it was a very different experience than in the city. City reporters were much harsher, much more political, much more kind of trying to see if they could trip her up on something. We would always try to get the down-state reporters to come upstate with us, to see that this is a woman who knows farming issues, who really understands rural issues and economic development issues." On one upstate campaign stop, when a couple of reporters from New York City had joined them, Finney recalled, "We went to a farm and Hillary literally got up on top of a milk box and she had a megaphone, and she started talking about the dairy compact, and these guys were like, 'How does she know about that stuff?' Hello, Arkansas?! I mean, a lot of these issues she's familiar with because of coming from a rural state. We would put extra time on the schedule for rope lines, because one of the things Hillary liked was that she could actually talk to people that way. People would come away and they'd say, 'She's so nice.' I'd think, I'm so glad you see what I get to see. I think that broke down a lot of the those biases against her among people who didn't really know her."

On the eve of Clinton's formal announcement in April 2015 that she was running for president, after a month of nonstop terrible media coverage, Clinton's approval rating stood at a healthy 53 percent. In early head-to-head polls, she ran 15 points ahead of the two leading Republicans. Democrats favored Clinton over Elizabeth Warren (who would decline to run) by a 52-point margin. The May *New York Times*/CBS News poll found that 82 percent of Democrats and 72 percent of liberals believed that Clinton "shares the values that most Americans try to live by."

But the drip, drip, drip of negative coverage, particularly regarding her email server, eroded support for Clinton over the summer.

Nate Silver of *FiveThirtyEight* analyzed Clinton's media coverage and found that negative stories about her were among the top three stories of the day for a total of twenty-nine days over just a two-month period, while only one day in that period featured a positive headline about Clinton among the top stories. Silver wrote in mid-September, "Candidates can get caught—or entrap themselves—in self-reinforcing cycles of negative media attention and declining poll numbers. Hillary Clinton looks like she's stuck in one of these ruts right now."

At the same time, Vermont independent senator Bernie Sanders was striking a chord with white progressive Democrats with his rousing attacks on Wall Street, the big banks, and big money's power over politics. Vice president Joe Biden continued to flirt with a run, egged on by pundits and political reporters who desperately wanted a more competitive and interesting primary to cover. Five months into Clinton's 2016 campaign, her approval rating had dropped dramatically and polls showed the race tightening. Although early polls are unreliable predictors of far-off elections, Sanders seemed to pose a real threat to her in the two earliest contests, Iowa and New Hampshire.

But the first Democratic candidates' debate on October 12, 2015, turned things around for Hillary, as well as showed a party united on core progressive values. Sanders brought down the house and won the affection of Democrats across the spectrum when he came to Clinton's defense on the email controversy. "I think the secretary is right," he said. "And that is, I think the American people are sick and tired of hearing about your damn emails." The media nearly universally pronounced Clinton the debate winner, praising her as "knowledgeable, relaxed, funny, totally relatable and, most importantly, presidential," in *Washington Post* columnist Chris Cilliza's words. Politico's headline blasted, CLINTON CRUSHED IT. In perhaps the most hilarious tongue-in-cheek assessment, columnist Dana Milbank wrote, "She was, in short, a man among boys."

Within the week, Clinton's status as the frontrunner had stabilized with a roughly 15- to 20-point national lead over Sanders and close to 30-point lead over the still-waffling Biden. Nine days after the debate, Biden called a press conference. With Obama at his side, Biden thanked Obama for lending him the Rose Garden and announced that he would not run for president. By that time, polls of New Hampshire, the first primary state, indicated that Clinton had narrowed her deficit there against Sanders. With Biden out, Clinton's support among Democrats nationally neared 60 percent.

It seemed that reporters, pundits, and election handicappers had underestimated Clinton—as they so often do with women candidates in general and Clinton in particular. That wasn't surprising to Mikulski. "The national media tends to discuss that which is not important," she told me, with Olympian detachment. "No really, the national media discusses what's important to them—which is conflict, crisis, and cranky. If it's got one of those three C's, then they go for it."

MEANWHILE, THROUGHOUT ALL the premature obituaries in the summer and early fall of 2015, Clinton had spent her days doing what presidential candidates do: meeting with voters in the early primary states and raising money to fund a campaign. Making a campaign visit to the early primary state, Clinton pledged to the South Carolina Democratic Women's Council that she would fight for equal pay, paid family leave, and a raise to the minimum wage. About her Republican opponents who denied the very fact of the gender wage gap, she quipped to applause, "What century are they living in?" Even when she flexed her populist muscle, as she often did on the trail, Clinton subtly cued gender, by noting that the twenty-five most highly paid hedge fund managers earned more than all the nation's kindergarten teachers combined—"My new least favorite statistic," she called it.

In Clinton's first major economic speech in July 2015, there were echoes of Beijing, as she highlighted the cost for women and their families of the nation's inadequate public policies for parents and children. Women's labor force participation had plateaued, which had resulted in the United States plunging from seventh to nineteenth place in the world. She explained, "Studies show that nearly a third of this decline relative to other countries is because they're expanding family-friendly policies like paid leave and we are not. We should be making it easier for Americans to be both good workers and good parents and caregivers. Women who want to work should be able to do so without worrying every day about how they're going to take care of their children or what will happen if a family member gets sick." Clinton told attendees at an early fund-raiser that she was going to put women's reproductive rights at the forefront of her campaign.

Nothing showed the evolution from Clinton '08 to Hillary '16 more than when Clinton joyously played the gender card. After Republican Senate leader Mitch McConnell said Clinton couldn't win the presidency by playing the "gender card alone"—a remark meant to insinuate there was no substance in the discussion of a woman president beyond crass identity politics—Clinton retorted: "There is a gender card being played in this campaign. It's played every time Republicans vote against giving women equal pay, deny families access to affordable child care or family leave, refuse to let women make decisions about their health or have access to free contraception. These aren't just women's issues, they are economic issues that drive growth and affect all Americans." "Here's our #gendercard," her campaign tweeted, with an image of bullet points for affordable child care, paid family leave, earned sick days, and equal pay.

I asked Center for American Progress head and Clinton's 2008 domestic policy chief Neera Tanden what she thought were the pros and cons of raising women's issues on the campaign trail. "I don't see a big con," she replied. "I think the culture has changed a little. You see it in social media. There has been a real rise of awareness—with the tweets from everyday sexism or the viral videos. I think there is greater awareness because the economic challenges have made it more clear." She mentioned a recent survey showing that men weren't turned off when candidates talked about supporting equal pay for women. "They understand that their family's economic success depends on how women are treated," she said.

"I started working for Hillary in the fall of 1997, and my first big job was working on President Clinton's child care initiative, which Hillary was kind of the architect of—she helped drive it. When she was First Lady, she was the point person in the administration pushing on all of these issues. She was the engine behind the child care initiative. She was the one talking about after-school care and all of these issues that bring the perspective of what it's like to be a working mother to the country's public policy debates." Tanden continued, "These are issues she's been concerned about her whole career. She addressed them even though no one was particularly pushing her to. My hope is that this time around the public demand will match her own interest and create a dynamic in which if she wins, she can have strong support to actually enact real policy change. I think that will be a foundational change."

What really makes the difference is a budding feeling that Hillary is a historic candidate, that her candidacy embodied the aspirations of American women—and not just feminists of the older generation.

At the end of the first quarter of fund-raising, Clinton's campaign reported that women made up more than 60 percent of its donors. That was noteworthy. Typically women represent just over a quarter of all political donors, according to the Center for Responsive Politics. I asked former Los Angeles city controller and Clinton administration official Wendy Greuel, who was spearheading a women's fund-raising drive in California for Clinton, what was motivating this surge in women donors. "I think there are three categories," she said. "One is women who were supportive of Hillary in 2008 and have just been itching to get back into it to help her get elected. There's a second group of women who say she is the most qualified candidate that's ever run for president. And then there is a third group who says, 'You know, it's time for a woman to be president. It's just amazing that it's 2015 and we haven't reached that yet.' And they want to make sure that it happens in 2016."

"Everything has changed since 2007," EMILY's List president Schriock told me. "As I travel around, there is a real interest, particularly among young women, to see women in leadership positions. They don't really get why this hasn't happened. Like hello! It's sort of a no-brainer. It's time. Our research is showing us that young women, in a really powerful way, want to see this happen. It doesn't necessarily make it the reason to vote for somebody. But it's definitely an inspiring factor that's going to energize folks to get more engaged."

"I personally think Hillary Clinton would make a stupendous president," NARAL president Ilyse Hogue said. "We would be lucky as a country to have her. She's passionate, she's skilled, she's proven her mettle on the entirety of issues that we face. I think there is enormous enthusiasm." The mood among Democrats had shifted since the divisive 2008 primary, she believed. "We're seeing a move toward 'Okay, it's time for a woman president.'"

"It absolutely is time," Hogue went on. "I think having a woman president, generally, and Hillary specifically, would do a lot to set the tone around policies that match where real women's lives are now. There is a symbolic nature to a woman's presidency—that we as a nation have moved into the 21st century. There are countries all over the world that have had women running them for a long time. But I also think the sheer experience of having grown up as a woman and a mother in a country where we have some of the most regressive policies in the world opens up this perspective at the top about how half of the country lives."

Gerntholtz, who has worked on global women's rights and empowerment since Bill Clinton was president—she served on South Africa's postapartheid Commission for Gender Equality— had a somewhat different take. "For me, it's striking that it's still a topic of conversation here that you might have a woman president. In some ways, the U.S. is really way behind on the curve."

Women have held the top political post in one-third of the world's nations. Ten of the sixteen democracies in the G20 have chosen women to head their governments. India, Pakistan, Israel, and the United Kingdom are all nuclear powers, and all have elected women prime ministers.

Why is America so far behind? It's our history.

Chapter 6

A BRIEF HISTORY OF WOMEN'S POLITICAL INEQUALITY

"A woman in politics is like a monkey in a toy shop. She can do no good, and may do harm."

—UNITED STATES SENATOR, NEW HAMPSHIRE, 1814

VICTORIA WOODHULL, THE first woman to run for president, spent the night of the 1872 presidential election in New York City's Ludlow Street Jail. She would remain there for the next thirty days, unable to raise the $16,000 bail to defend herself against federal obscenity charges for revealing a sex scandal involving the nation's most famous preacher, Henry Ward Beecher.

Granted, spending Election Day in jail did not affect Woodhull's electoral chances. A beautiful divorcée who practiced free love, conducted séances, and published the first U.S. translation of Karl Marx's *Communist Manifesto*, Woodhull was the candidate of an

obscure third party that hadn't qualified for the ballot in a single
state. President Ulysses S. Grant was reelected in a landslide.

ONE HUNDRED AND forty years after Woodhull's symbolic run,
America still has not elected a woman president. Who is to blame?

The roots of our presidential gender gap stretch all the way
back to the Founding Fathers. When Thomas Jefferson wrote in
the Declaration of Independence that "all men are created equal,"
he did not in fact intend to include women. His fellow Founding
Fathers, likewise, passed over in silence the question of women's
political rights. The U.S. Constitution, written in secret by fifty-
five men behind closed curtains in the summer of 1787, spelled out
exactly how "we the people" would govern ourselves. It included
not a word on women's right to self-government.

Indeed Jefferson, America's third president, held remarkable
ideas about the "good ladies," whom he believed were "too wise to
wrinkle their foreheads with politics." Instead, he wrote, American
women valued "the tender and tranquil amusement of domestic
life," and "were contented to soothe and calm the minds of their
husbands returning ruffled from political debate." Jefferson left
6,700 books to the Library of Congress and founded the University
of Virginia but once said that he had never given a thought to wom-
en's education. He refused to appoint women to federal offices when
he was president, saying it would be "an innovation for which the
public is not prepared, nor am I."

As every American schoolchild knows, colonial Americans
declared independence from England, fought the American

Revolution, and created a new republic to recover individual rights to freedom and self-government. But in the eyes of the law, a woman ceased to exist as an individual once she got married. Under the English common law doctrine of coverture, she was legally dependent on her husband and could not own property, keep her own earnings, or make contracts. In the eyes of philosophy, women were inferior. At the mercy of their emotions, women were unfit to exercise political rights. The creator made women "weak and timid, in comparison with man, and had thus placed her under his control, as well as under his protection," a delegate to Virginia's constitutional convention said. In other words, freedom for man meant the consent to be governed. Freedom for woman meant the consent to be married, and once she did, her actual freedom vanished.

American patriots added their own peculiar gloss to these legal and philosophical ideas that they had brought with them from Europe. The infant republic, surrounded on all sides by enemies, depended for its survival on women's submission to the biological division of labor. John Adams insisted that the family was "the foundation of national morality," and ignored his wife Abigail Adams's call to "remember the ladies." (Abigail's famous letter included a pointed criticism of Virginian slaveholders as well.) John spent most of the war away while Abigail, alone, managed their farm and educated their four children—including John Quincy, America's sixth president—all while surviving British attacks, a smallpox epidemic, and an outbreak of dysentery that killed her mother. Benjamin Franklin, one of the most renowned scientists and Enlightenment thinkers of the age, believed that "every man that is really a man is master of his own family." A good wife consented to this arrangement with "a becoming obedience." It's worth noting that Deborah Franklin, his wife, was his business partner. On another occasion, Franklin wrote a patriotic satire in which he likened women who refused to bear children to a British troop of pig castrators dispatched across the Atlantic to exercise their art on American men.

IT'S HARDLY THAT the Founding Fathers didn't know better.

In 1776, when Abigail Adams accused her husband John and his fellow patriots of hypocrisy—"whilst you are proclaiming peace and good-will to men, emancipating nations, you insist upon retaining an absolute power over wives"—she might have been a step ahead of her time. But by the early 1790s and Washington's presidency, "the rights of women are no longer strange sounds to an American ear," one congressman wrote. "They are now heard as familiar terms in every part of the United States."

The expression *women's rights* was made popular in the United States by Mary Wollstonecraft, a London political activist and writer, in her 1792 essay, "A Vindication of the Rights of Woman." Wollstonecraft's essay was widely known and circulated in the United States. In fact, more Americans owned a copy of "The Rights of Woman" than owned patriot leader Thomas Paine's "The Rights of Man." Following Wollstonecraft's example, Americans wrote many poems, plays, and essays exploring women's rights. (Like many women before 20th-century advances in medicine,

Wollstonecraft died of complications from giving birth, just seven years after her famous pamphlet was published. The daughter who survived, Mary Shelley, grew up to write the novel *Frankenstein*.) In "On the Equality of the Sexes," one of the most influential patriot writers, Judith Sargent Murray, wrote, "The 'Rights of Women' begin to be understood. Our young women are forming a new era in female history."

Plenty of men and women on both sides of the Atlantic were perfectly able to see the gap between America's stated ideals and the reality. A nation supposedly founded on self-evident truths about human equality was giving political rights to some people while depriving others of their most basic human rights. (That recognition, in fact, catalyzed the first movement in world history to abolish slavery, and during the Revolutionary era all the northern states set in motion the end of slavery.) One important legal thinker could not help but point out that women were taxed without consent, like "aliens, children, idiots, and lunatics." Even teenagers debated women's political rights. In a 1793 graduation speech, one girl accused her fellow countrymen of the sort of behavior that had gotten the British kicked out of the colonies in the first place: "The Church, the Bar, and the Senate are shut against us. Who shut them? Man; despotic man, first made us incapable of the duty, and then forbid us the exercise." One New York woman wrote about the "curious fact that a republic which avows equality of right as its first principle persists in an ungenerous exclusion of the female sex from its executive department." A sympathetic character in one play called *The Rights of Woman* says, "This constitution is unjust and absurd. Lawmakers thought as little of comprehending us in their code of liberty, as if we were pigs, or sheep."

To be sure, the belief that women were inferior to men remained common in early America. However, it is not quite accurate to say the Founding Fathers were merely men of their era who shared its prejudices and couldn't have been expected to embrace women's equality. After all, they were men of the Enlightenment who valued rational inquiry. And they were men of unusual talent, creativity, and intellect. Franklin was considered throughout the capitals of Europe to be one of the world's leading scientists. General George Washington defeated the world's most powerful empire with a ragtag volunteer army. Jefferson was the president of the American Philosophical Society. And really, with so many people talking about women's rights, you didn't have to be Galileo or Einstein to discover that women had the same natural right to liberty, equality, and the pursuit of happiness. Thanks to Mary Wollstonecraft, Judith Sargent Murray, and untold numbers of Americans whose names are lost to us, anyone who cared to listen could consider its truth.

ON THE OTHER hand, despite what the Declaration of Independence said, a good portion of America's Founding Fathers did not in any modern sense believe that all people were equal. George Washington, John Adams, Alexander Hamilton, and the men who joined them in the Federalist Party were absolutely certain that government should be run by society's natural leaders. Themselves.

Indeed, Washington and Adams spent the weeks leading up to America's first presidential inauguration absorbed with how best to impress the common people with their own superiority. Vice President Adams felt tremendous anxiety as he pondered how to address George Washington. What about "His Most Benign Highness," Adams thought. Washington preferred "His High Mightiness, the President of the United States and Protector of Their Liberties." The Senate split the difference and recommended that Washington and all future presidents be called "His Highness the President of the United States of America, and Protector of Their Liberties." While the Senate met behind closed doors and kept no transcript of the debate, Virginia congressman James Madison— America's fourth POTUS—became alarmed. After all, America had just won a revolution against another King George. Madison maneuvered to have the House vote on calling the president, simply, the president of the United States, and the Senate was stuck with the decision.

The debate has a distinctly *Monty Python and the Holy Grail* feel about it. But as the eminent historian Gordon Wood observed, "Although America becoming a monarchy might seem absurd, in 1789 it did not seem so at all." When Washington won unanimous election, for example, his future secretary of war wished him a "reign long and happy over us" and told him, "You are now a King, under a different name." Washington typically traveled to public events like a European monarch, riding in a cream-colored coach pulled by four white horses accompanied by servants wearing livery uniform. Adams—who never fought in

the Continental Army—wore a sword when he presided over the
Senate. In Europe, a sword was a symbol that you were a titled
aristocrat.

These kind of inegalitarian ideas were reflected in state laws
about who could and could not vote. The year Adams became president, after Washington's two terms in office, only 23 percent of the
American population was eligible to vote. Even a white man—if
he belonged to the wrong religion, or didn't own enough property, or didn't pay taxes—might not be enfranchised, depending
on which state he lived in. In other words, women weren't the only
ones excluded from political rights.

That changed over the next thirty years. By the time America's
sixth president, John Quincy Adams (Adams's son) was defeated by
Andrew Jackson, nearly all white men had gained the right to vote
and hold office. If the heart of democracy is rule by the people, by
the 1830s the United States was the most democratic nation on the
face of the earth.

However, expanding the vote to all white men went hand in
iron glove with taking rights away from others.

Consider New Jersey. The state's 1776 constitution enfranchised all "free inhabitants" who owned at least fifty pounds worth
of property, and free black men and unmarried women who owned
property did in fact vote. Was that just sloppy drafting? No, the
legislature later demonstrated, when it added the words *he or
she* to a bill, to clarify that the state constitution had intended to
enfranchise women who owned property and paid taxes. A report
in a state newspaper confirmed that the legislature acted "from a

principle of justice, deeming it right that every free person who pays a tax should have a vote."

So some widows and single women in New Jersey were able to and did vote. President Jefferson's party in New Jersey put an end to it. In 1807, Jefferson's Democratic-Republicans accused their opponents, the Federalists, of dressing up as women so that they could vote more than once. In the end, the Federalists and the Democratic-Republicans struck an ugly little deal. Federalists agreed to disfranchise propertied women in exchange for Democratic-Republicans agreeing to disfranchise free blacks. (Free blacks tended to vote for the Jeffersonian party in New Jersey.) Together, Democratic-Republican and Federalist white men passed a law restricting the vote to white male tax-paying citizens.

As the New Jersey case shows, some free blacks and some women had the right to vote in the early republic. But nearly all the new constitutions adopted during the Jacksonian era's expansion of the suffrage explicitly said the right belonged to "males," "white male citizens," or "white men." In the new, more democratic constitutions, not a single state enfranchised women, even though women's legal and political rights were discussed at the constitutional conventions. Several states disfranchised free black men.

At the same time, day-to-day politics became more thoroughly a world of men, by men, and for men. On election days, party leaders marshaled their voters, who then marched military-style to the polls with their rifles over their shoulders. Riots were commonplace and everyone drank. A lot.

This was no place for women.

EVEN AS THE founding generation drew the line against the Rights of Woman, women's contributions to the Revolution left their mark, and new ideas about gender took root. Americans in the decades between the Revolution and the Civil War came to understand their society as if it were made up of two distinctive ecosystems, each with its own natural laws and dominant being. Politics, the market, and the military, where competition and conflict prevailed, were the domains of man, the competitive and self-interested sex. The home, the nursery, and the church were the domains of woman, the nurturing and benevolent sex. Because of women's biological connection to child-rearing, women came to be seen as the selfless and morally superior sex.

In other words, many outdated stereotypes—that men are biologically driven to compete and women are biologically driven to nurture; that women's place is in the home and men are naturally suited to be public leaders; that women are more spiritual, more peaceful, more virtuous—took root during the first decades of our nation's history.

Such Mars-Venus thinking rings harsh in a 21st-century ear. Indeed, these ideas have been the very pillars of women's inequality in politics and the economy. Only in the last few decades have they been toppled, and resistance to gender equality in some quarters remains. Still, this cult of domesticity (as historians have called it) was a decided improvement over the colonial past—when men did hold the power of patriarchy in a legal sense and women were occasionally burned to death as witches.

Not only did women gain substantial new powers in the home in the early republic, but together these ideas about women's moral superiority, selflessness, and natural connection to children led to a new political role for women. True, no American woman could vote or hold office, but they had a more important calling: to raise their sons to be good American patriots and citizens. Metaphorically speaking, women were mothers of the republic. The infant nation desperately needed them in the home with their sons and daughters, molding and educating future American leaders and future American mothers, not in the voting booth or in Congress.

IN 1829, HARRIET Beecher Stowe organized the first women's petition to Congress in the nation's history. Stowe was outraged at President Andrew Jackson's plan to expel several Indian nations from their home states. Explaining herself in religious terms and disavowing a political motive—women "have nothing to do with any struggle for power"—Stowe spearheaded an effort that brought in 1,500 signatures against Indian Removal.

By this time, traditional gendered notions of women's essential role as wives and mothers had erased almost all trace of the Revolutionary era's debates about women's rights. Yet in a nation founded on high ideals about human potential and awash in religious fervor, the belief in women's moral superiority could be politically potent. Social reform movements spread like prairie grass throughout the free states in the early 19th century, and women made up the foot soldiers in most of them. As historian Rosemarie

Zagarri noted, women's activism was "an extension of their feminine role, not a challenge to it."

Women's moralistic cast of mind was especially congenial to the movement to abolish slavery. As abolitionist William Lloyd Garrison saw it, participating in party politics was tantamount to a "pact with the devil," given that both parties allowed slaveholders to dictate what could be said or done in the United States. By the late 1830s, abolitionism was the number one reform cause in the Northern free states. Tens of thousands of ordinary women participated in the movement, while individual women such as Sojourner Truth, Harriet Tubman, Abby Kelley, Angelina and Sarah Grimké, and Lucy Stone emerged as nationally recognized movement leaders. Such higher, selfless motives could spur women to violate gender conventions. In 1838, Angelina Grimké became the first American woman to address a legislature. And the moral stance of purity and virtue should not be confused with a lack of courage. When Abby Kelley became the first woman to speak at a mixed-sex abolitionist meeting in 1838, a pro-slavery mob attacked the meeting with stones and torches and burned down the hall where they met.

Men welcomed women's labor for the abolitionist cause. Up to a point, that is. In 1840, a number of men walked out in protest at the American Anti-Slavery Society convention when a woman, Kelley, was elected to their committee. Later that year at the World Anti-Slavery Convention in London, American women delegates Elizabeth Cady Stanton and Lucretia Mott were forced to sit behind a curtain so they could not be seen.

These sorts of experiences in the anti-slavery movement got wo-men thinking. Stanton and Mott returned home from London deter-mined to create a reform group to champion the rights of women. Women were circulating petitions to Congress, raising money for the cause, attending public meetings and rallies, giving speeches, and writing pamphlets and books—in short, doing everything men did in politics. Except, of course, voting and holding elective office.

"If I were to give free vent to all my pent-up wrath concerning the subordination of women, I might frighten you," abolitionist Lydia Maria Child wrote to Massachusetts senator Charles Sumner in the late 1840s. "Suffice it to say, either the theory of our govern-ment is false, or women have a right to vote."

In 1848, sixty-eight women and thirty-two men gathered in Seneca Falls, New York, for the first American women's rights convention. Stanton was already convinced that the right to vote was the key for "woman to be free, as man is free." The Seneca Falls Declaration of Sentiments reached back to America's found-ing ideal. "We hold these truths to be self-evident: that all men and women are created equal," it began, and closed with a full-throated demand for women's equal rights: "Now, in view of this entire disfranchisement of one-half the people of this country, their social and religious degradation . . . we insist that they have immediate admission to all the rights and privileges which belong to them as citizens of the United States."

American equal-rights feminism was born in the movement to abolish slavery. But abolitionism also reinforced the notion that women were the metaphorical mothers of the republic, as well as nourished the seed of an alternative claim about women's place in America's democracy. Women deserved a political voice not because they were equal to men, but because they were better than men. Women had little interest in competing on an equal footing in the political arena, so this line of thinking went. Rather, women would sweep in like Jesus to the Temple Mount, banishing the corrupt partisans and cleansing the seat of power of sin and sinners.

On one hand, the metaphor of women as mothers of the republic offered women leverage to influence the most critical public debates of their time. Women had no political rights, per se, but women spoke with moral and spiritual authority, and men had to listen. On the other hand, such zealotry about women's purity of purpose and moral superiority made them prone to interpret the inevitable give-and-take of politics in terms of good versus evil. These gendered ideas of virtue and purity ill-equipped women to compete on the partisan political playing field, the place where real political power was won or lost.

In any event, with the conflict between the North and South deepening over slavery, women would just have to wait.

IN 1872, SEVEN years after the Civil War ended and the Thirteenth Amendment abolished slavery, Susan B. Anthony and fourteen other women tried to vote for president. Anthony was arrested and indicted. At Anthony's trial the next year, as she began to testify on her own behalf, the presiding judge, Supreme Court justice Ward Hunt, interrupted her and would not let her speak in her own defense. He instructed the jury to convict her and, afterward, read a speech he had written before the trial had started. He then made the mistake of asking Anthony if she had anything to say.

"I have many things to say. You have trampled under foot every vital principle of our government. My natural rights, my civil rights, my political rights, my judicial rights, are all alike ignored. Robbed of the fundamental privilege of citizenship, I am degraded from the status of a citizen to that of a subject; and not only myself individually, but all of my sex, are, by your honor's verdict, doomed to political subjection," Anthony said, and as she continued he ordered her to sit down. Then he ordered her to stand, and he fined her $100 and the cost of the prosecution. (She never paid the fine.)

"Man is, or should be, woman's protector and defender. The natural and proper timidity which belongs to the female sex evidently unfits it for many of the occupations of civil life," Supreme Court justice Joseph Bradley wrote a year after Anthony's conviction in *Bradwell v. Illinois*, ruling that Myra Bradwell had no right to practice law because she was a woman. The "harmony" of the family itself would be threatened by Bradwell or any other woman "adopting a distinct and independent career from that of her husband," the court argued. "The paramount destiny and mission of woman are to fulfil the noble and benign offices of wife and mother. This is the law of the Creator. And the rules of civil society must be adapted to the general constitution of things . . ."

The Founding Fathers who wrote the United States Constitution had been silent about women's right to self-government. After the Civil War, their heirs clarified that the omission had not been an oversight.

In 1868, for the first time in our history, Congress wrote the word *male* into the Constitution. Section Two of the Fourteenth Amendment said, essentially, if a state deprived any male of the right to vote, it would lose congressional seats proportional to how many male citizens were disfranchised. Or, looked at from another angle, there would be no punishment for denying women access to the ballot box. In 1869, Congress passed the Fifteenth Amendment, declaring that "the right to vote shall not be abridged or denied by the United States on account of race, color, or previous condition of servitude." (It was ratified in 1870.) When Anthony tried to vote in 1872, it remained perfectly legal for states to deprive citizens of the vote on the basis of sex. Every state did.

The movement for woman's suffrage, which began before the Civil War, remained vibrant into the 1880s. But activists were rebuffed at every turn. They lost every vote in the U.S. Senate. In some states, they won votes in one house of the state legislature only to lose in the other. In Iowa, Maine, and Massachusetts, men voted down woman's suffrage amendments to state constitutions. In 1880, the Supreme Court conceded in *Minor v. Happersett* that women were indeed citizens of the United States but also ruled that national citizenship didn't confer the right to vote.

Granted, there were some baby steps forward in the last decades of the 19th century. Some states expanded women's rights to make contracts, own property, and sue for divorce. Local governments in sixteen states and territories gave women the right to vote in a few lady matters, such as in school board and municipal elections. The territories of Wyoming and Utah enfranchised women.

In Wyoming, where men made up six out of every seven residents, they thought the right to vote might attract brides. In Utah, voting rights for women gave Mormon polygamists an edge over the growing population of single non-Mormon men attracted to the territory's silver mines.

Yet resistance to women's political equality remained intense. The anti–woman's suffrage camp made two main points against giving women the vote. One, they said, women were too virtuous for the sordid business of politics and women didn't want to vote anyway. Two, giving women the vote would destroy the family, and with it, civilization itself. "This lunacy"—woman's suffrage—"of all lunacies is the most destructive," one man said at the California state constitutional convention. "It attacks the integrity of the family; it attacks the eternal decrees of God Almighty; it denies and repudiates the obligations of motherhood."

After Colorado (1893) and Idaho (1896) adopted woman's suffrage, no other state did until 1910. Congress took no votes on the federal woman's suffrage amendment. Six referenda were held and all lost. Michigan and New Jersey courts ruled that even partial suffrage was unconstitutional. Among suffragists, the years 1896 to 1910 were known as "the doldrums."

From the Civil War through the first decade of the 20th century, the Republican Party was America's dominant party and as such took the lead in denying political rights to women. Soon it was the Democrats' turn.

In 1917, President Woodrow Wilson took the United States into World War I to make the world "safe for democracy." But he wasn't quite ready to admit that the nation might be safe with women voting. Wilson came around, though. In January 1918, the president endorsed the woman's suffrage amendment "as a war measure," and the next day the Democratic-controlled House voted to approve woman's suffrage by a one-vote margin. But most of those votes came from Republicans. Wilson's own party split. Democratic resistance in the Senate delayed congressional passage until 1919.

In 1920, seventy-two years after Seneca Falls, forty-six years after Woodhull ran for president and Anthony was arrested for voting, the Nineteenth Amendment was ratified. Drafted by Susan B. Anthony, it said simply that the right of citizens to vote "shall not be denied or abridged on account of sex."

These, then, are the milestones in women getting screwed, politically speaking.

For most of American history, no woman became president because American law, gendered cultural norms, and the United States constitution denied women the most basic political right: the right to vote. Of course no woman would become president of the United States until women could vote.

But there is more to the story. Plenty of men have policed that highest glass ceiling. But women haven't always been hoisting each other through the cracks.

AFTER THE CIVIL War, the founders of American feminism put themselves on the wrong side of the global democracy project of the day.

The troubles began when Republicans pushed through the Fourteenth Amendment in 1868. "What was outrageous to women's suffrage advocates was that it introduced the word *male* into the representation clause, which basically said, if you deprive any man of the right to vote, you're going to lose some representation in Congress. But presumably if you deprived women of the right to vote, you didn't lose anything," Eric Foner, the leading historian on this era, explained. "The aim of the Fourteenth Amendment was to encourage southern states to give black men the right to vote. But it did not actually give anybody the right to vote. Nonetheless, the feminist movement was upset because it did introduce this gender distinction in the constitution which hadn't existed previously."

Woman's suffrage was raised explicitly soon after, as Republicans prepared a constitutional amendment to enfranchise freed slaves. Elizabeth Cady Stanton and others argued for including women in a broad expansion of the suffrage. But most people in the anti-slavery movement and most Republicans in Congress rejected the idea as politically impractical.

"The question whether they should have expanded it to include women is a difficult historical issue. On a moral level, absolutely, of course they should have. On the political level, the movement for women's rights was obviously not strong enough to force that issue into Congress," Foner continued. "The things that had gotten black men support for the right to vote did not apply to women, black or white—black military service was very important in this. Lincoln himself, at the end of his life, had said black soldiers ought to have the right to vote. There were people in Congress, like Charles Sumner, who in principle supported women suffrage, but said, 'No, this is the Negro's hour'—by which they meant the black man's hour. Frederick Douglass, who was certainly a feminist and had been there at Seneca Falls, said the same thing."

It's important, however, to note that the split wasn't necessarily on race or gender lines, according to Foner. For instance, Robert Purvis, a leading black abolitionist, said, "I do not want my son to have the right to vote unless my daughter also has it." Sojourner Truth also challenged Douglass. Foner continued, "Douglass said black men need the right to vote because it's the only way to protect black people against violence. She said, 'Well, aren't black women also victims?' To which Douglass said, 'Well yes, of course, but they're victims because they're black, not because they're women, and black men can protect them.'"

Stanton said, "It's not the 'Negro's hour.' It's the Constitution's hour. You don't amend it every day. And if this moment passes, it will take a century to reopen the door." Stanton drew from the debate the lesson that women "must not put her trust in man," and when a woman's suffrage referendum came up in Kansas, Stanton chose to make a strategic alliance with Democrats, who supported women's suffrage but were simultaneously mounting a racist campaign against black suffrage. Kansas voters were presented with two separate referenda, one on black suffrage and one on women's suffrage. They rejected both. When Congress took up the Fifteenth Amendment, enfranchising black men, Stanton, Anthony, and other mothers of American feminism actively opposed it.

"I tell students that this is a debate where both sides were right in a certain sense," Foner continued. "They both had irrefutable arguments, but unfortunately the politics of the situation pushed in one direction. The public consciousness of the desirability of women voting had not developed to a sufficient stage."

Still, no matter how just the cause of universal suffrage was, the battle between onetime allies took an ugly turn when Stanton began to express an unsavory brew of racism, nativism, and elitism. "Think of Patrick and Sambo and Hans and UngTung, who do not know the difference between a Monarchy and a Republic, who never read the Declaration of Independence, making laws for Lydia Maria Child, Lucretia Mott, or Fanny Kemble," she said one time. At another, she asserted that African American women would be better off as "the slave of an educated white man, than of a degraded, ignorant black one."

No 21st-century feminist can look back on this chapter in women's rights with pride, so it is worth noting that the men in Congress shared these prejudices. And unlike women, they had power to act on them. The Fifteenth Amendment says specifically that the right of citizens "to vote shall not be denied or abridged on account of race, color, or previous condition of servitude." Congress in fact considered and rejected broader language, barring discrimination in voting and officeholding based on "race, color, nativity, property, education, or religious beliefs." The Fifteenth Amendment, ratified in 1870, was silent about the right to hold office. It tacitly allowed poll taxes and literacy tests, the key means that Jim Crow states employed to deprive African Americans of their constitutional right to vote. But Congress's intent was not to consign African Americans to second-class citizenship in the future. Rather, northern and western Congressmen wanted to keep their states' own restrictions on voting. Rhode Island, for example, kept many immigrants from voting by requiring that anyone born in another country had to own real estate. Massachusetts imposed a literacy test. California allowed European immigrants to vote, but barred Chinese immigrants from doing so.

The conflict over black suffrage alienated women's rights advocates from their close allies in the anti-slavery movement, and it also split the women's movement itself. Angry that some suffragists (women and men) supported the Fifteenth Amendment, Stanton and Anthony broke away in 1869 to create their own organization, the National Woman Suffrage Association. Other advocates of woman's suffrage, such as Lucy Stone, supported the vote for black men and the Fifteenth Amendment, and they formed the American Woman Suffrage Association after Stanton split the women's rights movement into two camps. Both sides ended up weakened for the battles ahead.

Anthony and Stanton had maintained a belief in universal suffrage even as they gave vent to elitism. Subsequent women leaders dropped the egalitarianism and embraced the elitism. Carrie Chapman Catt called the immigrants pouring in from southern and eastern Europe in the 1880s and 1890s "a class of men not intelligent, not patriotic, not moral. It is they who nominate officials at the polls through corrupt means, it is they who elect them and by bribery." Racism in the white women's suffrage groups prompted black women to create their own suffrage groups in the last decades of the century.

Although this kind of anti-democratic prejudice was widespread among the white Protestant middle class in the Gilded Age, on merely a pragmatic level it was self-defeating for women suffragists to add their voices. After all, women weren't going to win the vote without men's votes. And it was exactly these working-class and immigrant men who made up the majority of voters in many of the most populous states.

The first wave of American feminists laid the foundation for winning the vote. But by bickering among themselves and breaking with longtime partners, they diluted their political influence and set back the cause. By 1890, the two organizations created by the schism over black suffrage had each become so small and ineffectual that they merged again into a new organization, the National American Woman Suffrage Association (NAWSA). In 1893, the *New York Times* wrote, "The cause of woman suffrage does not seem to have made the least progress in this part of the country in the last quarter of a century, if indeed it has not lost ground."

SURELY WOMEN LEARNED a lesson about how to maneuver in the national political arena? Unfortunately, no. Instead, they devoted most of their political energy to America's first disastrous war on drugs: Prohibition.

As we saw, the idea of women's moral superiority had fueled social reform movements throughout American history. This moralizing women's politics reached its pinnacle with the Women's

Christian Temperance Union, founded in 1874 by Frances Willard. The WCTU was far and away the largest and most influential women's organization that had ever existed in the United States, and if ever there was an identity politics of women, this was it. Men were barred from membership and officeholding in the WCTU. As the historian Mary Ryan wrote about this era, "Woman citizens increasingly pleaded their causes based on their womanly virtues and preeminently on their stature as mothers." Increasingly these notions colored the case for woman's suffrage. As one man who supported woman's suffrage put it, "When our mothers, wives, and sisters vote with us, we will have purer legislation, and better execution of the laws, fewer tippling shops, gambling halls, and brothels."

On Willard's prompting, the Anti-Saloon League (the WCTU's male counterpart in the temperance movement) launched a campaign in 1913 to win a constitutional amendment outlawing liquor. By 1915, twenty-three states were dry, thanks to the grassroots organizing done by WCTU women activists. In 1919, the Eighteenth Amendment was ratified.

In short, when women got involved in politics on a mass scale, the nation got Prohibition. That was no way to win friends and influence people.

Not until the early 20th century did the women's suffrage movement start to gain traction, thanks to an infusion of new blood and new ideas. It was the Progressive Era—one of the great waves of social reform in the nation's history, which brought us the direct election of senators, food safety, and laws banning child labor, among many other essential innovations in policy and law. Progressive women leaders, such as Florence Kelley and Jane Addams, persuaded NAWSA to pay attention to working-class and immigrant women and their need for the vote to win for themselves better pay and safer working conditions. "No one needs all the powers of the fullest citizenship more urgently than the wage-earning woman," Kelley said in 1898. (By 1900, women made up one-fifth of the labor force.) Some second-generation suffragists were themselves more attuned to progressive ideas. Elizabeth Cady Stanton's daughter, Harriot Stanton Blatch, publicly opposed her mother's support for literary tests for immigrants, and in 1906 NAWSA dropped its call to make education a requirement for the vote.

By this time, the woman's suffrage movement had grown into a mass movement, one that brought together women of all classes and ethnicities and used a variety of techniques to pressure men to share political rights with women. One group, led by Alice Paul, employed militant tactics learned from British suffragists. In New York, suffragists followed the blueprint of the Democratic Party machine and organized by precinct. In California, suffragists went door to door and flooded the state with pamphlets. Women trade unionists became more active in the movement, eventually winning over the American Federation of Labor. In 1912, 5,000 suffragists, dressed in white, marched through the streets of Washington, DC.

With broader support and creative organizing, victories began to mount. In 1910, the Republican president William Howard Taft endorsed woman's suffrage. In 1912, the Progressive Party, with former president Theodore Roosevelt at its head, did too. Between 1910 and 1914, women won the vote in Washington, California, Kansas, Montana, the territory of Alaska, and four other states. Still, the movement continued to suffer many defeats. Men voted suffrage down in state referenda in Ohio, New York, Michigan, Massachusetts, and the Dakotas. As late as 1915, no state in the Northeast or the Midwest had granted the vote to women.

In 1916, as the United States entered World War I, suffragists tried to punish Wilson at the polls. In 1917, they chained themselves to the White House fence. In jail, they went on hunger strikes and were put in isolation cells and force-fed. They marched and demonstrated and lobbied throughout the country. By 1917, NAWSA's membership stood at around 2 million. With the multipronged attack, the dominoes began to fall. In November 1917, New York State adopted woman's suffrage, after the immigrant and labor-backed New York City Democratic political machine stopped fighting it.

In January 1918, when the House voted to approve woman's suffrage, the deciding votes came from congressmen representing states that had recently adopted state woman's suffrage amendments—in other words, from politicians who needed women's votes to keep their jobs. But the amendment stalled again that summer, with a defeat in the Senate. Not until suffragists burned Wilson's high-minded speeches from the Peace Conference at "watch fires" on the White House lawn, toured the nation in their prison garb, and defeated two anti-suffrage Democratic senators did Wilson prevail upon members of his own party in the Senate to support the vote for women. On June 4, 1919, the Senate approved the Nineteenth Amendment, and on August 18, 1920, it was ratified.

But for all the suffragists' bravery in defying gender norms to win political rights for women, the movement as a whole was unwilling to challenge the racial status quo. To reach the three-fourths threshold required to ratify a constitutional amendment had taken affirmative votes from four southern border states, where Jim Crow laws denied the right to vote to African American men and women.

"In order to get southern votes for women's suffrage, the activists sort of made a deal with the segregationists, saying 'this will not affect black women in the south. The laws barring blacks from voting will continue in force,'" historian Eric Foner said. From the vantage point of the struggles after the Civil War, he continued, "The irony is that if you fast-forward fifty years, you get a reversal of the situation, which is to say that women's suffrage had become more acceptable than black suffrage. Women suffragists made their own compromise fifty years later."

IN 1920, FOR the first time in U.S. history, women would vote in a presidential election—and every other election for local, state, and federal office. But at the moment of triumph, the leading women's organizations refused to step up to the main stage of American politics: running and supporting candidates for elective office. The National Woman's Party, the group behind the radical hunger strikes, remained controlled by Alice Paul, and she steered it away from party politics. To add to the problem, Paul was an autocratic leader who took pride in the group's "complete disregard for popularity." NAWSA's Carrie Chapman Catt also disavowed party politics, and in 1919 she converted the 2-million-member organization into the League of Women Voters. The nonpartisan League refused to endorse any political candidate, even when the candidate was one of its own members. With thousands of members who had on-the-ground experience canvassing voters, lobbying elected officials, organizing demonstrations, and speaking at mass rallies— that is, everything a political candidate did and more—the League mystifyingly decided that its job was solely to educate women about politics. Some suffragists turned down posts in presidential administrations, insulted by the tokenism they thought animated the offers. Movement purists accused women who ran for office of selling out.

At first, Democrats and Republicans courted the more than 30 million new women voters with promises about women-focused legislation. Both parties offered positions in party leadership to women leaders, appointing prominent feminists and suffragists to their governing councils, the Democratic and Republican National Committees. But when the predicted gender gap did not materialize, showing that women weren't going to demand anything for their vote, politicians lost interest in the women's vote and women's issues.

In short, at the decisive moment of opportunity, when American women could have coasted into political leadership on the twin engines of experience and leverage, when they could have easily won seats in state houses and Congress, and so stepped onto the ladder leading to the governor's mansion, the Senate, and ultimately the

White House, the leaders of the women's movement suffered a case of arrested development. Here stood the greatest number of potential women candidates ever in American history—women with the education, the campaign experience, and the interest in politics to launch successful campaigns. But their leaders kept them out of the real action. As one Republican woman suffragist said, it was like "going back to kindergarten days."

Chapter 7

THE REPUBLICAN DILEMMA

"THERE ARE THOSE who make the contention that no woman should ever aspire to the White House, that this is a man's world, and that it should be kept that way," senator Margaret Chase Smith said, as she announced her candidacy for the 1964 Republican presidential nomination to a surprisingly raucous gathering of the Women's National Press Club. "It is contended that as a woman I would not have the physical stamina and strength to run and that I should not take that much out of me even for what might conceivably be a good cause, if even a losing cause. So because of these very impelling reasons against my running, I have decided that I shall." Forty-four years after American women won the right to vote, Senator Smith became the first credible woman candidate for president and the first to win votes from delegates at a major party convention.

In 1960, on the 40th anniversary of the Nineteenth Amendment, the political gender divide was stark. Not a single state had ever elected a woman in her own right to be governor. White men made up 96 percent of Congress. A total of seventeen women served in the House and only one in the Senate. To be fair, few women had the typical qualifications to be elected to Congress, where nearly half of the men were lawyers and half were war veterans. Women earned only 2 percent of law degrees and were barred by law from combat roles in the military. Millions of American women—black women in the Jim Crow South—could not even vote. Selma and the Voting Rights Act still stood five years in the future.

The one sitting U.S. senator was Margaret Chase Smith. Change came fast for women after that 1960 nadir, and Smith's presidential bid, although daring, should be seen in the context of a nascent feminism that would crest over the next decade. The year before Smith ran, in 1963, Congress passed the Equal Pay Act, America's first law ever requiring equal pay for women. In 1964, Congress passed the Civil Rights Act, barring discrimination in employment on the basis of race, color, religion, national origin, and sex. In 1965, the Supreme Court ruled in *Griswold v. Connecticut* that state laws banning contraceptives for married couples violated their right to privacy and were unconstitutional. In 1970, some 50,000 people marched to celebrate the 50th anniversary of woman's suffrage, and in 1972, Congress passed the Equal Rights Amendment. In many ways, 1972 was a tipping point year. Congress also passed Title IX, guaranteeing gender equality in education—the foundation for girls and women's athletics today. Both political parties adopted bold feminist planks in their platforms, and Shirley Chisholm, the first African American woman ever elected to Congress, ran for president in the Democratic primary.

Advances in every area of life—work, politics, family, and education, to name only the most important—were achieved thanks to the many women's movements of second-wave feminism. Whereas before, discrimination against women was legal and accepted, now women won equal rights. (Future Supreme Court justice Ruth Bader Ginsburg was the intellectual force behind many of the legal victories that dismantled gender discrimination. As founder of the ACLU Women's Rights Project and general counsel, she argued many of the landmark cases before the Supreme Court.)

The stories of these movements have been told many times, from many perspectives. For our purposes, suffice it to say that second-wave feminism accomplished two fundamental tasks on the road to gender equality: one, eliminating nearly all legal discrimination by sex, and two, transforming the hearts and minds of Americans about women's role and place in the world. It had taken 200 years, but finally the nation seemed ready to apply its founding ideal—all men are created equal—to women.

That America could at some time elect a woman president is imaginable only because of these changes. Consider that in 1937, 64 percent of Americans said that they would not vote for a woman for president even if she were qualified "in every other respect." In 1964, when Smith ran, just half of the country said they would vote for a qualified woman nominated by their own party. The quantum leap took another decade, but since the nation's bicentennial in 1976, our willingness to vote for a woman president has never fallen below 75 percent. In 2014, support registered at 95 percent. (Although, it does make you wonder what that other 5 percent was thinking.)

Likewise, in 2014, it looked nearly certain that the Democrats would nominate a woman. Yet it also looked highly unlikely that any viable woman candidate would emerge from the Republican presidential primary race. Where were all the missing Republican women?

IN THE 2012 presidential election, the women's vote was absolutely decisive in Barack Obama's reelection. Barack Obama won women by an 11-point margin. He received 7.5 million more votes from women than his Republican opponent Mitt Romney did, and nearly 10 million more women than men voted in the election. Although Romney won men overall, he did so by a narrower margin and there were fewer of them, so it wasn't sufficient to overcome Obama's greater advantage with women. To put this in perspective, if women had so much as split their votes fifty-fifty, Mitt Romney would be America's 45th president, having won the election by a 4-million-vote margin of victory.

Add to the GOP deficit with women voters the fact that Democratic women in Congress outnumbered Republican women three-to-one, and you get a sense of the scale and scope of the Republican dilemma. The party had a woman problem, and that woman problem was devastating at the presidential level.

Shocked and dismayed at the scale of the party's 2012 loss, Reince Priebus, the chair of the Republican National Committee (RNC), commissioned a report by veteran party leaders and operatives to figure out what went wrong. Things were so bad that the project quickly became known as the "autopsy." Saying that the GOP at the federal level had marginalized itself, the RNC report warned, "unless changes are made, it will be increasingly difficult for Republicans to win another presidential election in the near future."

Straightforwardly acknowledging how bad the problem was with women, it said, "our inability to win their votes is losing us elections." It did not recommend any policy change or new measures regarding the rights or well-being of women, but it did advise the party to recruit more women candidates and elevate women within the party hierarchy. "Additionally, when developing our Party's message, women need to be part of this process to represent some of the unique concerns that female voters may have. There is growing unrest within the community of Republican women frustrated by the Party's negative image among women, and the women who participated in our listening sessions contributed many constructive ideas of ways to improve our brand with women throughout the country and grow the ranks of influential female voices in the Republican Party."

Few people have done more than Katie Packer Gage to take that concept of a new brand and message into the real world of political campaigns. She came to that place out of hard experience, as deputy campaign manager for Romney. After his defeat, she and Ashley O'Connor, Romney's advertising director, did their own autopsy among themselves. "One of the things that we kept coming back to is that the Democrats had really done a pretty good job of defining Romney with women in a way that we felt was really inaccurate. They did it early, and it was enough to define him with women in a way that was not very flattering and made it very hard for us to make the kind of emergence with women that we needed. It obviously wasn't the only reason we lost, but it was something that we felt like maybe we could help fix, and prevent the Republicans from making the same mistake moving forward."

Although the Romney campaign had catalyzed Gage and O'Connor's thinking about different ways to influence women voters, Gage emphasized that it wasn't something that could be implemented at the time. "We were at the table, and Ashley and I own the loss as much as anybody does. We are in no way suggesting that we had a different plan that would have resulted in a victory and nobody listened," she said. "A lot of the things we thought were based on gut instinct. And when you're talking about multimillion-dollar decisions in a presidential campaign, we weren't really inclined to step up and go, 'No, no, no, no, no, let's do it differently,' because we didn't really have data to back it up."

In 2013, Gage, O'Connor, and Republican pollster Christine Matthews created an all-women political firm for Republicans, Burning Glass Consulting. "The idea behind it was, what would we do differently in political campaigns if only women were voting? How would we conduct research? How would we create mail copy? How would we create television ads? All focused specifically on the way women digest information. Beyond even just the issues that they care about. How do they make their decisions?" Gage continued, "We talked with people in academia, people in the research community, and looked at how Madison Avenue goes about selling their products to women. We came to the conclusion that political campaigns were really behind the times. Political campaigns were born out of a process that was designed by men, for men, to communicate with men. Women are now 53 percent of the electorate, and there's nothing in campaigns that pays any attention to that. But yet, if you look at how Ford sold the car, or how

Gillette sold the razor, they have very specific marketing techniques that they use to communicate with women."

Gage recalled how she first started to question how the GOP was communicating with women while she was commuting between the Romney headquarters in Boston and her home in Virginia during the campaign. "I was watching TV in those two places. At one point I said to our ad guy, 'I'm not seeing our ads. I feel like I'm seeing the Obama ads, but I'm not seeing our ads.' And he said, 'Well, you're probably not watching the evening news. More women watch the evening news than any other show.' I'm sure he had data to back that up, but I was kind of like, this just doesn't make sense to me, because most women I know don't really have time to sit down and watch the evening news. That's when they're cooking dinner. Their kids are doing homework. They're running back and forth to soccer practice. The TV might be on in their home, but I don't think they're sitting watching it. And I don't think Madison Avenue thinks they are either. Otherwise, you would see tampon ads during that time, and I've never seen a tampon ad in the evening news. I see car ads. I see insurance ads. I see Cialis ads."

Besides changing advertising to target women, Gage went on, Burning Glass also concluded that the conventional approach to focus groups was wrong for women. (Campaigns use focus groups to test messaging, to dive deeper on opinions that emerge from large-scale polls, and generally to figure out how candidates can tap into the real concerns of voters.) "All of the focus groups that we did in 2012 took place in a boardroom environment, where every-body's sitting around a boardroom table, and it's very sterile and anonymous," Gage recalled. "And we thought, that's not really how women sit around and talk. A big part of how women make their decisions and come to their conclusions about issues and about candidates is sitting around talking to friends. They don't do that around a boardroom table!" To capture these distinctive women's ways, "to get more real feedback," Gage continued, "we started doing our focus groups in a living room–type environment, where we serve cappuccino and wine. We try to do things to draw women out and make them feel like they were among friends. We find that we got a really different result from that."

The focus groups helped them glean another key insight about women: They change their minds after they've had time to think, Gage said. "A lot of women don't have the luxury of sitting around worrying about the fiscal cliff and things that are happening in Washington, DC, which pollsters like to ask them about. So, often-times, the first time they really contemplate an issue is in a focus group. You're trying to understand how they feel about an issue, but they've spent about ten seconds focusing on it." So Burning Glass implemented follow-up interviews a week later, when possible. "Women are much more open to completely shifting their opinion based on new information. Men are much less likely to change their mind. Once they've come to a conclusion, even if it is not based on a lot of information, they'll look for ways to defend that conclusion. Everybody that we talk to says, 'Yeah, that doesn't surprise me at all.'" Gage continued, "We thought, here we had made multimillion-dollar decisions in the 2012 campaign based on information coming out of focus groups, and finding out that these women may have changed their mind a week later. It's so obvious that it's almost like a crime that nobody's really focused on it before."

Gage exuded confidence, but the problem facing the GOP was bigger than a cappuccino-fueled focus group could solve. In the 2014 midterm elections, even though the GOP won control of the Senate, it lost women by a greater margin than it had in the 2010 midterms. Six months into its control of the 114th Congress, only 32 percent of Americans rated the Republican Party favorably. Only 36 percent of women identified or leaned Republican, compared to 52 percent who identified or leaned Democratic, according to the Pew Research Center 2014 report on partisan identification, which was based on a whopping 25,010 interviews. (To get a sense of how definitive these results are, keep in mind that highly reliable polls typically are based on a sample of roughly 1,000 interviews.) The 16-point pro-Democratic lean among women, furthermore, has a dramatic electoral impact because the GOP can't make up the deficit with men. Not only do fewer men vote, but men also split their allegiances roughly evenly between the two parties.

Why aren't more women Republicans? Nonpartisan surveys and academic studies consistently find that women are more liberal than men and that women officeholders are more likely to take liberal positions on a range of issues, not just conventionally women's issues. This is true globally as well. The GOP is the party that stands for low taxes and small government, yet women favor more government provision of services and more government spending than men do, according to American National Election Studies surveys going back to the 1980s. So as the conservative party in the United States, the GOP starts at a disadvantage with women.

Women's liberal leanings are particularly salient in contemporary American politics, as the fallout from the 2008 financial crisis has elevated the problem of income inequality to the top of ordinary voters' concerns. In a 2015 *New York Times*/CBS News survey on income inequality and workers' rights, supermajorities of women supported government policies to reduce inequality and boost wages. Seventy percent of women said the gap between the rich and poor was a problem that needed to be addressed now, with 63 percent saying government should do more to reduce that gap. Seventy-three percent of women thought money and wealth in the United States should be more evenly distributed, 72 percent favored raising taxes on millionaires, and 75 percent favored raising the minimum wage. Women's support for policies to aid working parents was overwhelming; 85 percent favored requiring employers to provide paid leave to parents of new children and employees caring for sick family members, and 89 percent favored requiring employers to provide paid sick leave. Women were significantly more progressive than men and Republicans on most of these questions. Only a minority of Republicans supported these measures, and the difference between women and Republicans ranged from 19 points on raising millionaires' taxes to 29 points on economic fairness questions, such as the distribution of money and wealth and government action to reduce the gap between rich and poor. In short, something more than a way of talking to and about women seemed to be at the bottom of the Republican's women voter problem. The

Republican Party was out of synch with the views of the majority of American women.

THE REPUBLICAN PARTY not only wins less support from women voters, but also lags behind on women in elected office. In the 114th Congress only 9 percent of House Republicans are women, compared to 35 percent of House Democrats. A record number of Republican women serve in the Senate: six. Democrats had hit that mark sixteen years earlier and currently have fourteen women senators, many of whom had served as heads of powerful committees when Democrats controlled the Senate. Only one woman entered the 2016 Republican presidential primaries: Carly Fiorina, a former CEO of a Fortune 20 company, who had never held a single elected office.

"I would have thought Republicans would have had women at the forefront sooner, given the fact that from my experience, Republicans were anxious and receptive to having women in their ranks, and at the highest levels. It's regrettable," former U.S. senator Olympia Snowe told me.

"How long now have we been talking about a gender gap in the Republican party?" Republican pollster Wilma Goldstein said, recalling discussions after the 2012 debacle. "So finally, finally, finally the party gets around to thinking, 'Well, yeah, maybe it does exist and maybe we ought to do something about it.' So what do they do? They have an election for leadership. They don't pick a single woman! So we start screaming saying, 'For God's sake, what's the matter with you? You know the problem. We just got our butts kicked,' or language somewhat like that anyway! You don't think a woman can do anything? They make up this job for Cathy McMorris Rodgers, and we have some hope that that'll be something, but it hasn't really worked out."

Goldstein was convinced that the men at the helm of the GOP did not highly value women leaders. "If you're not one of the boys, you don't get to sit at the table and make the decisions," she continued. "If we don't keep fighting for more women members in Congress, there aren't going to be any more women members of Congress. The men don't care. We have to be the ones that care. We have to be the ones to make sure that it continues to happen." In a similar though more measured vein, former New Jersey governor Christie Todd Whitman thought the party just "paid lip service" to women in leadership.

Republican women agreed that they would like to see more women elected in their party, but most did not think that resistance to women from the party's leadership was the source of their current deficit. Margaret Hoover, a pro-choice conservative and head of American Unity Fund, a PAC supporting pro–LGBT rights Republicans, observed, "I have a hard time saying Mitch McConnell is sexist. He has one of the most dynamic and aggressive wives that I've ever known." McConnell, the Senate majority leader, is married to Elaine Chao, former secretary of labor in the George W. Bush administration. Hoover continued, "I've seen Kelly Ayotte taken up under the arm of John McCain and Lindsey Graham on the foreign relations stuff. I know that she's valued. I've seen some of these newer members really be ushered into leadership far more quickly than many men, frankly because there aren't a lot of women. I think if there's sexism, it's that we're not robustly going out and recruiting more women candidates and supporting them through primaries. That's what we should be doing, and frankly, I don't see the Republican Party doing that."

Despite a general sentiment that more women representatives would be better, few Republican women in high leadership or with significant influence in the party or conservative movement make it a priority. According to political scientist Ronnee Schreiber, a specialist on conservative women, although conservative women would like to see more women in office and admire conservatives like Ayotte, McMorris Rodgers, and South Carolina governor Nikki Haley, they do not devote resources and energy to electing women. Burning Glass Consulting, for example, has carved out a niche in the women's space and, uncharacteristically for Republican firms, is composed of an all-women team of principals. Gage told me they were very supportive of more women in office but did not actively recruit women to run. "I would love to see women at parity. I don't think that there's a situation where either side is trying to keep women down. I think it's more of an issue of trying to encourage women to do it and giving women the tools to help them emerge from primaries," she said. "Our overall goal is changing the way that the Republican Party is viewed by women. And certainly, having more women mouthpieces, more women that have the letter R next to their name on television, is a really important part of that."

On a key measure, donating money and bundling contributions for women candidates, Republicans fall dramatically behind

Democrats, a fact lamented by Republican women. There are only a handful of PACs devoted to electing women and no Republican counterpart to EMILY's List. Some efforts have been made over the years, the most successful being the WISH List that Candace Straight and others created in 1992. (In 2010 the WISH List merged with another PAC, the Republican Majority for Choice.) Although the WISH List provided critical support to some of the women Republicans elected in the 1990s, it never was able to scale the way EMILY's List did on the Democratic side. Over its eighteen years, it raised a total of only $3.5 million for socially moderate, fiscally conservative Republican women candidates. Since its founding, EMILY's List has raised more than $400 million. The most active, Republican-leaning women's PACs tend to be oriented toward electing anti-abortion politicians, and they show no particular favoritism to women candidates. The pro-life Susan B. Anthony List, for example, raised $2.1 million in 2014, and a good chunk of its funds went to men.

Republican women candidates face a further disadvantage, which in part explains the dearth of funding and the missing candidates. People who vote in GOP primaries tend to be very conservative, and many academic studies have found that these conservative primary voters perceive women candidates to be more liberal than the men they run against. (As an aside, this would seem to demonstrate a gender bias, except that the facts support their perception: On average, women are more liberal than men.) This makes it more difficult for Republican women to advance to the general election. They do not fare as well in primaries as Democratic women do, the scholarship confirms. Apparently, as a recent study demonstrates, less conservative Republican women have factored their lower odds of victory into their calculations about running for office. Political scientist Danielle Thomsen, in "Why So Few (Republican) Women?" suggested that the "partisan imbalance in Congress" between Democratic and Republican women was partly because moderate Republicans were less likely to run, and women were overrepresented among moderates. In other words, Republicans who felt they did not fit ideologically with the party's primary voters did not run because, in a rational cost-benefit analysis, they perceived their chances of winning to be slight. Thomsen also found that conservative women were underrepresented in the pipeline, and proposed that as more conservative women ran for local and state office, the numbers of Republican women in the U.S. Congress would gradually rise.

Many political operatives and academics alike believed the main reason for women's underrepresentation was that not enough Republican women ran for office, and that had a direct bearing on its pool of potential presidential candidates.

"I think women sometimes bring different viewpoints to the table. That's important," Chriss Winston, the head of President George H. W. Bush's speechwriting office, told me. "Sure I'd love to see more women. I'd love to see a woman president. Not Hillary Clinton! Which has nothing to do with her being a woman. Philosophically, she'd be more of the same as Barack Obama." Winston is a conservative who sharply disapproved of Obama's policies, especially the Affordable Care Act. "I would never vote for someone because of their sex. I just don't look through that prism. I think most Republicans don't see things through these demographic prisms the way Democrats do."

Others expressed a similar mix of desire and disclaimers. "I think Republican women would be as excited to have a woman president as Democrats," Maria Cino, former deputy chairwoman of the RNC, said. "As long as the person was qualified, up for the job. I think everybody would be thrilled to have a woman president. I don't know that there are many woman left who would say, 'Oh no, it's a man's job.' But I do go back to qualifications. I do think there are a lot of qualified women coming up through the ranks." As important, she emphasized, was for women to aim for the highest nonelected leadership positions in government. "Not everyone wants to be elected. We sometimes forget about that side, having women in the room when serious policy decisions are being made. It would be great to have a woman chief of staff at the White House. It'd be great to have more cabinet members that are women. A little-known secret is that sometimes the chief of staff is as powerful as a member of Congress. I served as a chief of staff and I had a great relationship with the member of Congress I worked for. We had been friends since high school. We ran it as a team. I know he valued my opinion," Cino told me. For someone who started a PAC to elect women, Cino attached a surprising number of caveats to her support for more women in elected office.

"My guess is that if you polled most women who self-identify as Republican, primary voters would probably say, 'No, we just want more qualified people.' I don't think you have a lot of Republican women voters who are really pro-women people, if you hear me,"

Margaret Hoover said. "But I think if you ask Cathy McMorris Rodgers and any elected Republican woman in the House of Representatives or in the Senate whether it was important to elect more women, they would all say yes."

Across the ideological spectrum within the GOP, women agree that more women would be better, and they hope to see progress toward gender parity in American government. Still, the GOP lags far behind on women's leadership. Why? To be sure, the GOP's deficit of women politicians is a legacy of decades of anti-feminism within the conservative political movement. The Republican base currently includes groups, especially the religious right, that historically have opposed women in public leadership roles, as I explained in my book *Delirium*. Right-wing women's organizations like the Eagle Forum and Concerned Women for America, even though they were led by powerful career women, insisted that women's proper place was in the home. Their position on women has changed somewhat, but only in the last five or so years.

Today, the ambivalence Republican women express about dedicating energy and resources to women's political advance no longer stems from any doubt about women's capacity or right to hold political office. Nevertheless, their genuine interest in women's leadership does not come close to matching the intensity of their Democratic counterparts. Within the GOP, there is less institutional support for women candidates, less priority accorded to gender parity, and it has to be noted, more questioning about women's qualifications.

So what explains the difference between Republican and Democratic women? Their views are a logical outcome of the individualistic ideology that makes them Republicans in the first place. Republicans are suspicious of collective action based on shared identity and group claims, because they believe that individual rights are sacrificed in the process. They reject progressive claims that institutional and structural barriers prevent some people from getting ahead. Across the many factions within the party, Republicans believe that America is a land of opportunity, that any individual can make his or her own way as long as the government gets out of the way, and that the driven and the talented will rise if they work hard. As Chriss Winston said, "My grandfather was an illiterate immigrant who worked in the fields as a boy in Iowa. My father fought in World War II and went to law school on the G.I. Bill. In two generations, we went from illiterate farmworker to the White House. I don't believe the American Dream is dead."

What matters is the individual, not whether the individual is a man or woman.

NOT ONLY ARE Republican women ambivalent about promoting women politicians, they are divided among themselves about whether women as women have distinct interests. "I have a hard time understanding exactly what a woman's issue is—other than issues that relate directly to female reproductive rights," Hoover said. "Certainly biology makes women's reproductive issues specifically women's. But all these other issues that people call women's issues? It's slightly offensive to characterize them as women's issues. Like flex time for work, that's bullshit. Men and women are both raising children now, so I feel like that should just feature as a family issue, not a woman's issue," Hoover said.

"I don't ever use the phrase *women's issues*. I have a very visceral reaction to that, because I don't think that we should be confined to certain issues," Gage said. "When people say, 'What are the issues women care about?' I say, 'Well, what are the issues men care about?' Women care about all kinds of issues. I just don't think that we should be shoved into a silo where we're only allowed to talk about reproductive issues. We should be also allowed to talk about national security and the economy and education."

"All issues are women's issues, and that's true. But clearly, there are some issues that affect women disproportionately," Snowe countered. Republican women who first entered politics when gender discrimination was codified in law and commonly practiced in day-to-day life seem more prone to think that women still have distinct interests concerning specific issues. Snowe recalled, "When I first came to the House of Representatives, I was determined to go to bat for women, because if we didn't, who would? I felt I had a unique responsibility and obligation."

Snowe was first elected in 1978 and for a decade she served as co-chair of the bipartisan Congressional Caucus on Women's Issues in the House with Democrat Pat Schroeder. "There were so few of us serving in elective capacity that I thought it was paramount to champion those issues that mattered profoundly for women. There should be concern by everybody, because it matters to everybody in the country, obviously. Nevertheless, laws did affect women adversely. Oftentimes, a lot of my women colleagues would feel that if we did not insist that these issues be on the front burner, rather than languishing on the back burner, they would not get addressed." Christine Todd Whitman, who first ran for the U.S. Senate in 1990 (and lost) and in 1994 was elected governor of New Jersey, concurred that there were distinct women's issues, such as pay equity, that remained unresolved. A strong critic of the rightward direction of the Republican Party since the Bush administration and a keen observer of American political life, she suggested that outside pressure rather than work within the party might be a more effective way to make progress for women. "Each party has had its separate women's wing, but those have never been integrated enough into the mainstream. To make a real difference on critical issues, you need a bipartisan organization that would focus on them, raise money, and lobby."

Whitman and Snowe are moderates, an increasingly rare breed in the GOP. (Wilma Goldstein, who was nicknamed "Red Wilma" in the 1970s by conservatives, quipped that moderate Republicans like her were so few "we could hold a meeting in a closet." Both Whitman and Snowe have published books critical of the increasingly rightward tilt of the GOP in the 21st century.) Most Republicans self-identify as conservative, and on principle, conservatives do not think that promoting gender equity is the government's business. Women leaders in Republican-affiliated conservative women's groups, political scientist Ronnee Schreiber explained, do not believe that most challenges women face could or should be addressed by the federal government. "They would say that women's economic challenges were individualized, not the result of wage discrimination or the structure of the economy. They would say that Democratic women and feminists perceive of women as victims who need government intervention to help them."

Other conservatives do not go as far as to deny the persistence of gender discrimination. They just do not think there is a practical solution that is consistent with their preference for less regulation and low taxes. "Republicans are certainly not against equal pay for equal work," Winston said. "As a Republican woman I look at those kind of claims and just roll my eyes. I do! Do you think I would work in a party that was against equal pay? The answer is no!"

Yet Republicans at the state and federal level have blocked equal pay legislation on many occasions, and that opposition has been a fruitful line of attack for Democrats. When I raised this with Winston, she answered, "Republicans might just not like the particular brand of legislation. The measures that the Democrats have brought up always have poison pills in them of one kind or another." Was there any legislation that would be acceptable to her, I asked, giving the example of the proposals on the table for paid maternity leave, which polling shows has wide bipartisan support? "I understand why those policies would be appealing. I was at the Department of Labor when I had my son. I took off a couple months and when I was facing going back, it was really heartbreaking. Financially if I had more paid leave, I would have taken it. So I'm sympathetic. But having said that, I don't think the country can handle more taxes on small business. I just don't think the country economically can afford it. At some point, you kill the goose that lays the golden egg. When you put more and more demand, particularly on small businesses, at some point they create fewer jobs. There are always trade-offs. Somebody pays for that and it's usually business. At this point, less regulation is the way to go. It's a very big philosophical difference between the parties."

Hoover, who describes herself as a conservative with social libertarian views, said, "I'm pro-choice. I'm pro–LGBT freedom because I just think that consistently extends the idea of individualism to public policy. I'm a free marketer on economic policy. I like less government intervention. I like slightly less regulation to the extent that there is regulation. I'd like it to be smarter. I think that's the constant challenge in regulation."

Straight, who has arguably done as much as anyone to promote women in the GOP, succinctly expressed the sentiment that binds most Republican women to the party. "I'm a Republican because I believe in limited government," Straight said. "I believe that you can spend your money better than the government can spend your money. So that's why I'm a Republican."

Together, reluctance to promote women as women, combined with skepticism that there are distinct women's issues that could be addressed by government action, render it difficult for the GOP to tackle what even the most optimistic Republican concedes is a problem with women.

"OFTEN I WOULD say I felt like a cast member on *Survivor*," Snowe told me, with a laugh, when I asked her about Republican women's views of the current party. "I was a minority, within a minority, within a minority. I was a moderate Republican, Greek

American woman, from New England. I've talked to a number of Republican women who feel that they no longer identify with the current Republican Party. We've lost a lot of Republican women who would otherwise have been involved members of the party."

Snowe believed that these women absolutely had a hunger to see more women in office, but internal party dynamics thwarted them. "They don't vote in the primaries, because they don't feel that they have choices. You get more of an ideological base in these primaries. There are so many Republican women who I know just do not connect with the current Republican Party, which no longer represents who they are or why they became a Republican initially."

To add to Republican women's minority status within America's two-party system, Republican women are weakened by divisions among themselves. None more so than on social issues, especially on abortion.

"My observation is that many of my friends who are more moderate on social issues have left the Republican Party," Straight said. "I have not. I continue to fight. I'm confident I'll always be a Republican. It doesn't mean I'll always vote for a Republican."

That broad feeling of disaffection, of not having a home any-more in the party, put the presidential race up for grabs. Straight, who was a strong supporter of New Jersey governor Chris Christie in the GOP primary, acknowledged that with so many men in the field, the GOP nomination was wide open. "If we pick somebody from the far right such as Ted Cruz, I believe a lot of women will ditch on the party and not vote for him," she speculated. "Whoever we pick, if they go too far to the right, women will not vote for them. Mitt Romney probably went too far to the right. He had a huge gender gap. If it's Ted Cruz, I don't know, Hillary could win all fifty states!" She chuckled. "If it's somebody else, it could be a very close race."

I asked Snowe if the women whose alienation she described might defect to Hillary Clinton in the presidential election. "Well, it's possible. It all depends on who is nominated and how the Republican presidential primary unfolds—in the topics for debate and the positions that are taken," Snowe answered. "I was engaged in numerous battles on the Republican Party platform at the national convention, not to say that Republican Party platforms are reflective of all Republican views, or that you have to even embrace it. In fact, oftentimes you say, 'I disagree with much of it.' But the point is, it becomes an overall reflection of the party. It's a statement. It creates an image and tenor that characterizes the party. Those battles can obviously alienate a broad segment of Republican women. Certainly on the choice issue, that has been the case."

As Straight and Snowe both suggested, the veto power held by anti-abortion activists in the party base weakened the GOP's appeal to a broader universe of women. But it also limited their ability to increase the numbers of Republican women in elected office. "You have to be very conservative today in order to run in the Republican primary," Snowe said. She thought more women would run if the party broadened its appeal. "That's where it stands today. You have a very narrow universe of women." Straight agreed. "To get through primaries is very difficult as a pro-choice Republican," she said.

"My main beef is that there are fewer Republican women in federal elected office because of the pro-life litmus test and the lack of financial support for pro-choice Republican women to get through to the general election." Hoover said. "The pro-life activists have a monopoly on the primary process. I really think that is like the 800-pound gorilla in the room. Nobody is talking about it. Everybody says, 'We need more women, we need more women,' but nobody's identified why we don't have them. And it's not that they don't know. I think they're terrified. They're just terrified of enraging the base, of like awakening a beast."

Chapter 8

THE POLITICS OF
WOMEN'S BODIES

IN NOVEMBER 2014, Republicans won seven Senate seats to gain control of the Senate. By the end of election night, they controlled both houses of Congress, as well as many state houses. They had picked up governorships in two of the nation's bluest states, Maryland and Massachusetts.

What a difference two years made. Clearly Republican candidates had learned the lesson Katie Packer Gage and others had taught post-2012 about how to talk to and about women. In key races, Republican candidates had soft-pedaled their views on women's reproductive health. Colorado's Cory Gardner, a sponsor of a thrice-rejected state personhood amendment to endow fertilized eggs with full constitutional rights, said he had changed his mind and that he had been wrong. Iowa's Joni Ernst, an advocate of personhood amendments as well as the impeachment of President Barack Obama, simply refused interviews with the major state newspapers and painted her opponent, an incumbent Democratic senator, as out of touch with regular Iowans. Wisconsin governor Scott Walker, who had already signed four laws restricting access to abortion, ran an ad misleadingly implying that he believed that abortion should be a "decision" between a woman and her doctor.

But past history suggested the pendulum would swing back. Since 1992, when George H. W. Bush lost his reelection bid to Bill Clinton after running sharply to the right, a familiar pattern had played out within the Republican Party. After a major loss, the establishment would express contrition, blame the right for the party's defeat, and promise to rededicate themselves to fundamentals—national security, taxes, the economy—to earn back the affection of mainstream voters. Meanwhile, the religious right would go into stealth mode. Activists would tone down their rhetoric, while their favored candidates would avoid talking about their intention to ban abortion and oppose gay civil rights. And then, when Republicans won back power, goaded by the party base, Republican elected officials would typically overreach. For instance, in 2011, after the Tea Party powered the GOP to control over the House on a message about jobs, they tried to defund Planned Parenthood and threatened a government shutdown if their demand was not met.

Considering the robust pattern, it was a good bet that a moment would come when social issues would rise to the top of the Republican agenda. In June 2015, as the 2016 presidential campaign was swinging into gear, the Supreme Court ruled in *Obergefell v. Hodges* that same-sex marriage was a constitutional right. With three-quarters of Democrats, two-thirds of independents, and one-third of Republicans supporting gay marriage, much of the nation rejoiced. The night of the ruling, the Obama administration lit the White House in rainbow colors. All the Republican presidential candidates publicly expressed their disapproval of the ruling in favor of marriage equality.

The subterranean rumblings on the right, however, did not erupt in full force until the following month. In July 2015, an anti-abortion front group, the Center for Medical Progress (CMP), released secretly recorded, deceptively edited videos that falsely accused Planned Parenthood of "harvesting" and "selling" fetal organs for profit. In fact, Planned Parenthood was providing fetal tissue for medical research, a practice made legal by a 1993 bipartisan congressional vote, and was only being reimbursed for its costs. Objective analysis of the CMP videos and reviews of Planned Parenthood procedures seemed to conclusively show that Planned Parenthood followed all established legal procedures. Regarding the accusations of profiteering, the unedited videos themselves showed that to be false.

Republican party leaders seized the moment to demonstrate their pro-life bona fides to the anti-abortion GOP base. House Republicans impaneled several committees to investigate Planned Parenthood and some members talked of shutting down the federal government rather than allow the group to receive government money. (The public funds at issue were Medicaid reimbursements to cover the cost of providing birth control, cancer screenings, and other health services to low-income women. Since 1979, the Hyde Amendment has prohibited the federal government from paying for abortions, except in cases of rape, incest, or serious threat to the mother's health, so no government funds were going to abortion services.) Republican Senate majority leader Mitch McConnell fast-tracked a Planned Parenthood defunding bill sponsored by freshman Iowa senator Joni Ernst. Journalists reported that Ernst had been tapped by leadership in order to put a woman's face at the head of the charge. Ernst's bill failed, but only one Republican voted against it. Jeb Bush, who as a governor had defunded Planned Parenthood in the state of Florida, said, "I'm not sure we need half a billion dollars for women's health issues." Soon after, Bush said, "Planned Parenthood is not actually doing women's health issues," a claim the *Washington Post* called "patently incorrect."

For their part, Democrats up and down the party issued statements underscoring their support for women's health, abortion rights, and Planned Parenthood. Presidential candidate Bernie Sanders issued a pro–Planned Parenthood press release and later told *Fusion Media*, "I think a lot of this attack, to be honest with you, comes from people who simply do not believe that a woman should have the right to control her own body." Hillary Clinton released a video calling out the GOP for retrograde views. "If this feels like a full-on assault on women's health, that's because it is. Unfortunately these attacks aren't new, they're more of the same," Clinton said on the video. "We're not going to let them get away with it. We're not going back. We're going to fight back. I'm proud to stand with Planned Parenthood. I'll never stop fighting to protect the ability and right of every woman in this country to make her own health decisions."

Three days after the Senate vote, the 2016 Republican candidates met for their first televised debate of the campaign season and clamored for attention from right-wing primary voters. Every candidate, from front-runner Donald Trump to also-ran Rand Paul, vowed that if they were president, Planned Parenthood would be defunded. Ted Cruz, architect of the 2013 government shutdown, vowed to shut down the government rather than allow Planned Parenthood funding to go forward. Marco Rubio testily insisted that he was against abortion in all cases, even for rape victims. In the second Republican candidates debate, Carly Fiorina said the CMP videos showed "a fully formed fetus on the table, its heart beating, its legs kicking while someone says we have to keep it alive to harvest its brain." Her poll numbers soared briefly, but then fell back into the single digits when it was definitively proven her statement was a lie and voters began to scrutinize her mixed record as a CEO. On the eve of the third debate, Ben Carson likened women who had abortions to slave owners. That same week showed him taking first place in polls of likely Republican primary voters.

By early fall, as the 2016 GOP primary shaped up with more than a dozen candidates trying to break out from the pack, it was looking as if the Republican Party was going to reprise its part in 2012's election year controversies over women and their bodies. And now as then, public opinion surveys indicated they were undermining their party with the general public. In the midst of the controversy, an NBC News/*Wall Street Journal* poll found that the public viewed Planned Parenthood more favorably than any national politician, every single GOP presidential candidate, and both political parties. A month later a Pew Research Center poll showed that 64 percent of independents and 83 percent of Democrats believed that "any budget agreement must maintain funding for Planned

Parenthood." The same poll found that only 19 percent approved of Republican leaders in Congress. Despite a historic nuclear deal with Iran, multiplying crises in the Middle East, the burgeoning Black Lives Matter movement, the hottest year on record, and a host of other pressing issues, abortion and women's health were at the top of the candidates' agenda. The delirium was once again in full bloom.

"I KNOW FROM looking at polling that women and men were highly aware of the attacks on women going into the 2012 election," Planned Parenthood president Cecile Richards told me. Long before the summer 2015 sting videos, many states had passed laws that eliminated the organization's public funding or imposed medically unnecessary regulations on clinics that forced them to close. In 2013, as these laws were first making their way through Republican-controlled state houses, I spoke with Richards. Why, I asked, did she think Planned Parenthood had been singled out?

"Planned Parenthood is the largest reproductive health care provider in the country," she answered. "So, I do think some people are motivated by an idea that if they could just get rid of Planned Parenthood, they could really end reproductive health care access for millions of women. I also think—it's a motivation that I can't fully understand—but for those people who believe that life was better in America when women were not in the workforce, when we were staying home exclusively to raise children, Planned Parenthood, I think, is an enormous symbol of the progress that women have made over the last several decades. I didn't fully appreciate this until a few years ago, when it was the 50th anniversary of the birth control pill, and I started reading up on it," she continued. "It's fascinating to see the demarcation in this country of when women started being able to finish college, go into graduate programs, explore the professions, be astronauts, you name it. Just when the pill was approved by the FDA, you can begin to map so much more equity for women. So I think some folks think maybe we can put the genie back in the bottle."

"We've been doing polling on women's issues for a long time and I have elected a huge stable of female candidates," Democratic pollster Lisa Grove said. In 2012, she was a lead pollster for the Obama reelection campaign, charged specifically with improving the president's vote with independent women in competitive swing states. "What we kept finding was outrage. They're like, 'Hello, Republican member of Congress. You were supposed to deliver on the economy and instead what you've been doing is dithering in a place that's mine.' Republicans thinking that they can adjudicate things like access to birth control not only makes our base Democratic voters fired up, it really creates a lot of animosity with swing voters. They think it's none of your business."

In 2012, according to the nonpartisan Sunlight Foundation, Planned Parenthood's political action committee was the single most effective PAC of the 2012 cycle, with a 98 percent success rate. (By comparison, Karl Rove's PAC American Crossroads had a 1 percent success rate.) "Over almost 100 years of history, you touch a lot of women, a lot of families, a lot of communities. One in five American women will have attended or been a patient in some way, shape, or form at a Planned Parenthood over their lifetime," Dawn Laguens, vice president of Planned Parenthood's political action committee told me. Laguens thought they had been successful because they had gotten a message out simply using Mitt Romney's own words. "And boy, when they found out what Mitt Romney's statements were, they fled from him. 'Wait, is he against Planned Parenthood? He wants to overturn *Roe v. Wade*?' Women know that the gains women have made—on wages, on education, on health, and so on—are directly tied to their reproductive rights. They recognized all this as a worldview. All these things, I think, piled up to a real view of going backward for women."

Katie Packer Gage, Romney's 2012 deputy campaign manager, sharply disputed that characterization of her former boss. "The Democrats tried to convey that Mitt Romney wanted to take away birth control, which was the craziest thing," she said. (In fact, Romney had publicly campaigned against the Affordable Care Act mandate that health insurance had to include contraception at no cost. Romney had also endorsed a Rubio-sponsored bill to allow employers who claimed a "moral objection" to deny their employees' birth control coverage.) "But I do think that the Democrats did a very effective job of depicting Republicans as these old, white, rich cavemen that wanted to get involved in your personal life."

Voters do not care much about women's reproductive issues, Gage argued, as many Republicans do. So she thought the GOP could attract women voters by redirecting attention to other subjects, like the economy or jobs. "The reality is that you're not going to change the opinions of a lot of these people—particularly on issues like abortion—that people think are life-and-death," she said. "There's about a third of women that are somewhere in the middle. They might be pro-life but don't feel like you should tell anybody else what to do. They might be pro-choice, but it's not really a critical issue for them. And Republicans can cobble together enough support from women if they just don't come across like angry, nasty cavemen."

Gage and her business partners have set themselves the job of civilizing the cavemen, so to speak. "We've spent a lot of time talking to candidates about how you can be pro-life and still convey an awful lot of compassion for women who find themselves with an unplanned pregnancy. You don't have to come across like some of our candidates have in the past. We were very strong advocates of engaging in the primary process this time around so that we didn't have people, like Richard Mourdock and Todd Akin, who come across in a way that's so off-putting—even to conservative women—that it hurts the whole party brand." Gage was referring to the cases where Missouri GOP Senate candidate Akin had said rape victims do not get pregnant from "legitimate rape," and Indiana GOP Senate candidate Mourdock had said if women did become pregnant from rape, it was because "God intended it." Both had been favored to win their races before they made the remarks, and both lost.

As we've seen, Gage's company came into being to improve the GOP's performance with women, and it was instrumental in devising the party's new message on abortion and birth control for the 2014 election cycle. Even Republican candidates with extreme records on women's reproductive health successfully avoided being tarred as anti-women—despite much effort by Democrats to rekindle the war-on-women message. When you factor in the "pro-life litmus test," as Margaret Hoover put it, it becomes more apparent why a change in tone or branding was the only option, as Gage acknowledged.

"There are some places where, on the issues, candidates just are where they are," Gage continued. "But you can address the way they talk about it, and talk about solutions to reduce the number of abortions that are occurring, and like I said, show compassion. One of the things that I communicate to candidates is that a lot of Republicans talk about abortion as if that's the only really sucky choice that a woman has. The reality is, if a woman has an unplanned pregnancy, all of her choices suck. So, when you talk about it and communicate, 'Well, you've got all these other great options but you're picking the bad one,' it doesn't show any real understanding or compassion for the situation that they found themselves in. And just changing the tone and conveying like, 'Look, I understand that a woman facing an unplanned pregnancy is a woman in crisis, and we need to put our arms around her and show her some support.' When we talked to women in focus groups, they're like, 'Yeah. I could get behind a candidate that disagrees with me on that issue if he sounds like he cared.'"

Others, however, thought that women wanted something besides a politician's arms around them. "When we were talking in 2012 about the war on women, what conservatives didn't understand is that for women, these issues represented not just the issue itself, but an idea of fundamental respect," Karen Finney, a former Clinton administration communications aide and an MSNBC contributor during the 2012 campaign, recalled. "There was this catalytic effect. Young women particularly got much more engaged than they had been and started to recognize that these rights they had taken for granted, that you had to keep fighting for them. The way Republicans talk about these things makes a lot of women think that you have no idea who we are and what we do and how we live our lives."

"The attacks on women are not just about losing access to a specific right or a specific health care benefit, but a total disregard for women," Richards said. "You see that in the stories women tell. My mom told me once—she told me more than once—that people do things for their reasons, not for your reasons. She was talking about politics, but I think that's true in general." Richards began her career as a union organizer in Texas and Louisiana working with immigrant women garment and hotel workers. "Back in those days, even though I could be organizing someone who's making $3.25 an hour and really had huge economic issues, for them it was as much about respect and dignity as it was about their economic situation. I think that's what we've seen in politics recently with this outpouring about what has been happening to women."

"There are reasons that we fight for abortion access and decision making in the hands of the individual," Ilyse Hogue, president of NARAL Pro-Choice America, said. "Those reasons are about common values of autonomy, self-determination, equality, and justice. And we don't do ourselves any favors when we don't actually lean into our values." Like Finney and Richards, she thought that larger questions of women's place and status in America were at stake in the conflict over abortion and birth control. "The opposition has become brazen and is willing to say things out loud that they only used to whisper behind closed doors. It really is an agenda based on a very antiquated view of women—about women's roles, where women belong, who has control in society, all the way down to inside the home. That's offensive to a lot of people. And it's also not real. It so does not reflect where the majority of the country is right now."

The alarm over women's reproductive rights was not limited to Democrats. "When family planning comes under attack, you know we're in trouble," Republican senator Olympia Snowe told me. "I literally thought this was the retro debates of the '50s. I felt like I was going backwards."

The 2012 battles over the contraception mandate had been the last straw for Snowe, a senator known for her willingness to cross the aisle, her legislative acumen, and her veneration for the Senate as a deliberative institution. The Senate had in her view become so dysfunctional—dramatized by taking up legislation by Marco Rubio and Roy Blunt to allow employers to deny birth control to employees if they had a "moral objection" to it—that she decided not to run for reelection that year. (She was virtually guaranteed a victory—that is, if the right wing of the Maine Republican Party didn't knock her out in the primary.)

"The Republican Party had the basic principles of individual freedom and opportunity, which stands in stark contrast to the party that now is denying women the capacity to make decisions—very difficult, personal decisions," she continued. "Now it extends to family planning. It totally contradicts the basic principles of the Republican Party. It's a massive government intrusion in my estimation."

Likewise, it was a big change from where the party had been. When Snowe first ran for Congress in 1979, she recalled, "The national Republican Party was prepared to endorse me, even though I was a pro-choice Republican. That was not even a subject that came up in our conversation or on our agenda. They were just anxious to have more women within the Republican ranks. Sort of goes into the category of Ripley's Believe It or Not!"

Other pro-choice Republicans felt that the way politicians were trying to placate the pro-life base by focusing on women's reproductive rights was not just contrary to Republican ideals, but also disastrous from a purely political perspective. Candy Straight, who is personally pro-choice but supports pro-life candidates, shortly after the 2014 midterms told me, "You can't be pessimistic about the outlook for the Republican Party. It was a huge failure of the Democratic Party not to win those governors' races in Maryland and Massachusetts in 2014." Still, she warned presciently before Congress convened, power itself could prove to be a mixed blessing. "Republicans control both houses. If all they do is introduce legislation relating to taking away reproductive rights from women and nothing else, I think there will be a backlash against them. I hope they concentrate on other issues. But right now the jury's out."

When I asked Margaret Hoover what she thought was attract-
ing women, especially those in their twenties and thirties, to the
Republican Party, she answered. "Nothing is drawing women to
the Republican party."

Her response frankly surprised me. In that case, I asked, what
was keeping them away?

"I think it comes down to abortion and the way the Republican
Party handles it. Truly, honestly, I think the kids—the millennials,
the youth—they're not absolutists when it comes to some of these
social issues. The majority of people are still not for overturning *Roe
v. Wade*. In other words, I think they wouldn't have an abortion for
the most part. I think they'd probably advise their friends probably
not to have abortions. But they don't want it to be illegal and they
don't want the federal government telling them they can't."

SO NOT ONLY was there fundamental disagreement about wom-
en's reproductive rights, but also contradictory assessments about
how much Americans cared about the issue and how much it influenced the outcome of elections. Who was right?

Let's start with the evidence from nonpartisan public opinion
surveys. According to Pew, a solid majority of Americans under
the age of seventy thought abortion should be legal in all or most
cases, and Democrats held a 19-point advantage over Republicans
on the question of which party was better at dealing with policies
on abortion and contraception. Public Religion Research Institute
(PRRI) found in 2014 that 55 percent favored legal abortion
in all or most cases. A 2015 *Vox* poll found that 67 percent of

Americans opposed overturning *Roe v. Wade*, a finding consistent with more than thirty years of surveys on the Supreme Court's 1972 ruling. Sixty percent thought the trend to "make it harder for women to get abortion care" was going "in the wrong direction." A separate PRRI large-scale survey of millennials confirmed that 55 percent favored the legal right to abortion, and 56 percent opposed making it more difficult to get an abortion. Large majorities of millennials—81 percent—supported increased access to birth control for women who couldn't afford it, and six in ten believed that privately owned corporations (like Hobby Lobby) should be required to provide no-cost contraception in employee health plans. (PRRI also found that the pro-choice and pro-life labels had become largely irrelevant to millennials, particularly for Hispanics, African Americans, and Asian Pacific Islanders.) Gallup, which polled the ambiguous pro-choice versus pro-life identification, found pro-choice identification ahead, 50 percent to 44 percent, the highest level of support in seven years.

In short, according to the most respected nonpartisan public opinion firms, Republicans were out of step with the American people on the right to legal abortion, and even more out of the mainstream on contraception access.

But in the cold reality of elections, such a wide gap between the public and a party matters only if people vote those views and reject candidates who don't share them.

On one hand, Gage was correct that in most elections the majority of voters did not base their vote primarily on a candidate's position on legal abortion. Nonetheless, abortion has been a decisive issue in several recent presidential elections, and in every case, the candidate favoring the legal right to abortion has prevailed. Several independently conducted peer-reviewed studies by political scientists reached the conclusion that support for abortion rights was an important factor in Bill Clinton's victory in the 1992 and 1996 presidential elections. Exit polling from the 2012 election showed a spike in those favoring legal abortion, to a near-record 59 percent, compared to only 36 percent who favored outlawing abortion. A study by political scientists Melissa Deckman and John McTague on the 2012 election found that support for the birth control mandate was a key predictor of women's vote choice for Obama. Controlling for other factors, a woman who supported the mandate was 23 percentage points more likely to vote for Obama. (Men who were supportive also were more likely to vote for Obama, but not to the same degree.) It was likely a contributing factor to the three-point increase in the gender gap between 2008 and 2012. Deckman and McTague concluded, "Insurance coverage for birth control appears to have been a decisive factor for many voters, especially women."

Thus the 2012 election was, in part, a referendum on the Republican presidential ticket's proposed rollback of women's reproductive rights. Yet even as Obama was reelected and Democrats preserved their Senate majority, the GOP emerged from that election with control of twenty-five states, a result partly of gerrymandering by Tea Party Republicans after their 2010 midterm victory. In the nine months after the 2012 elections, more than 450 provisions were introduced in the states to restrict access to abortion and birth control. In the first three weeks of the 114th Congress, Republicans introduced eleven new restrictions on abortion. The Republican-controlled House of Representatives passed several anti-abortion bills, including a twenty-week ban on abortions that required pregnant rape victims to report to police in order to be allowed to abort. In the first quarter of 2015 alone, state lawmakers introduced an additional 332 provisions restricting abortion access. All told, between 2010 and mid-2015, Republican state lawmakers passed nearly 300 restrictions on access to abortion and birth control.

The evidence mounted that the battles over women's health made abortion a more salient political issue and in fact increased support for reproductive rights. Pew tracked a 9-point increase between October 2014 and July 2015 among those who thought Democrats were better than Republicans at "dealing with policies on abortion and contraception." In 2015, when Gallup reported that for the first time in seven years, Americans were "pro-choice," it seemed to indicate that the anti-abortion laws had provoked a backlash, particularly among women and among Democrats. Pro-choice identification had increased by 12 percentage points—to 68 percent—between 2001 and 2015. A gender gap had opened up between men and women in the three years after the 2012 election. Fifty-four percent of women identified pro-choice, compared to 46 percent of men. (It is often assumed that the gender gap reflects opinion about abortion, but historically there has been no significant difference in men's and women's views of abortion.) A new generational gap was evident as well, with those under the age of thirty-five the most pro-choice, and those over fifty-five the least. Fifty percent of independents identified pro-choice. Two-thirds of all voters indicated that abortion was an important factor in how they voted, with 21 percent saying they would only support a candidate who shared their view. Only a quarter of voters said abortion did not matter at all to them. Gallup speculated that the pro-choice trend seemed to be part of a "broader liberal shift in Americans' ideology" and thus has staying power.

ALL ROADS RAN back to *Roe v. Wade*, and so to the presidential race. "The stakes in 2016 for reproductive freedom are significant. The politics are such that we don't have any pro-choice Republicans running. That didn't use to be the case," Ilyse Hogue said, when I asked her about the presidential election. "The Supreme Court is high on our minds. The court showed with the Hobby Lobby decision how out of touch they are with the everyday reality of women. That was just an inkling of where they could go with the cases coming before them. And there are a lot of cases coming. We would be blind if we weren't concerned about retirements." Four justices are in their late seventies and eighties, including women's rights champion Ruth Bader Ginsburg. "Absolutely, the next president will have a disproportionate effect on the makeup of the court."

"In imagining *Roe v. Wade*, who would have thought in the 21st century we would be fighting these issues to the extent that we are?" Snowe said. "In many ways, we have rolled back many significant rights. So that's the big challenge and that's the big battle, frankly. When I think about where we were when I began in

Congress in '79, it's almost hard to believe. If I were to have pro-jected thirty-five years out, I never would have come to the conclu-sion that those rights are threatened as much as they are today."

Early on Cecile Richards foresaw how reproductive rights might play out in the 2016 presidential race. "Some of us thought after the 2012 election that there would be a toning down, particularly among the Republican leadership—some rethinking that, 'boy, this is just not a fruitful avenue.' But the evidence, at least in the state legislatures and by some in Congress, is directly opposite. I think, unfortunately, there is a part of the Republican Party right now that is not representative of the mainstream, but that is hell-bent on going after women and women's rights. They are a very vocal, activist minority, and they are driving the Republican Party agenda. So I will not be surprised if these issues are front and center again in the 2016 elections."

"It wasn't that long ago that we had a lot of pro-choice Republicans—in the '90s and '80s and '70s," Margaret Hoover said. "And by the way, Barry Goldwater's wife helped open a Planned Parenthood in Arizona. You had pro-choice Republicans all throughout the West and all throughout the Northeast. It was the Reagan coalition—the synthesizing of the evangeli-cal Protestant base with the conservative movement—that made this issue part of the party platform. This is really recent history. There's no reason some really smart, organized people can't change it. We just haven't organized ourselves." Hoover was critical of the Planned Parenthood PAC and NARAL for putting all their cards on Democratic candidates. "A winning strategy really would be to have robust pro-choice candidates on both sides. Win the issue, don't win the party. I think it's a bad strategy to only bank on one party, because what happens when your party is out of power?"

Going on public opinion alone, Hoover was right that there was opportunity to draw the Republican Party back into the mainstream. Polling has consistently shown that at least three in ten self-identified Republicans think that abortion should remain legal. But the Republican presidential contest offered mounting evidence of a swerve even further to the right and no sign that the focus on women's reproductive health would abate.

"Women's reproductive rights in this country are at a crisis point," Hogue continued, as we talked about the implications of 2016 for women's health and rights. "I think it's going to take a long time to undo the damage, but I think we have a lot of the necessary elements in place. I am, perhaps, uncharacteristically optimistic. When the pendulum has swung so far in the direction against us, if we play it right, it doesn't stop where it was before. We have an opportunity for an evolutionary leap in how the culture understands what women need to thrive."

Under Hogue's leadership, NARAL was still defending access to abortion yet also expanding to advocate for stronger protections for pregnant workers, guaranteed universal access to the most effective forms of contraception, and paid parental leave. "You start to look at other elements of what reproductive freedom means to people in the 21st century. There is a continuum. We see this with the post-*Roe* generation—dedication to preserving legal abortion is matched by a holistic understanding that I'm the same woman when I'm trying not to get pregnant as when I do get pregnant and I have kids. So, how do abortion rights fit into a broader agenda?

"For years we played on a right-wing frame, which is that voters care about jobs and the economy, not social issues. It's the biggest straw man out there. I've traveled all over this country, and I have not met a single woman who is like, 'My womb is over here and my job security is over here.' These are not two separate issues." PRRI's millennial poll confirmed Hogue's impression; 64 percent of young women and 55 percent of young men said that access to contraception was "critical" to women's financial security. And two-thirds of millennial women felt that there was still significant discrimination against women in the workplace.

Hogue continued, "Most people I interact with—not just women by the way—really understand that their ability to have control over when, how, and if they have kids has everything to do with their economic security. That's where the conversation is going—and really needs to go. It's easy to take it there. For the vast majority of the up-and-coming voting population, that's their lived experience. You're not trying to teach anyone anything. In fact in many ways, the institutions are catching up with where people are."

Chapter 9

BREAKTHROUGH

I T WAS AN early fall night, and a couple dozen women in their twenties were gathered around a portable fire pit, chatting over wine and Trader Joe's appetizers in a concrete backyard in San Francisco. The conversation careened back and forth from tech start-ups and coding trainings to the upcoming midterm elections and global feminism. Cold gusts of wind whipped smoke from the haphazardly built fire first this way, then that. There were no tongs or poker in sight. Apparently the roommates hosting the monthly meeting of Women Get It Done had never been Girl Scouts.

I had joined them to gauge how young women felt about politics in general and a woman president in particular. When talk turned to women's status in politics, several chimed in that women were better at compromise and collaboration and getting things done, not just in politics but across the board. "It's abysmal. Women only hold 25 percent of offices in this country. We are 50 percent of the population. That's not equal representation in any way, shape, or form," a twenty-three-year-old who worked in politics said. "Do I think more women need to be in office? Yes. A wonderful example of why was the birth control hearings that the House held. I personally do not think that a bunch of old, conservative, white men know what it's like to be a young woman in her twenties who is trying to focus on her career and not have a family immediately. That's not to say that I don't want a family eventually!"

That afternoon I had met the group's cofounder, Kate Maeder, at her office, where the self-described data geek specialized in data analysis and microtargeting for a progressive political firm. Precinct maps and campaign posters covered the walls and a plastic basketball hoop hung on the door. Maeder is tall with wavy shoulder-length hair, hazel eyes, and a smile with a touch of mystery about it. Maeder recalled the genesis of Women Get It Done. In May 2012, she met friends on a Saturday afternoon for a picnic at Dolores Park and got to talking with two other women. "We were all pissed. No one was mentoring us in the workplace. There were no groups we felt we could belong to. I'm an organizer at heart, and I realized there was a real void. Young women felt so much discontent and frustration," she said.

It was striking that a group of go-getter, young, progressive women in San Francisco felt they had no group to belong to. If any city in America has an old boys' and old girls' progressive club, it is San Francisco. The new lean-in brand had been created nearby. Quickly the three turned to six, and then grew more, and they started holding salon-style gatherings. They named their group Women Get It Done and gave it a tagline: More of a fight club than a sorority. "To my surprise, a lot of people wanted to join. We grew and grew," Maeder went on. "And then in July 2013 Ready for Hillary reached out to us. They had been a DC-based group up to that time. They asked, 'Can you help us throw our first grassroots fundraiser?' I want to dedicate my life to empowering women and getting more women elected to office, so it was right in line with my passion." They came up with the idea of asking for a $20.16 donation, which was then replicated throughout the country. By the summer of 2015, WGID had formed a board, and groups were meeting in Los Angeles, Oakland, and Washington, DC.

At the meeting that night, Maeder was leading the discussion, and she brought it around to Hillary. Were they excited about her running for president? Did they support her? Applause and a chorus of voices went up, it seemed from nearly everyone. "I'm so fucking ready for her to get shit done," twenty-five-year-old Emma Gibbens said. "Hillary Clinton is our patron saint. She's our patroness," a Wellesley graduate said, which everyone loved. (Clinton's first step into the national spotlight was from the Wellesley stage. Chosen as the first student commencement speaker at the prestigious women's college, she had given a powerful political protest speech and had been profiled in *Life* magazine as a voice of her generation.)

When Maeder asked if there were any other women they looked up to or would support if Clinton didn't run, six or so voices went up for Elizabeth Warren. Four or five Kirsten Gillibrand fans drowned them out. Still, about three-quarters of the women said they would volunteer on Clinton's campaign, and several talked about quitting their jobs to join it.

"I want a woman president for so many reasons," Danielle Mulein told me later. Mulein, a political junkie and marketing manager at a firm that worked with women corporate executives, had volunteered for a congressman in high school and, after college, had worked in Colorado for Obama's 2012 campaign. She jokingly called herself a professional feminist. "I think that there is a real search and a hunger for more women in political office and particularly for a woman president. I find that people feel like what we're doing now isn't working. They're beginning to get fed up with the fact that all of these white guys, all these older men, are running the show in Washington. That doesn't correspond with the general public. I think there is this idea that having a woman would break down so many barriers for other people, for those who are minorities. There are so many different avenues that will be opened once we have a female president that I do find that a lot of people have that hunger. They want a change."

DOES AMERICA'S RECENT fascination with women's leadership—seen everywhere in pop culture from best-selling books like Sheryl Sandberg's *Lean In* to the TV hits *Scandal* and *Veep* to Beyoncé's feminist MTV Video Music Awards performance—extend to the political realm? If women are not punished at the ballot box for being women, as we have seen, are they rewarded? Are women especially attracted to women candidates?

"We did polling right after the 2012 election to find out what independent women were thinking about the election," EMILY's List president Stephanie Schriock told me. "One question we asked was, I'm paraphrasing, 'Did you know a record number of women were elected, and do you think it matters?' Really for the first time in our polling they said yes by a large majority. It does matter. It's going to make things better. That was a huge change."

In America's last presidential election, as we saw, women favored Barack Obama by 11 points and women's votes were decisive in his reelection. The gender gap—the difference between women and men's vote—was near a historic high at 10 points. Moreover, women made up 53 percent of all voters in 2012. (Women have cast a greater number of votes than men in every presidential election since 1964.)

Women's votes matter, and as long as women outnumber men at the polls, they matter disproportionately. So what do women want? What are their hopes and their fears, their ambitions and their frustrations? Does it matter to American women that the nation elects a woman president?

A bevy of public opinion surveys and academic research indicates that women voters do care. Sixty-nine percent of Democratic women hoped to see a woman president in their lifetime, according to a large-scale Pew Research Center 2014 survey on women in leadership. In an earlier poll by ABC, 69 percent of Democratic women said that electing more women to Congress would be "a good thing." In the Pew survey, four in ten women said that having more women in top positions in government would do a lot to improve the quality of life for all women. The academic scholarship confirms that women are motivated by and enthusiastic about women in political leadership. Various studies on the United States and other countries, for example, have shown that women candidates and lawmakers inspire women to participate more in political life, to vote at higher

levels, and to feel more confidence and trust in government. If anything, the effect is stronger in the United States than it is in other
countries. In a large study comparing democratic nations, the United
States was one of only two nations where girls showed a statisti-
cally higher rate than boys of anticipated involvement in politics as
adults. When Gallup asked for open-ended responses regarding "the
best or most positive thing about a Hillary Clinton presidency," one
in three Democrats and one in six independents volunteered that it
would be that she would be the "first woman president."

"In 2016, we will have the most pro-woman-candidate electorate we have ever had," Democratic pollster Celinda Lake said.

Advancing women's political leadership has been one of Lake's
passions since she began her career fresh out of graduate school on
the 1984 Mondale-Ferraro presidential campaign. "I love polling. I
love learning people's opinions on why they think about things and
I have a lot of affection and respect for the voters," Lake, a legendary workaholic, said about her motivations for doing this work.
"I'm very motivated by social change. I want to see more women
and people of color represented in the political system."

I met Lake at her company's office just off of K Street in
Washington, DC, one evening two months before the 2014 election. Lake was wearing a loose-fitting bohemian blue dress and a
striking silver and turquoise necklace. She seemed to be hardwired
to her iPad. Lake grew up in Montana—like Stephanie Schriock.
When I asked her what was in the air out there, she said, "I'll show
you what is in the air." Above uncountable stacks of papers and
books, photos and professional awards, sculptures and knickknacks

from her many travels, hung what she called her "most inspiring" poster—a faded black-and-white photograph of a few dozen women in cowboy hats on horseback, captioned: Cowgirls at the Round-Up, 1911. To Lake, it was no coincidence that women from the West were so prominent among today's champions of women in politics. "I do think there was something in the West," she said. "In Montana we had the first woman in Congress. Many of the western states gave women the franchise earlier. I do think in general women in the West have played an important role."

So what were voters thinking about the next presidential contest, I asked, especially regarding the possibility of electing a woman president?

"I think the context of 2016 is kind of a harmonic convergence," she said. "The groups of voters who want women candidates will be the most dominant that they have ever been. People who vote for women candidates tend to be college-educated women, unmarried women under fifty-five, women of color, and they'll all be at their biggest proportions ever in the electorate." Also, she continued, "I think people are very eager for someone who can bring people together, who can compromise, who says, 'Let's get things done.' And that's a trait traditionally associated with women." Voters were looking for leaders who understood their lives, and women had an advantage there too. "People think that current politicians are very much out of touch."

Finally, there were two groups who were especially invested in electing a woman president and viewed 2016 as a historic opportunity. "I think there is a growing pool of people," Lake continued, "of baby boomer women, who worry they'll never see a woman president in their lifetime, and younger women, who think it's about time we had more women in leadership." She added, "I think Hillary Clinton is a unique iconic figure. She is particularly well suited to the moment—she has all the strengths of women candidates and doesn't have the weaknesses."

Discontent with the nation's political dysfunction was one of the key background facts in Lake's analysis of 2016 as a "harmonic convergence." Lisa Grove, another prominent Democratic pollster, also believed that women candidates had an advantage in this context. Voters had hoped for change in 2008 and 2012, Grove said. "They're frustrated that things seemed to stay the same. Yet they're more inspired and have more optimism when they think about women candidates running. In female voters' minds, women tend to be running for the right reasons."

Grove and her firm had worked with EMILY's List on polling and focus groups of independent women during the 2014 cycle. As part of the study, participants were asked, "When you think of our nation's leaders—specifically the people in Congress—what is the first image that comes to mind?" One woman sent in a photo showing a sloth hanging upside down off a leafy tree branch. Another said she pictured "a bunch of old men with their arms crossed and grouchy looks on their faces." Still another offered an image of a young, clean-shaven, white professional, his hands cupped in front of his face, chomping on a pile of $100 bills.

"People looked at Congress and other legislative bodies, and they said three things," Grove told me. "They're old, they're white, and they're gendered—they're old white guys. So women, by virtue of their gender, are change agents. I think women are just better at the 'I feel your pain' message and can do it in a way that is more authentic. It's an important part of the psychological connection that needs to be made between a voter and a candidate."

On the one hand, in recent years women voters have shown enthusiasm for Democratic women candidates (when the candidate's values lined up with their own and the candidate ran a good campaign—by no means a given in all cases). Women wanted more women in government and they were frustrated at the lack of parity. But like most political operatives, Grove believed it was a bad idea for candidates to appeal to women as women too explicitly. Instead, she thought women candidates should highlight the assumptions voters already held about women leaders. "Women have these bios of service. What that says is, 'You get what life is like for me.' Even if they don't have these bios, the default for women is, 'You understand what my life is like.' You don't have to be Patty Murray wearing tennis shoes for people to think you've walked in my shoes." Murray, one of the Democratic women senators elected in 1992's Year of the Woman and a onetime preschool teacher, had campaigned as "a mom in tennis shoes."

Likewise, Grove believed that progressive policies on women's issues, such as on equal pay, raising the minimum wage, and paid family leave resonated with women—with independents as well as Democrats. "They say, 'Okay, you know what? I'm willing to buy into these candidates and believe that there are people who get what life is like for me and want to make it better," she said. It showed that Democrats were in touch, she thought, and that they understood what women needed to be able to determine their own destiny, both on health and economic well-being.

"On the left, the idea of electing the first woman president right after the first African American president would be something great. It certainly plays a factor among Democrats," Robert Jones, the head of the nonpartisan Public Religion Research Institute (PRRI), said, putting Grove and Lake's admittedly partisan interpretation in perspective. "On the right, the biggest baggage Hillary has is not that she is a woman but that she's Bill Clinton's wife."

Political scientist Ronnee Schreiber, whose specialty is women on the right, agreed. When I asked her how they viewed the possibility of a woman president, she said with a laugh, "Their main goal will be to make sure that Hillary Clinton does not become president!" She added that they would love to see women like Kelly Ayotte, Nikki Haley, or Cathy McMorris Rodgers run in the future.

Still, Republican women universally said they looked forward to a Republican woman presidential candidate. "I think if there were somebody that was eminently qualified and capable of being president that was running, women on the Republican side would be just as excited," Republican consultant Katie Packer Gage told me. "I don't think women on the Republican side are as willing to overlook other shortcomings just to have a woman."

I asked if that meant she thought Democrats were willing to overlook shortcomings in their candidates.

"Sometimes, yeah," she chuckled.

"What about the case of Sarah Palin?" I asked.

"I don't think you saw Republican women jumping all over that thing, 'Let's go. She's a woman. Vote for her.' I think that there were a lot of Republican women who held their nose and did not think she was particularly qualified. That's part of why we lost," Gage said. "I don't think that there was this big outcry from Republican women saying, 'Support Sarah Palin because she's a woman.' She just happened to be a woman. I'd like to see the day where we have a woman candidate, somebody like a Joni Ernst—I don't mean her for president now. But in her case, when she was running for the Senate in Iowa, the fact that she was a woman was the fourth or fifth thing that qualified her."

"I think we've got a pretty good bench," Chriss Winston said. "Do I think Fiorina's going anywhere? No, I don't. I like her, and so on, and wish she'd won that Senate race in California, but she didn't. Which is not helpful as a stepping-stone for the presidency."

The GOP's apparent woman problem at the presidential level, as Gage and Winston observed, was partly because none of the party's top-tier women officeholders chose to run for president in 2016. Moreover, as Gage's remark suggested, Republican women seemed to be particularly sensitive to the ways in which Palin had set the party back. Margaret Hoover praised women who she believed had presidential potential. "Kelly Ayotte is just as qualified as Scott Walker. Susan Collins and Lisa Murkowski are far more savvy in the ways of Washington and how to get things done than half the Republican contenders on the right." But she emphasized that someone like New Mexico governor Susana Martinez, whom she admired, needed more experience. "She is an incredibly capable governor. But there's a long way to go from being a small western state governor to being a leader of the free world, to use a term from the Cold War. We saw that with Sarah Palin, right? You're really not ready to be a good president if you're just a governor of a small western state—you're really not. You're not versed in the issues, you're not speaking about national politics, and you're not going to be effective at working with Congress. There are just a hundred thousand reasons why Susana Martinez probably isn't ready to run for president. Truly, I think she would say that. And I think she should be a national figure. She should be heralded by the party. She should go work in the cabinet and really get exposure into national and international issues. I think that she has a great future."

But there was more to it than the absence of candidates or the Palin hangover. Public opinion surveys suggested that Republicans had only a marginal interest in promoting women's political leadership in general. Only 20 percent of Republican women were excited about electing a woman president, compared to 69 percent of Democratic women, according to a Pew analysis. The Pew report's authors noted, however, that for many Republicans "this view may be more about the prospect of a Hillary Clinton presidency than about a major milestone for women." Two-thirds of Democratic women thought electing more women to Congress would be "a good thing," but only a quarter of Republicans—women and men—thought so.

As we saw, Republicans labored after 2012 to improve their standing with women. But as in 2008, when enthusiasm to elect the first black president helped power the momentum of Obama's presidential bid, the GOP was likely going to find itself again on the wrong side of a potential historic milestone: the election of America's first woman president.

"I THINK GENDER is to Hillary Clinton's advantage but I don't think she has to say much. She shows up with the right body parts, people get it," Grove said. "Generally speaking, we get all our partisans and we get some independent women, and we've got enough to get across the finish line. I do believe that she may have to do some persuading with certain types of men, independent and very light blue male voters, to make it clear that she is the right candidate. That has to do with more Clinton-residue, perhaps, than her gender."

Grove raised an important concern, one that has bedeviled women candidates in recent years, especially as they aim for the highest offices. If women draw too much attention to the fact that they are women, do they risk alienating men?

Women win elections at rates similar to men, as we've seen. That would be impossible if men, in aggregate, did not support women candidates. Still, since the 1990s, the gender gap in voting and party identification has widened. The most recent large-scale analysis, by Pew, showed women identifying or leaning Democratic by a 16-point margin, while men were evenly split. In every demographic group—ethnic, racial, religious, age—women vote and identify more pro-Democratic than men. And there is substantial evidence from public opinion surveys and academic research that men do not view women's economic or social equality as a priority.

In recent polling, half as many men as women said that having more women in top leadership positions in government would do a lot to improve the quality of life for all women. Although a majority of Democratic men said they wanted to see more women in Congress, they did so by 15 percentage points less than Democratic women. And in a striking example of persisting gender bias, in Pew's survey on women's leadership, 27 percent of Republican men said that men make better political leaders than women. (Only 11 percent of Democratic men said men made better leaders, less than those who said women made better leaders.)

The verdict is mixed about how men feel about women candidates and respond to campaigning that highlights women's issues. On the one hand, men vote for women and generally hold the same views on social issues and gender equality. Political scientist Brian F. Schaffner found in a 2005 paper that there was no tradeoff when candidates—male or female—appealed explicitly to women. Campaigning on women's issues made women more likely to vote for a Democratic Senate candidate and had no effect on how men voted. Early polls by major news outlets on the 2016 election consistently showed Democratic men supporting Hillary Clinton by a 40- to 60-point margin. Before Massachusetts senator Elizabeth Warren definitively made it clear she would not run, and before Vermont independent senator Bernie Sanders entered the Democratic primary, Warren consistently polled second or third, ahead of Martin O'Malley and about even with Vice President Joe Biden. True, once Sanders rose into second place in the polls, he showed disproportionate support from white men. But men overall still preferred Clinton. In sum, the polls indicated that Democratic men had no qualms about electing women. Rather, party identification and ideology were the determining factors in their choice.

On the other hand, men historically have been less supportive than women of women candidates. Differing views on two areas are thought to be the main sources of the gender gap. One, men are generally less supportive of social welfare policies and more conservative on the role of government. Two, although men broadly share women's liberalism on reproductive rights and gender equality, they place less importance on these issues, and so don't tend to vote on them.

The most recent findings in public opinion, however, powerfully suggest that how men feel about women leaders and gender equality is in flux.

According to Lake, there are notable age, ethnic, and racial gaps among men themselves. Latino, African American, unmarried, and young men—members of what Lake calls the Rising American Electorate—tended to view women candidates positively. There were a number of reasons for that, Lake said, "The Rising American men are younger, so they're less into traditional gender roles. They're less religious and they're unmarried, so they don't have this traditional view of the role of women. They're people of color, so they're used to women's leadership in their communities." Likewise, in Grove's polling for the EMILY's List Madam President campaign, she found that these same groups showed enthusiasm for a woman presidential candidate. When asked if a woman running for president would make them more likely to pay attention to the campaign, 60 percent of Hispanics and 71 percent of African Americans said yes.

Lake and Grove are Democrats, granted, but their conclusions about age and ethnic differences among men were consistent with those of nonpartisan public opinion surveys. In ABC's survey on women in Congress, which we saw above, 54 percent of nonwhites said it would be good to elect more women, but only 38 percent of whites did. (That survey also indicated that so-called identity politics was not at the root of the enthusiasm, as a far lower share—29 percent—of nonwhites said it would be good to elect more nonwhites to Congress.) Pew's annual report on party identification supported Lake's portrait of the Democratic leanings of various demographic groups: African Americans were pro-Democratic by 69 points; Asian Americans by 42 points; Hispanics by 30 points; the religiously unaffiliated by 36 points; unmarried men by 17 points; and millennials by 16 points. A majority of all these groups identified or leaned Democratic. By contrast, 55 percent of white men without college degrees identified or leaned Republican, and only 33 percent identified or leaned Democratic. Mormons and white evangelical Protestants constituted the only demographic groups less Democratic than these less educated white men.

In short, not all men. As it turned out, the only men who appeared as if they would be cool to a potential Democratic woman presidential candidate were non-college-educated, older white men. But of course, white men had been unenthusiastic about Democratic presidential candidates for decades. The last Democrat to do well with them was the southern evangelical Jimmy Carter, who won 47 percent of their vote. Since 1988, Democrats have averaged just 38 percent of the white male vote—and they won the White House in four of those seven elections.

"HILLARY RUNNING IS just like a dream come true," WGID member Emma Gibbens told me. "I feel like to my generation and my mother's generation, Hillary is our icon. Me and my mother bonded over Hillary. We bonded over seeing a really intelligent woman at these higher levels. She was like the true trailblazer." Gibbens grew up in small towns in Alaska and Northern Minnesota and first got active in politics as a teenager, volunteering on Al Franken's 2008 Senate election campaign. As a college student and member of the College Democrats in Madison, Wisconsin, she had helped lead the massive demonstrations and sit-ins protesting Republican governor Scott Walker's policies. After graduation, Gibbens worked on local election campaigns in Wisconsin, before moving to California in 2012, where she was now working for a tech company on digital field canvassing tools. She was a progressive, so she was sympathetic to those who felt more enthusiasm for Democrats other than Clinton. "I understand where some people are coming from when they want Elizabeth Warren to run and they're not super invested in Hillary," she continued. "But that aside, Hillary still is completely one of the most intelligent, best situated women to run the country, so I'm absolutely ecstatic for her to run."

College students Denai Joseph, Andrea Chu, and Jordan Long had lined up at three in the morning at Clinton's Los Angeles book signing. "I love her," Joseph said. "She's a feminist. She's someone who has broken barriers for many people. And as someone who is a political science major and tries to venture into the world of politics, I want to know that is something that is feasible. She's an inspiration to me in that sense." Chu struck a similar note. "I think she's done a lot of groundbreaking work, especially as a woman in politics. She's such a great example for other young women who want to do this same kind of work," she said. Long, who was still wrapped in his UCLA Bruins blanket from their night camping out on the sidewalk, said, "Why has it taken us so long to have a female president? Other countries have done it, so why should the United States be in the background of that? We should be leading."

Tiffany and Chloe Majdipour, sisters aged nineteen and twenty who were University of California students and gender studies majors, woke up at 4:00 AM to come to Clinton's book signing. "We're really big fans of Hillary. She's an amazing woman. I'm inspired by her," Tiffany said. "Our mom loved her, so we loved her. I think it's just like the parents loved her when she was the First Lady and they just passed that on to their kids. I think the younger generation can relate to her. As you can see here, there's so much diversity here. You just can't help but love her. " Her sister Chloe added, "She's so qualified. She's ready and we're ready!"

The testimony of these millennial women and men about how Clinton inspired them was at odds with a commonly held assumption going into the 2016 election. Namely, that Clinton was too old, familiar, and boring to excite millennials. "Mrs. Clinton would love for young trendsetters to champion her cause and to replicate Mr. Obama's success at converting his cultural currency among young voters into hard votes," journalist Jason Horowitz wrote. "The question is then whether she can get young people excited about her candidacy. A temperature-taking in Washington Square Park was not promising," he concluded, in an unintentionally self-parodic tone, after six interviews conducted for a *New York Times* style section piece headlined "HILLARY CLINTON AIMS TO CAPTURE THE COOL."

How young people would vote was no joke. Once feted for sweeping Obama into the White House with their enthusiasm and optimism, after 2010, they were blamed for the Democrats' resounding defeats in the Congressional midterm elections during Obama's presidency. Certainly these impatient—read immature— kids would yawn at Hillary Clinton. The disenchantment and apathy of millennials, the media narrative went, endangered the Democrats' hold on the White House going forward.

Nothing generated more passion among Women Get It Done members than when I asked them if they thought the media accurately portrayed their generation.

"I wasn't eighteen at the time Hillary Clinton was in the primaries in California, unfortunately, so I could not vote for her then," Abby Ellis, a junior staffer in Senator Dianne Feinstein's office, said. But she was able to vote by November. "The 2008 campaign was just the most revolutionizing experience. Part of that was seeing how dysfunctional the government was, plus growing up in a conservative family in Southern California, all I wanted to do was change it. I did vote for President Obama in 2008 largely because I believed in change, and that he could change the government. Discrediting millennials is really doing a disservice to our generation—"

"—We're an optimistic generation," Kate Maeder interjected.

"—We are, we're very hopeful," Ellis continued. "Millennials aren't the ones who messed it up."

Moreover, they were under no illusions about how difficult it was to make change, and they were far less naive than pundits assumed. Like many Americans old and young, Gibbens felt frustrated about the nation's political dysfunction. "Everyone is pretty disgusted with the gridlock in Washington. It's just at a complete standstill—like, pass any freaking bill, my God!" she said. She believed that Clinton was the best person to tackle the problem. "I think that Hillary would be really instrumental in getting the country moving again—passing actual legislation. This is real and relevant and affects people's lives. I think that she would be able to reach across the aisle and also maybe get our own party in line. I mean she will get shit done when she is in office as the president."

Still, both Democrats and Republicans believed with good cause that the 2016 election could hinge on millennials. Feminist Majority Foundation president and Clinton supporter Eleanor Smeal was confident the results would be favorable. "They're idealistic, yet more savvy. They understand politics at what I would call a retail level, as well as at a theoretical level," she said. "They were trained well by Obama's campaigns. They know more because of the Rachel Maddows, Twitter, the blogs. They're far more knowledgeable about what is happening. We are going to have a groundswell, I can tell you right now!"

Others were less sanguine, because historically young voters have a disturbing tendency to sit out elections. When young adults vote at high levels, elections since the 1990s showed, Democrats won. When instead the young stayed home, older men and women made up a larger share of the electorate and tipped elections to the GOP. (Americans older than sixty-eight were the only age cohort that did not lean Democratic in 2014, according to Pew.) Bill Clinton and Barack Obama both inspired a voter surge among men and women under thirty; the youth vote was unusually low in 2000, when Republican George W. Bush narrowly defeated Democrat Al Gore. Most agreed that low turnout among young people was a significant factor in the GOP's victories in the 2010 and 2014 midterms. According to Pew, "Over the past decade, younger Americans have been the Democratic Party's strongest supporters in both vote preferences and partisanship, while older Americans have been the most reliably Republican."

The unique ethnic diversity of millennials—they were 40 percent nonwhite—and their progressive views on social issues combined to make them the most Democratic generation. Given that only the Democrats were poised to nominate a woman for president and that two out of three women in Congress were Democrats, the fate of women political leaders was anchored to millennials also.

So Democrats were right to worry how motivated millennials felt about the party and its candidates. Yet despite Republican efforts to attract millennials, Democrats and Hillary Clinton continued to hold a large advantage ahead of 2016. According to Pew, millennials identified or leaned Democratic by 16 percentage points. According to a large survey of millennials conducted in October 2014 for *Fusion Media*, 50 percent said they would likely vote for

Clinton in the general election against any Republican, while only 33 percent said they were likely to vote for the Republican nominee. Moreover, 58 percent of the Democratic millennials surveyed favored Clinton in their party's primary, compared to 9 percent who favored Warren and 2 percent for O'Malley. (Sanders was not polled, as he had not yet declared his candidacy.) Clinton did particularly well among the groups Lake identified as part of the rising American electorate; she won the support of 72 percent of young black voters, 63 percent of young Hispanic voters, and 54 percent of young women voters.

Millennials were a very Democratic generation, but beyond that, Clinton had unseen advantages with them—particularly with women. As Gibbens and the Majdipours described it, mothers and daughters had bonded as they witnessed Clinton's rise and her resilience. It was a story I heard in different varieties again and again.

When you think about it, it wasn't at all surprising. The oldest millennials were just on the cusp of adolescence when Clinton gave her historic speech on women's rights in Beijing. The youngest millennials were just starting their first American history classes in elementary school when Clinton put her first 18 million cracks in the highest glass ceiling. All millennials were too young to have witnessed firsthand the searing anti-feminism of the 1992 campaign, or Hillary's Icarus-like rise and fall over the Clinton effort at health care reform, or the endless hearings over Whitewater and other manufactured scandals. Not once in two years of interviewing did anyone under forty mention the name Monica Lewinsky to me. As they packed up for college and entered their first jobs, Clinton was

America's top diplomat, serving in the cabinet of a president for whom they had enormous respect.

In short, millennial women admired Clinton, were excited about her presidential candidacy, and often felt personally inspired by Hillary Clinton as an individual. To them she was an "icon"—a word many women used to describe her. Even more powerfully, Clinton embodied their hopes for themselves as women and their generation of women. Clinton was a model of their American dream, their burning impatience as young women to share equally in the highest offices and honors the nation had to offer.

Once again, as she was when she was a trailblazing First Lady in the 1990s, Hillary Clinton served as a Rorschach test for ideas about women's place in the nation. This time, however, the hopes seemed to overpower the fears. More "yes, we can" than "how dare she."

"THERE'S A BIG gap for women in political roles. I think that having Hillary in office as president would both inspire a lot of women and give us a role model to see, 'Oh hey, we can do it. This is where we can go. This is how we get there.' Just having that image up there makes a world of difference, because you can see something and aspire to see it," Gibbens said. "I hope the ripple effect would be many more women running, and that we would reach equal parity in Congress way before 2121." She was referring to a recent study that calculated that at the current slow growth rate, women would not hold 50 percent of the seats in Congress for more than 100 years. She continued, "I think electing a woman president would absolutely make a huge difference."

"We desperately need a woman as a president. It's a sad statement but it's very true. We need somebody who is going to show kids and young women that this is something that they can accomplish," Danielle Mulein said. "Thus far it's really hard to tell a young girl, 'Hey, you can be president,' if there has never been a female president before. How is she going to be able to say, 'Yes, I can totally do this one day,' if all of the people who have been president before don't match up with what she looks like and who she is?"

"I have younger siblings, and I think the most important thing for us is to get a woman president, because of the ripples throughout the country," Maeder said. She is the oldest daughter in a family of thirteen. "That would be the most empowering thing we can do for young girls."

The "role model effect" is real and powerful, according to research by political scientists David Campbell and Christina Wolbrecht. In a 2006 study, they found that teenage girls were significantly more likely to see themselves as potentially running for election as adults in places where viable women candidates ran for election. Campbell and Wolbrecht even discovered how the role model effect in these cases worked: Parents of daughters talked about politics more when they could point to specific examples of successful women politicians. In other words, what parents literally saw as possible for girls powerfully shaped what girls conceived as possible for themselves. In a companion study, Wolbrecht and Campbell analyzed data from more than twenty nations and discovered similar results. The greater number of women who held political office, the more that adolescent girls envisioned themselves as politically active adults. "A highly visible woman politician in the future—perhaps even at the top of a major party presidential ticket," they speculated in 2006, "has the potential to generate significant interest in political activity among adolescent girls with possible long-term effects on the political engagement of women."

Many women who have held political office report that girls, their parents, and young women look to them to see what opportunities are in fact open to women. Amy Klobuchar served as Minnesota's first woman attorney general and then its first woman senator. "While you had women in the Senate already, there was the whole state, Minnesota, with 5 million people, and I never saw a woman in either of those jobs," she recalled. "I was the first woman in those jobs. When you do that, it makes other women—and especially girls—think anything is possible. That is something that is intangible, but it matters. If people see that we can have a woman president, then why can't a woman be CEO of a certain company? Or why can't we have more women on a corporate board? You're using more talent that way, and I think nothing would encourage that more in America than having a woman president."

Hawaii representative Tulsi Gabbard, who is the first Hindu American to have been elected to Congress, told me, "I can't tell you how many times I've met these young girls who are nine or ten years old, who come up to me and say that they want to be the president of the United States." The relative dearth of role models means that women politicians attract a specific kind of attention from girls and young women, even when the identification might be a stretch. "I am so inspired every time, for example, I meet a young Indian girl. I have no Indian heritage or ethnicity in my family." Gabbard was born in American Samoa and moved to Hawaii as a child. "But there is an affinity and a sense of connection between many Hindus and Indian Americans here in the United States. These girls' parents tell me that their ambition has been inspired by seeing someone who they can connect with, who they can relate to, who they feel understands them."

It's not just impressionable girls and their doting parents who are hungry for models of women's political leadership. "America is seen as a premier country, both economically and in terms of its democracy, and to have a woman leading that Number One entity is a big deal," Irene Natividad, president of the Global Summit of Women, said. In her travels around the world while Clinton was running in 2008, women leaders would press her for news. "The vice president of Vietnam, she would say to me, 'So how's Hillary doing?' Or I would see Ursula von der Leyen," a German cabinet minister, "and she would ask, 'How's Hillary?' It was as if they had something riding on her candidacy," Natividad recalled. Ironically, even though the U.S. lagged far behind many advanced democracies on women's political leadership, women around the world looked to us to set an example.

"I travel a great deal, and anybody who knows I have had any relationship to Hillary Clinton, they all say to me, 'We're praying. We're hoping she's going to be president. Because if she wins, we all win,'" Melanne Verveer, head of the Georgetown Institute for Women, Peace, and Security and former U.S. ambassador for

Global Women's Issues, said. "There is a sense that if she makes it, we make it. I don't know how to put it differently. There's this transference of, 'My God, if a woman could be president of the United States, that will lift all of the rest of us up.' And it is true. Madeleine Albright broke ground, just by virtue of being secretary of state. And then Condi broke ground. And then Hillary Clinton followed. That role modeling comes across."

Verveer continued, "If you're a woman and you never see yourself in that position, you almost don't even aspire to get there because you don't think it's possible. Madeleine Albright tells a story about her granddaughter. They were sitting around the table and talking about how she was secretary of state, and the kid looks up and says, 'I don't understand what the big deal is. It's a girl's job.'" Verveer laughed. "Well, not that many years ago, nobody dreamed it possible a girl could be in that job. So yes, it has a profound impact.

"I think young women have less of a doubt that they will see one of their contemporaries in the presidency. So I think they're feeling much spunkier about the prospects, which is a good thing."

Chapter 10

WHY WOMEN'S LEADERSHIP MATTERS

W HY DOES IT matter if women hold political power? Are their countries better off when they do? What might a woman president accomplish that none of the forty-four men who have served accomplished? To put a fine point on it, why should a woman be president?

In theory, a government composed of only men could fulfill every interest, demand, and concern of the 51 percent of the population that are women. Democratic president John F. Kennedy signed into law the Equal Pay Act, America's first ever law banning sex discrimination in wages and salaries. Republican president Ronald Reagan nominated the first woman, Justice Sandra Day O'Connor, to the Supreme Court. Vice President Joe Biden, when he was a senator, authored the landmark Violence Against Women Act. In short, men with power have at times championed the interests of women citizens and voters.

But, as John Stuart Mill, one of the first great theorists of modern democracy—and not incidentally an early champion of women's political equality—wrote, "In the absence of its natural defenders, the interest of the omitted is always in danger of being overlooked." Or as a popular expression in Washington goes, if you are not at the table, you're going to be on the menu.

"WHEN THE AFFORDABLE Care Act was first brought to our caucus, Senator Mikulski stood up in the meeting and said, 'Wait a minute. This bill is not moving in its present form,'" Maryland Democratic senator Benjamin Cardin recalled. Only the day before the scheduled vote, Democratic Party leaders in the Senate had approached Barbara Mikulski to inform her that they had removed a key provision on women's preventive health care that she had sponsored. Mikulski was furious. After all, the Senate Committee on Health, Education, Labor, and Pensions had voted overwhelmingly to include the provision in health care reform, and here leadership—which did not include any women—had imperiously nixed it without consulting her or anyone else. Mikulski immediately reached out to all the Democratic women senators. She said to them they could not tolerate it, and that she was going to make a stand at the caucus meeting.

When I asked Mikulski about it, she said, "You have to know where we were."

It was November 2009 and passage of health care reform was touch-and-go. That was the context in which party leaders tried to assure Mikulski and other supporters of the dropped provision. She told me, "They said, 'Oh, don't worry, when we do this you'll be included.' It was our position that we hear that all the time—that the bill will take care of you. My modus operandi is that often when public policy is made it means one size fits all. And that usually means we don't take into consideration women or perhaps some minority populations."

Democrats largely agreed that health care reform had to end gender discrimination. Health insurers often refused to cover basic women's preventive health care, such as mammograms or contraception, and a major part of reform was to guarantee that insurers would cover essential preventive health care services without a copay. The question was how to define what made up those essential provisions. Mikulski explained, "My analysis and experience was that it never would happen unless we explicitly stated the benefit package." The provision that was dropped put responsibility for identifying women's preventive health in the hands of the Institute of Medicine, a division of the National Academies of Sciences, Engineering, and Medicine. Mikulski went on, "I wanted to avoid a political squabble, to make sure that it wasn't done by politicians, that it wasn't done by special interest groups, etc."

Mikulski recalled what happened at the caucus meeting: "I said to Harry Reid, 'If you're going to move this bill, you have to include the women.' The Democratic women insisted that there had to be a women's health amendment and we had the support of men. It wasn't our initiative only—it wasn't girls versus boys. In fact there was tremendous support from the men." Making a stand within the caucus and organizing the women senators paid off. The day after Thanksgiving, Reid called Mikulski to say they were going to try to put the provision back in the bill, and promised her that it would be the first amendment to be debated and put to a full Senate vote.

Looking back, Cardin blamed the omission on "insensitivity," that no one recognized that "too many males and not enough women were involved in developing that bill."

A senior Senate aide who was aware of the maneuvering was more blunt: "Had there been one chairwoman of the committee, that would not have happened."

In short, every person who held power to decide what stayed in and what was cut from the most significant legislation in a generation was a man. This episode just shows how many tables there are in Washington, and how vigilant women need to be about claiming their seats.

"On an average day you go to a Democratic chiefs of staff meeting and you're the only woman in the room," Tara McGuinness, at the time an executive at Center for American Progress, told me. "It's not until you're sitting in one of these precious seats that you realize there haven't been many women in them. It's these remarkable moments when you realize the leadership of women makes a huge difference."

"I think the challenge is to educate women and convey, 'We're not going to change things unless we have a seat at the table,'" Republican consultant Katie Packer Gage said when I asked her about her views on the gender gap in political officeholding. "And I do think that whatever your opinions, for instance, on the issue of rape in the military, the fact that you have Republican and Democrat women on both sides of the issue debating how to address it, I love. That's an issue that is very personal to women—even though men are often victims. And I think that there will be different solutions that are found to that because there are women working in a bipartisan way to come up with them. So, I think it's critical, and I hope that as more people are focusing on this, that we'll see more and more women getting into the mix."

The impact women legislators can have on the lives of women can be monumental and, as the case of the women's health amendment shows, women often bring a perspective to public policy that is missing when women are missing. "Sometimes women focus on issues that otherwise would not get the attention they deserve," Maine senator Olympia Snowe said. "When I served on the Senate Armed Services Committee, I fought for gender-integrated training. It's hard to imagine today, but back in the late '90s that was a major issue. Many in Congress, as well as in the military, were resisting the whole notion that women should be part of integrated basic training. It didn't make sense. They fight as they train. Can you imagine today an all-volunteer army without women? It couldn't happen. But I had to fight that mightily as a woman on the Senate Armed Services Committee. I was the one that led this effort as a woman, for women, and for our military. So I think women do bring a unique perspective. I think it's critical to have representation in our government that is more reflective of the demographics of our country at large."

Hawaii representative and Iraq War veteran Tulsi Gabbard shared Snowe's view. "I think it's a travesty that we don't have more women who've worn the uniform and more women who've served in combat representing our country at the highest levels of leadership. We need that," Gabbard said. "What inspires me is hearing from some of our female service members in different parts of the country. People who I've never had the chance to meet, who've sent me emails saying how much they appreciate just knowing that there is someone there in our nation's capital who understands their life and the challenges they have, and someone who they know has their back. It's a great responsibility to be able to be a voice for our female service members in Congress."

Likewise, women's representation matters because diversity is an asset to any institution. "When only men are making decisions, there is a great deal of societal wisdom and experience that's not part of the decision-making. That leads to okay, but not spectacular decisions," Democratic consultant Mary Hughes said. And, as Feminist Majority Foundation president Eleanor Smeal maintained, it was fundamental to our national values. "Our life experiences are different," she said. "We are in a representative democracy. Our life experiences should be represented. And it's about as simple as that. Now, someday it won't matter, because we'll have similar experiences. But right now it definitely matters."

AT MIDNIGHT ON October 1, 2013, the United States government shut down. Raising the stakes of the crisis, the U.S. Treasury was projected to reach the limit of its borrowing authority less than two weeks later. If Congress did not act to raise the so-called debt ceiling, the nation would default on its debt and throw global markets into a tailspin.

The night before, the Republican-controlled House of Representatives had sent the Senate, controlled by Democrats, a budget bill that defunded the Affordable Care Act and delayed implementation of several key provisions. At a stalemate, Congress could not pass a budget, and with no funds yet authorized for the fiscal year, the United States government stopped paying its bills. Every nonessential function of the federal government was shuttered. Although members of Congress continued to receive their paychecks, national parks closed, benefit checks to veterans went unwritten, and no student loans were issued. The high-stakes gamble linking the budget to the Affordable Care Act had been masterminded by freshman Texas Republican senator Ted Cruz, who advanced the theory that President Obama and Democrats would scrap health care reform rather than let the government shut down. When Cruz failed to persuade his fellow Republican senators to go along, in a monumental breach of Senate tradition, Cruz took his plan over to the House GOP Tea Party Caucus.

"I was sitting in my office on Saturday—it was the end of the first week of the government shutdown—and I was watching the debate on the Senate floor. The more I watched, the angrier and more frustrated I became," Republican senator Susan Collins told me. "Those who were arguing for the shutdown claimed that if we shut down government, it would somehow lead to a defunding of Obamacare. That, of course, was a ludicrous supposition, because there was no way that the president was going to agree to repeal what to him was his signature achievement. I felt that the shutdown was a disaster. I saw how it was hurting the economy in my home state of Maine and across the nation." Collins recounted. "In my judgment, we were not being responsible and we were failing the American people by not governing."

Growing increasingly alarmed as she watched her colleagues deliver chest-thumping speeches to a nearly empty Senate, Collins turned on her computer, drafted a three-point plan that she hoped would jump-start discussions to reopen the government, and walked over to the Senate to deliver her speech.

"When Susan gave the speech, I was in the chamber. There happened to be a lot of women hanging around. We felt like we shouldn't go home during the shutdown," Minnesota senator Amy Klobuchar recalled, leaving unsaid the fact that despite the crisis, most congressmen had left town for their usual weekend break.

Senator Barbara Mikulski was in the chamber too. "So there I was, the chair of the Appropriations Committee, and I stood up and said, essentially, good for Senator Collins for offering fresh ideas and a fresh approach," she told me.

Collins's cell phone started ringing as soon as she left the Senate floor. "The first three people I heard from were Lisa Murkowski, Kelly Ayotte, and Amy Klobuchar. I don't think that's a coincidence that women who heard my speech all said, 'I want to help, count me in, what can I do?'"

As the workweek began and the shutdown continued, it was clear to journalists, pundits, and most Republican senators that the GOP was losing the battle for public opinion. (Congress's approval rating plunged to an all-time low of 15 percent in the wake of the shutdown.) But in the House, Republican representatives escalated their demands. Obama and Democratic Senate majority leader Harry Reid refused to negotiate until the government reopened; they had been burned badly by the 2011 debt ceiling crisis. In the midst of what seemed to be stereotypically male behavior, Collins started working behind the scenes to organize senators—women and men—to forge a compromise.

Collins, as a member of the Senate's minority party who was not in leadership, had limited authority to devise the final plan, but she smartly leveraged the power she had. Mikulski recalled, "People like me who chaired committees and didn't want this shutdown—really, this was a Ted Cruz thing—we were able to say they're building everyday, some of those ideas are pretty good, we need to pay attention to the coalition."

The coalition of senators Collins forged presented their plan to Democratic leader Reid and Republican leader Mitch McConnell and also dropped a bombshell on them. Collins's group would hold a televised press conference about their plan—unless the leaders worked with them. "We told them that we were going to go to the Senate press gallery to unveil our plan," Collins said. "Needless to say, neither leader wanted that to happen, because they didn't want to lose control." The plan by Collins's coalition became the framework for reopening the government. Just hours before the Treasury would no longer be able to pay America's bills, the sixteen-day shutdown ended. Standard and Poor's estimated that the shutdown had taken $24 billion out of the nation's economy.

"In the Senate, a voting bloc of fourteen people is determinative," Mikulski said. "Collins got the ball rolling, and with Senator Klobuchar, they built a coalition of fourteen members. I thought it was just fantastic."

IN AMERICA'S POLARIZED and dysfunctional politics, getting along to get things done across party lines is a positive good in and of itself and something most Americans want. Yet what do women politicians substantively accomplish with their more collaborative style of governance? In other words, can they deliver? The resounding conclusion of the research is that they do. Congresswomen are as effective as their male colleagues, studies have shown. And they outperform men in some cases. One study found that women in Congress delivered more money to their districts—roughly 9 percent more in federal discretionary funding. Another found that women sponsored a greater number of bills. Women senators introduce more bills and win more support for them, and they successfully move more of these bills out of committee and enact them, compared to their male counterparts, according to Quorum's analysis of Congress during the polarized Obama years.

The value women add to the process is not limited to government, but extends to the private sector as well. Women possess more of the leadership attributes valued in today's globalized, networked economy. Although that claim might sound as if it was cooked up at the Feminist Majority Foundation, in fact, that is what McKinsey consulting discovered when it surveyed global business executives. Those executives said they believed that women more often displayed the top qualities of superior business leadership: participatory decision making; the talent for inspiring people; setting expectations; and intellectual stimulation. Various studies have found that businesses that include women in leadership perform better for their shareholders. A study by Catalyst, a respected nonprofit that conducts research on women's leadership, concluded that corporations with the highest proportion of women board members delivered a 26 percent higher return on invested capital, compared to corporations with no female board members.

A 2012 survey on 7,280 business leaders found that women leaders were rated more effective than men on twelve of the sixteen competencies that make for "outstanding" leadership. "Most stereotypes would have us believe that female leaders excel at nurturing competencies such as developing others and building relationships, and many might put exhibiting integrity and engaging in self-development in that category as well. And in all four cases our data concurred—women did score higher than men," Jack Zenger and Joseph Folkman, the study's authors, wrote in the *Harvard Business Review*. "But the women's advantages were not at all confined to traditionally women's strengths. In fact, at every level, more women were rated by their peers, their bosses, their direct reports, and their other associates as better overall leaders than their male counterparts."

Not only are women politicians at least as competent as men and, as we see in the resolution of the government shutdown, more collaborative. They also are more attuned to the interests, values, and concerns of women.

While men and women voters hold generally the same positions on issues involving women's rights, women legislators are more likely to vote in favor of feminist proposals. When a woman replaces a man in a Congress, a greater number of bills on women's interests are introduced from that district. Although men in

Congress are as likely as women to support measures promoting women's health, the more women in leadership, the more bills on women's health are passed.

And the list of women acting on behalf of women goes on. Compared to congressmen, congresswomen sponsor more bills protecting women's rights and LGBT rights. Democratic and moderate Republican congresswomen are more likely to advance legislation on child care and domestic violence. Even in legislatures with only a handful of women, women representatives often feel especially responsible for representing women and distinguish themselves by taking leadership on women's issues.

Moreover, even when men and women voters agree on a so-called women's issue, women legislators are more likely to champion it. Take recent legislation on equal pay for women. Democrats—men and women—unanimously voted in favor of the Lilly Ledbetter Fair Pay Act of 2009, sponsored by Mikulski. The only four Republican votes in favor came from the only four Republican women in the senate at the time, Collins, Murkowski, Snowe, and Kay Bailey Hutchison. Or consider reproductive rights. Although historically the difference in men's and women's opinions about the right to legal abortion has been slight, women in Congress have been more likely than men to support measures protecting access to abortion and contraception. The particular attention women legislators devote to women's particular concerns is true generally across race and ethnicity, and, importantly, minority interests are not sacrificed in the process. African American state legislators introduce as many bills advancing African American interests and women's interests, respectively, as their counterparts among black men and nonblack women. Similarly, when the interests of women and Latinos clash, it is Latinas who take the lead in adjudicating the conflict to forge a solution.

Similar results are found in the private sector. When women hold top leadership positions, women in their companies do better. American corporations led by women CEOs or board chairs hire more women as senior executives and pay female executives up to 20 percent more than corporations led by men. Corporate Women Directors International commissioned a study of women CEOs in thirty-six economies and found that in the companies headed by women, the percentage of women on boards and in senior executive roles was double that of their peers. The group's head, Irene Natividad, told me, "We did the study because I would always hear, 'Oh, women don't help other women.' I hate that remark."

Of course, given the diversity among women, acting on behalf of women can put women on opposite sides. As we have seen, conflicts over issues of sexuality and reproduction sharply divide Republicans and Democrats; Republican women disagree among themselves on many of the classic women's issues, such as equal pay and domestic violence; and many dispute the very idea of women's issues. Likewise, the bell curve of talent applies equally to women as it does to men. "I do not subscribe to the idea that the world's going to be a better place with women running it," Democratic consultant Karin Johanson said. "I just think it's a basic equity question. Some women are incredibly skilled and some women are mediocre. I suppose when I started I thought women would be better in office. I just care about basic fairness. We have a right to representative government. Why should women have to be better?"

The research on gender differences in governing is consistent and transcends national lines. Globally, women have taken the lead in making women's issues a priority. From Canada to Argentina, New Zealand to Scandinavia, women legislators are more active than men in promoting economic measures that enable women to participate equally in the workforce, such as providing paid family leave and making it illegal to pay women less than men for similar work. Political scientist Jennifer Piscopo examined 18,700 bills introduced by lawmakers in Argentina's lower house over a ten-year period and found that nearly three-quarters of women's rights bills were written by women. She found a similar pattern in Mexico—77 percent of the bills in the lower house related to women's rights were introduced by women. In both countries, most of the remaining bills were written by men in left-leaning political parties.

Women politicians have led the charge to eradicate legal discrimination in nations in which fundamentalist religion and patriarchy relegated women to subordinate roles and low status. It was women in the Rwandan legislature who won property rights for women; it was women parliamentarians in Turkey, working in concert with women's rights groups, who reformed the criminal law to remove references to chastity, virginity, and honor that discriminated against women. In overwhelmingly Catholic Latin America, where men have been timid about crossing the Vatican, women legislators have been more likely than men to champion expanded access to contraception and abortion.

In addition, women legislators have different priorities than their male counterparts on a broad range of issues, according to a substantial though less unanimous body of research. In the Scandinavian nations, women parliamentarians have been more likely than men to champion environmental protection and social welfare. In a study of twenty-two democracies (including the United States) women legislators voted for lower defense spending and fewer military interventions compared to men. Considering that global public opinion surveys show women on average are more liberal than men, the policies advanced by women legislators suggest they are acting with their women constituents' values in the forefront.

These aren't just isolated cases. In a comparison of thirty-one countries, political scientists Leslie Schwindt-Bayer and William Mishler found that governments were more responsive to women's policy concerns when more women were in the legislature. And the more women elected to political office, the greater the benefit for women specifically and gender equality in general. Even where popular opinion was strongly on the side of gender equality, the key determinant of how much got accomplished regarding women's issues was how many women lawmakers there were.

Likewise, the more women in legislature, the more confidence ordinary women had in the legislature. Importantly, men also responded positively to women's representation—expressing increased confidence in the legislature as women's representation rose. Simply put, women legislators got things done for women—and men.

The scholarship is unequivocal. To make progress toward gender equality, to tackle the "unfinished business of the 21st century," nations need women in power, and the more the better.

"WHAT I'VE FOUND almost to a surprising level is the issues that get debated are determined by the people who are making the decisions. Who is at that table decides what we are going to talk about as a nation," Center for American Progress head Neera Tanden told me. "Occasionally, you'll have something that grows from the bottom, like Occupy Wall Street. But if you're thinking about what bills we're going to pass or what the priorities of Washington are, it's who controls that budget process, it's who controls the State of the Union address. Who is at the table decides what are the top priorities, especially in Washington."

Liberian president Ellen Johnson Sirleaf, the first woman elected in an African nation to be head of state, shared the Nobel Peace Prize in recognition "of the great potential for democracy and peace that women represent." Under the leadership of Jóhanna Sigurdardóttir, the world's first openly lesbian prime minister, Iceland outlawed strip clubs, on the logic that it "is not acceptable that women or people in general are a product to be sold." (Sigurdardóttir had won election after promising to put an end to "the age of testosterone.") German chancellor Angela Merkel is universally seen as Europe's most powerful leader. Depending on your perspective, she either saved the European Union or set in motion its dissolution with her forceful response to the 2008 global financial crisis.

While it is clear from the global record that women lawmakers act with women's interests in mind, it is harder to make generalizations about women top executives, given that the culture, political institutions, and economies of nations are so varied. Irene Natividad, head of the Global Summit of Women, has met and worked with many of the world's women leaders. She observed that you tend to find a woman's name attached to bills that have benefited women, but, she said, "Women as presidents of countries—it's uneven. Kirchner for instance is not one of my favorite people," she said. (At the time we spoke, Argentina's president Cristina Fernández de Kirchner was presiding over a currency crisis and was the target of several investigations.)

Still, Natividad continued, "There is a group of women who never forgot that they were women who happened to be president. Michelle Bachelet is a great example. In a macho country, she was the one behind child care and pay equity."

Chilean president Michelle Bachelet, in her first term, opened thousands of new, free nurseries for infants and toddlers, in order to give their mothers the opportunity to work; on the eve of her second term in the presidency, she promised to open thousands more. Not only did Bachelet push through an equal pay law, she appointed a parity cabinet—that is, a cabinet with equal numbers of men and women—even though many in her own political party put up resistance. She made emergency contraception universally accessible, against major opposition from parties of the right and the church. In her major reform of Chile's pension system, she incorporated creative measures, such as child bonuses, to boost women's retirement earnings. (In employment-based pension systems, like Chile's and America's social security system, women tend to retire with lower pensions because of time out of the workforce to care for children.) And that was all in her first term. (The president is not allowed to serve consecutive terms, but after sitting out one term, during which she was the head of UN Women, Bachelet easily won reelection. She was and remains the most popular politician in the nation.) In her second term, which runs from 2014 to 2018, Bachelet is pushing for electoral quotas to boost the level of women's representation, as well as to liberalize Chile's highly restrictive abortion laws, put in place by Pinochet's military dictatorship. (Bachelet, it's worth noting, had been imprisoned and tortured by the military regime; her father was tortured and killed.)

Bachelet is an example of what seems to be a solid trend: When a woman who has a prior record of advancing gender equality steps into the top post, she uses the power of her office and expends political capital to advance women's full and equal participation in society. There is also a strong association between gender equality and women heads of government. For instance, Iceland ranked number one in 2014 on gender equality, and in twenty of the past fifty years the nation has had a woman prime minister or president. Finland and Norway ranked second and third, respectively, and in both, women were the top elected leaders for over a decade.

But of course, some women assume these top positions having had no significant past record of prioritizing gender equality. They give us perhaps an even more important insight into the question of women in power.

Consider the case of Europe during the 2015 Greek debt crisis. German chancellor Angela Merkel—arguably the most powerful European leader of the 21st century and a woman—was the single most powerful person among the leaders of Greece's creditors. Merkel took a hardline position. Many economists and other global leaders instead called for a balanced package of reforms, including debt relief, so as to allow the Greek economy to grow. Some in this camp sharply rebuked Merkel for her intransigence. Among these critics, the individual with the greatest influence over the actual talks was International Monetary Fund managing director Christine Lagarde—arguably one of the most powerful bankers in Europe and a woman. As Bloomberg News reported, "Now that Greece is eligible again for loans from the IMF, getting any more money from the fund may hinge on a test of wills between Christine Lagarde and Angela Merkel."

Unsurprisingly, no one suggested the world would be in better hands if men were at the helm of the high-stakes negotiations. No one said that Merkel and Lagarde were not qualified to lead. Many experts and pundits took sides, but no one thought that these women lacked the resolve or the toughness for executive leadership in a crisis in a traditionally "male" policy arena. And no one thought that the differences between Merkel and Lagarde had anything to do with their gender. Instead, observers understood that complex forces shaped the two women's positions: their national histories, their personal political histories, the powers of their particular office, the political and financial objectives of the institutions they led, and their appraisals of the economic stakes for the Euro zone. Both the IMF and the German nation, as Greece's largest creditors, stood to lose lots of money if they got it wrong.

This was a sign of progress. In a case in which there were no questions of gender parity or equity—except the obvious and largely irrelevant one that women make up half of all Greek citizens—women were at the head of the table of decision makers. And the gender of the key players was a nonissue. Europe, it seemed, had achieved what many people in the United States look forward to: At some point, having a woman in the top position wouldn't be remarkable because it was no longer rare.

And yet in one important regard, an American woman president will always be remarkable, in the true meaning of the term, because of the power the United States wields on the global stage.

"Having America have a woman president—America has always been known as the land of opportunity—I think helps internationally," Minnesota senator Amy Klobuchar said. "When we look at some of these issues like Boko Haram and sex trafficking, I think having a woman as president sends a message more than anything else about that kind of treatment of women. And every single time a country improves the way it treats women, we seem to have more democracy and more progress in the country."

That message—about a nation's values and women's opportunity—matters as much at home as it does abroad.

"The fundamental ideology of this country, one of the things that we bring to the world, is equality for girls and women,"

Democratic consultant Celinda Lake said. "That's going to ring hollow until our girls see a woman president."

In other words, there are bigger philosophical questions about democracy and the American Dream at stake.

EPILOGUE

A RTICLE TWO OF the United States Constitution on the powers and duties of the president is surprisingly open-ended.
That is because the framers knew who the president would be:
George Washington. Already the people of Revolutionary America
venerated Washington and spoke of him as the "father" of the
nation. The men who wrote the Constitution had confidence in
Washington and faith that his improvisations in the office would
set the nation on the right course.

Washington himself would have been happy to retire to his
Mount Vernon plantation, but he embraced his role out of a sense
of patriotic duty. In 1789, he faced two daunting challenges. First,
he had to project gravitas and authority, so as to impress on hostile
European monarchies that the infant nation was here to stay on the
world stage. Second, at a time when the men and women who made
up "We the People" identified themselves as citizens of a state, not
the United States, Washington sought to embody an ideal of an
American and craft a distinctly American model of leadership. John
Adams later said of Washington, "He was the best actor of the
presidency we have ever had."

In short, Americans have always understood that the president
is far more than just the CEO of the federal government. As the

primary authority in foreign affairs and as the ceremonial head of state, the president personifies national power. Occupying the one office elected by the people of all the United States, the president symbolizes national unity and embodies national identity. Our forty-four presidents stand as exemplars of our democracy, of the living American Dream, of our national narrative about equality and opportunity for all.

In the heat of the 2008 presidential race, presidential candidate Barack Obama once warned his supporters about what his opponents might say to win. "So what they're going to try to do is make you scared of me," Obama said. "You know, he's not patriotic enough, he's got a funny name, you know, he doesn't look like all those other presidents on the dollar bills."

With this quip Obama obliquely posed the question, can you envision me, an African American, as president of the United States? After all, three of the seven presidents pictured on America's currency were slave owners. Obama's comment plumbed the murky depths of our troubled history and our contentious contemporary politics. The backlash was as predictable as it was fierce.

In our national imagination, who seems presidential?

The Constitution says that the president must be thirty-five years old and a natural born citizen. And that is it. Although the pronoun *he* is used liberally in the text, nowhere do the Founding Fathers say that the president must be white or be a man. Indeed, the words *male*, *slave*, and *white* appear nowhere in the original United States Constitution.

American voters twice elected an African American president.

Is America ready for a woman president? Have the barriers that kept women out of the Oval Office for more than two centuries fallen?

We've seen how women's leadership in politics matters on a practical level, how it affects people's lives in tangible ways. We've seen that women are more apt to work across party lines and tend to approach governing in a more cooperative fashion. We've observed that the United States has some ways to go to close our gender gaps in pay, leadership, and other areas, and also that women elected officials pay more attention than men do to protecting civil rights and advancing gender equality.

As we've seen, women candidates at all levels of office are as likely as men to win election. We've seen that among voters, there is pent-up demand for a woman to be president, and that there is enthusiasm for the particular woman, Hillary Clinton, who currently has the best chance of becoming America's first woman president. And we've seen that for all intents and purposes, the double standard is dead. Gender bias is no longer the reason America hasn't yet elevated a woman to the Oval Office.

Yes, we can say to our daughters and sons that we have crossed a historic threshold. A woman can now be president of the United States. And that is progress.

ACKNOWLEDGMENTS

I WANT TO express my gratitude to all those who generously gave of their time and knowledge to participate in interviews for this book. All but a few agreed to talk on the record, and their names appear in the text and in the chapter notes that follow. I owe a special debt to several of these women and men. Wilma Goldstein and Candy Straight connected me to Republican women leaders, and without their help this project as I conceived it simply would not have been possible. Jeffrey Slavin, one of the first people I talked to about this project, helped guide me to the right people and gave me one of my first glimpses behind the scenes. Celinda Lake, Marcy Stech, Jess McIntosh, and Renee Cohen all opened doors for me among Democrats. Jennifer Piscopo, Occidental College political scientist, powerfully influenced my thinking on women in politics globally, read drafts of the relevant chapters, and introduced me to her network of academics specializing in gender and politics.

Special thanks to my agent, Dana Newman, who has championed this book from beginning to end. My editor, Dan Smetanka, has seen me through the ups and downs of two books. I am truly grateful for his incisive editing, but even more for his guidance, support, and mood-lifting wit. Thanks to Kelly Winton, managing editor, Megan Fishmann, publicity director, Charlie Winton, publisher, and to everyone else on the team at Counterpoint.

Many friends and family members have helped shepherd this project from intuition to finished book. My mother, Suzanne F. Cohen, among many of her talents, has been for me a source of inspiration and information on politics. L. Spencer Humphrey, publishing maven, provided invaluable professional advice in the early stages. Lisa J. Hacken read the full manuscript at the eleventh hour, providing indispensable editing. Torie Osborn and Jennifer Piscopo, both political women in their own ways, allowed me to bounce ideas off them for countless hours over the last two years. Thank you Nazila Shokrian and Susan Margolin, as always, for your steadfast friendship and encouragement. To all of you, dayenu.

This book is dedicated to my daughters, Helena and Camille, and to my stepdaughters, Morgan and Paloma. Whenever I wavered, I would remind myself of what is at stake for young women like you. Your confidence, kindness, creativity, and drive inspire me and give me confidence about our country's future.

My biggest thanks of all goes to my husband Jonathan Parfrey, for his friendship, wisdom, unwavering support, and unconditional love.

References

PROLOGUE

Interviews by author:

Ambassador Melanne Verveer. March 3, 2015.

Governor Jennifer Granholm. January 24, 2014.

Interviews with Twyla Hodges, Tony Cowser, Joe Boccolucci, Katelyn Rydzewski, and others at Hillary Clinton's book signing, Los Angeles. June 19, 2014.

Senator Benjamin Cardin. July 23, 2014.

Senator Kay Bailey Hutchison. November 24, 2014.

Published sources:

Baer, Denise, and Heidi Hartmann. "Building Women's Political Careers: Strengthening the Pipeline to Higher Office." Institute for Women's Policy Research, May 2014. http://www.iwpr.org/publications/pubs/building-women2019s-political-careers-strengthening-the-pipeline-to-higher-office.

Brown, Quinn Russell. "1,200 Turn Out for Hillary Clinton at Seattle Book-Signing." *HeraldNet*, June 18, 2014. http://www.heraldnet.com/article/20140618/NEWS02/140619196.

Clinton, Hillary Rodham. *Hard Choices*. New York: Simon & Schuster, 2014.

Pew Research Center. "2014 Party Identification Detailed Tables." April 7, 2015. http://www.people-press.org/2015/04/07/2014-party-identification-detailed-tables/.

———. "A Clinton Candidacy: Voters' Early Impressions." April 10, 2015. http://www.pewresearch.org/fact-tank/2015/04/10/a-clinton-candidacy-voters-early-impressions/.

———. "Women and Leadership." January 14, 2015. http://www.pewsocial trends.org/2015/01/14/women-and-leadership/.

Sandberg, Sheryl. *Lean In: Women, Work, and the Will to Lead*. New York: Knopf, 2013.

Verveer, Melanne, and Kim K. Azzarelli. *Fast Forward: How Women Can Achieve Power and Purpose*. Boston: Houghton Mifflin Harcourt, 2015.

Warner, Judith. "Fact Sheet: The Women's Leadership Gap." *Center for American Progress*, March 7, 2014. http://www.americanprogress.org /issues/women/report/2014/03/07/85457/fact-sheet-the-womens -leadership-gap/.

World Economic Forum. "The Global Gender Gap Report 2015." Insight Report. Geneva, November 2015. http://www.weforum.org/reports/ global-gender-gap-report-2015.

Chapter 1: OUTSIDE IN

INTERVIEWS BY AUTHOR:

Governor Christine Todd Whitman. December 11, 2014.

Governor Jennifer Granholm. January 24, 2014.

Jeffrey Slavin. April 10, 2013.

Lisa Grove. September 26, 2014.

Senator Amy Klobuchar. December 10, 2014.

Senator Barbara Mikulski. September 8, 2014.

Senator Benjamin Cardin. July 23, 2014.

Senator Kay Bailey Hutchison. November 24, 2014.

Senator Susan Collins. November 25, 2014.

Wilma Goldstein. October 23, 2014, and other dates.

PUBLISHED SOURCES:

Barakso, Maryann. "Is There a 'Woman's Way' of Governing? Assessing the Organizational Structures of Women's Membership Associations." *Politics & Gender* 3 no. 2 (June 2007): 201–27.

"Barbara Mikulski, Fact vs. Fiction." *Washington Post*, September 8, 1998.

Barsh, Joanna, and Lareina Yee. "Unlocking the Full Potential of Women in the U.S. Economy." McKinsey & Company, 2011. http://www.mckinsey.com/client_service/organization/latest_thinking/unlocking_the_full_potential.

Boxer, Barbara. "The 'Dean' of the Senate Women Determined to Make Life Better." *Politico*. December 12, 2013.

Ford, Lynne E. *Women and Politics: The Pursuit of Equality*. 3rd ed. Boston: Wadsworth, 2011.

Gillibrand, Kirsten, and Elizabeth Weil. *Off the Sidelines: Raise Your Voice, Change the World*. New York: Ballantine Books, 2014.

Itkowitz, Colby. "In Male-Dominated Congress, It's Male-Dominated Committee Hearings." *Washington Post*, September 11, 2014. http://www.washingtonpost.com/blogs/in-the-loop/wp/2014/09/11/in-male-dominated-congress-its-male-dominated-committee-hearings/.

Kim, Seung Min. "How Barbara Mikulski Led the Way for Women in Congress." *Politico*, March 3, 2015. http://www.politico.com/story/2015/03/barbara-mikulski-congress-retirement-115681.html.

Klein, Mariel. "Working Together and Across the Aisle, Female Senators Pass More Legislation Than Male Colleagues." *Quorum*, February 19, 2015. https://www.quorum.us/blog/women-work-together-pass-more-legislation/.

Mikulski, Barbara, et al. *Nine and Counting: The Women of the Senate*. New York: William Morrow, 2000.

Mitchell, Andrea. Interviewing Senator Kirsten Gillibrand on her book *Off the Sidelines*. Washington, DC, September 10, 2014.

Mundy, Liza. "The Secret History of Women in the Senate." *Politico Magazine*, January 5, 2015. http://www.politico.com/magazine/story/2015/01/senate-women-secret-history-113908.html.

Newton-Small, Jay. "Women Are the Only Adults Left in Washington." *Time*. http://swampland.time.com/2013/10/16/women-are-the-only-adults-left-in-washington/.

Pianin, Eric. "The Abrasive Lady from Baltimore Polishes Her Act." *Washington Post*, June 14, 1987.

Reingold, Beth. "Women as Officeholders: Linking Descriptive and Substantive Representation." In *Political Women and American*

Democracy, edited by Christina Wolbrecht, Karen Beckwith, and Lisa Baldez. Cambridge: Cambridge University Press, 2008.

Weber, Daniela, et al. "The Changing Face of Cognitive Gender Differences in Europe." *Proceedings of the National Academy of Sciences* 111, no. 32 (August 12, 2014): 11673–78.

Weiner, Rachel. "Barbara Mikulski, First Female Chair of Senate Appropriations, Returns to Minority." *Washington Post*, November 16, 2014.

Chapter 2: THE NEW GUARD

INTERVIEWS BY AUTHOR:

Bettina Duval. January 30, 2015.

Candace L. Straight. November 21, 2014.

Eleanor Smeal. May 22, 2013.

Ellen Malcolm. January 14, 2014.

Ilyse Hogue. September 10, 2014, and February 27, 2015.

Karen Finney. September 8, 2014.

Katherine Spillar. October 11, 2014.

Maria Cino. November 21, 2014.

Neera Tanden. January 16, 2015.

Stephanie Schriock. April 10, 2013, and February 6, 2015.

Tara McGuinness. April 4, 2013.

Wilma Goldstein. October 23, 2014, and other dates.

PUBLISHED SOURCES:

Albright, Madeleine. *Madam Secretary: A Memoir*. New York: Harper Perennial, 2013.

Allen, Jonathan, and Amie Parnes. *HRC: State Secrets and the Rebirth of Hillary Clinton*. New York: Crown, 2014.

Chozick, Amy. "Planet Hillary." *New York Times Magazine*. January 26, 2014.

Clinton, Hillary Rodham. *Hard Choices*. New York: Simon & Schuster, 2014.

———. *Living History*. New York: Simon & Schuster, 2003.

Dowd, Maureen. "Fireworks for Former First Lady and Future First Lad." *New York Times*, July 4, 2007.

———. "Quien Es Mas Less Macho?" *New York Times*, February 24, 2008.

Guttmacher Institute. "Laws Affecting Reproductive Health and Rights: State Trends at Midyear, 2015," July 1, 2015. http://www.guttmacher.org/statecenter/updates/2015/statetrends22015.html.

———. "State Policy Trends: Abortion and Contraception in the Crosshairs." http://www.guttmacher.org/media/inthenews/2012/04/13/index.html.

———. "State Trends for 2014 on Abortion, Family Planning, Sex Education and Insurance." http://www.guttmacher.org/statecenter/updates/2015/statetrends22015.html.

Jaffe, Alexandra. "Run, Hillary, run, say Senate's Dem women." *The Hill*, October 30, 2013. http://thehill.com/blogs/ballot-box/188687-report-democratic-women-senators-sign-letter-urging-hillary-clinton-to-run.

Kliff, Sarah. "Exclusive: NARAL President Nancy Keenan to Step Down." *Washington Post*, May 10, 2012.

Lanchester, John. "1979 and All That." *New Yorker*, July 29, 2013. http://www.newyorker.com/magazine/2013/08/05/1979-and-all-that.

Lawrence, Christopher. "Stephanie Schriock Is Transforming Women into Major Contenders." *Marie Claire*, August 18, 2014.

Leive, Cindi. "Career Advice from Hillary Rodham Clinton." *Glamour*, August 7, 2014. http://www.glamour.com/inspired/2014/08/hillary-rodham-clinton-career-lessons.

Ornstein, Norman J., et al. "Vital Statistics on Congress." Brookings Institution and American Enterprise Institute, July 2013. http://www.brookings.edu/research/reports/2013/07/vital-statistics-congress-mann-ornstein.

Romero, Lois. "Gatekeepers of Hillaryland." *Washington Post*, June 21, 2007.

Chapter 3: LEADING WHILE FEMALE

INTERVIEWS BY AUTHOR:

Betty Yee. October 14, 2014.

Cecile Richards. May 21, 2013.

Celinda Lake. April 5, 2013, and September 9, 2014.

Denise Feriozzi. June 13, 2013.

Ellen Malcolm. January 14, 2014.

Governor Jennifer Granholm. January 24, 2014.

Jonathan Parker. June 13, 2013.

Karin Johanson. April 9, 2013.

Katie Packer Gage. December 14, 2014.

Lisa Grove. September 26, 2014.

Maria Elena Durazo. February 12, 2015.

Mary Hughes. June 21, 2013.

Rose Kapolczynski. June 26, 2013.

Senator Olympia Snowe. February 3, 2015.

Stephanie Schriock. April 10, 2013, and February 6, 2015.

Tara McGuinness. April 4, 2013.

Wendy Greuel. July 8, 2015.

Wilma Goldstein. October 23, 2014, and other dates.

PUBLISHED SOURCES:

Baldez, Lisa. "Political Women in Comparative Democracies: A Primer for Americanists." In *Political Women and American Democracy*, edited by Christina Wolbrecht, Karen Beckwith, and Lisa Baldez. Cambridge: Cambridge University Press, 2008.

Brooks, Deborah Jordan. *He Runs, She Runs: Why Gender Stereotypes Do Not Harm Women Candidates*. Princeton, New Jersey; Oxford: Princeton University Press, 2013.

———. "Testing the Double Standard for Candidate Emotionality: Voter Reactions to the Tears and Anger of Male and Female Politicians." *Journal of Politics* 73, no. 2 (April 1, 2011): 597–615.

Cohen, Nancy L. "How to End California's Political Gender Gap." *Los Angeles Times*, August 20, 2014. http://www.latimes.com/opinion/op-ed/la-oe-cohen-california-politics-gender-20140821-story.html.

Dolan, Kathleen A. "Is There a 'Gender Affinity Effect' in American Politics? Information, Affect, and Candidate Sex in U.S House Elections." *Political Research Quarterly* 61, no. 1 (March 2008): 79–89.

———. "The Impact of Gender Stereotyped Evaluations on Support for Women Candidates." *Political Behavior* 32, no. 1 (March 1, 2010): 69–88.

———. *Voting for Women: How the Public Evaluates Women Candidates.* Dilemmas in American Politics. Boulder, CO: Westview Press, 2004.

Ford, Lynne E. *Women and Politics: The Pursuit of Equality.* 3rd ed. Boston: Wadsworth, 2011.

Fowler, Linda L., and Jennifer L. Lawless. "Looking for Sex in All the Wrong Places: Press Coverage and the Electoral Fortunes of Gubernatorial Candidates." *Perspectives on Politics* 7, no. 3 (September 1, 2009): 519–36.

Fox, Richard L., and Jennifer L. Lawless. "Gendered Perceptions and Political Candidacies: A Central Barrier to Women's Equality in Electoral Politics." *American Journal of Political Science* 55, no. 1 (January 1, 2011): 59–73.

Fridkin, Kim L., Patrick J. Kenney, and Gina Serignese Woodall. "Bad for Men, Better for Women: The Impact of Stereotypes during Negative Campaigns." *Political Behavior* 31, no. 1 (March 2009): 53–77.

Fulton, Sarah A. "Running Backwards and in High Heels: The Gendered Quality Gap and Incumbent Electoral Success." *Political Research Quarterly* 65, no. 2 (June 2012): 303–14.

Gillibrand, Kirsten, and Elizabeth Weil. *Off the Sidelines: Raise Your Voice, Change the World.* New York: Ballantine Books, 2014.

Hayes, Danny. "When Gender and Party Collide: Stereotyping in Candidate Trait Attribution." *Politics & Gender* 7, no. 02 (2011): 133–65.

Hayes, Danny, and Jennifer L. Lawless. "A Non-Gendered Lens? Media, Voters, and Female Candidates in Contemporary Congressional Elections." *Perspectives on Politics* 13, no. 01 (March 2015): 95–118.

Holt, Cheryl L., and Jon B. Ellis. "Assessing the Current Validity of the Bem Sex-Role Inventory." *Sex Roles* 39, no. 11–12 (December 1998): 929–41.

Huddy, Leonie, and Nayda Terkildsen. "Gender Stereotypes and the Perception of Male and Female Candidates." *American Journal of Political Science* 37, no. 1 (February 1, 1993): 119–47.

———. "The Consequences of Gender Stereotypes for Women Candidates at Different Levels and Types of Office." *Political Research Quarterly* 46, no. 3 (September 1, 1993): 503–25. i:10.2307/448945.

Karnie, Annie. "This Time Hillary Clinton Embraces the Gender Card." *Politico*, July 21, 2015.

Lawless, Jennifer L., and Richard L. Fox. "Girls Just Wanna Not Run: The Gender Gap in Young Americans' Political Ambition." Washington, DC: Women and Politics Institute, March 2013.

———. *It Still Takes a Candidate: Why Women Don't Run for Office*. Rev. ed. New York: Cambridge University Press, 2010.

———. "Men Rule: The Continued Under-Representation of Women in U.S. Politics." Washington, DC: Women and Politics Institute, January 2012. http://www.american.edu/spa/wpi/upload/2012-Men-Rule-Report-web.pdf.

Lawless, Jennifer L., and Kathryn Pearson. "The Primary Reason for Women's Underrepresentation? Reevaluating the Conventional Wisdom." *Journal of Politics* 70, no. 1 (January 1, 2008): 67–82. i:10.1017/S002238160708005X.

O'Regan, Valerie, and Stephen J. Stambough. "To Succeed or Not to Succeed: It's Based on Your Experience." Paper presented at the Western Political Science Association. Las Vegas, NV, April 2–4, 2015.

Oxley, Zoe M., and Richard L. Fox. "Women in Executive Office: Variation across American States." *Political Research Quarterly* 57, no. 1 (March 2004): 113–20.

Pew Research Center. "Women and Leadership." January 14, 2015. http://www.pewsocialtrends.org/2015/01/14/women-and-leadership/.

Sandberg, Sheryl. *Lean In: Women, Work, and the Will to Lead*. New York: Knopf, 2013.

Sides, John, and Lynn Vavreck. *The Gamble: Choice and Chance in the 2012 Presidential Election*. Princeton, NJ: Princeton University Press, 2013.

Spence, Janet T., Robert Helmreich, and Joy Stapp. *Masculinity and femininity: Their psychological dimensions, correlates, and antecedents.* Austin: University of Texas Press, 1978.

Stambough, Stephen J., and Valerie R. O'Regan. "Republican Lambs and the Democratic Pipeline: Partisan Differences in the Nomination of Female Gubernatorial Candidates." *Politics & Gender* 3, no. 3 (September 2007): 349–68.

Windett, Jason Harold. "State Effects and the Emergence and Success of Female Gubernatorial Candidates." *State Politics & Policy Quarterly* 11, no. 4 (December 1, 2011): 460–82.

World Economic Forum. "The Global Gender Gap Report 2015." Insight Report. Geneva, November 2015. http://www.weforum.org/reports/global-gender-gap-report-2015.

Chapter 4: GOLDILOCKS NATION

INTERVIEWS BY AUTHOR:

Bettina Duval. January 30, 2015.

Celinda Lake. April 5, 2013, and September 9, 2014.

Chriss Winston. December 11, 2014.

Eleanor Smeal. May 22, 2013.

Eric Foner. March 5, 2015.

Governor Jennifer Granholm. January 24, 2014.

Ilyse Hogue. September 10, 2014, and February 27, 2015.

Jeffrey Slavin. April 10, 2013.

John Neffinger. February 27, 2015.

Margaret Hoover. February 19, 2015.

Robert P. Jones. July 23, 2014.

Ronee Schreiber. October 24, 2014.

Rose Kapolczynski. June 26, 2013.

Senator Kay Bailey Hutchison. November 24, 2014.

PUBLISHED SOURCES:

ANES Feeling Thermometer Toward Presidential Candidates 1968–2008, ANES, http://electionstudies.org/nesguide/toptable/tab7a_2.htm.

Bartels, Larry M. "The Impact of Candidate Traits in American Presidential Elections." In *Leaders' Personalities and the Outcomes of Democratic Elections*, edited by Anthony King, 44–69. Oxford: Oxford University Press, 2002.

Brooks, Deborah Jordan. *He Runs, She Runs: Why Gender Stereotypes Do Not Harm Women Candidates*. Princeton, NJ: Princeton University Press, 2013.

Chavez, Linda. "Hillary Clinton Is Too Old to Run." *New York Post*, March 27, 2015.

Dallek, Robert. "The Medical Ordeals of JFK." *Atlantic*, August 2013. http://www.theatlantic.com/magazine/archive/2013/08/the-medical-ordeals-of-jfk/309469/.

Enos, Ryan. "No, Good Looks Don't Win Elections." *Washington Post*, November 13, 2013. http://www.washingtonpost.com/blogs/monkey-cage/wp/2013/11/13/no-good-looks-dont-win-elections/.

Fox, Richard L., and Jennifer L. Lawless. "Reconciling Family Roles with Political Ambition: The New Normal for Women in Twenty-First Century U.S. Politics." *Journal of Politics* 76, no. 02 (2014): 398–414.

Gallup. "Gallup Election Review: October 2007." Gallup.com. http://www.gallup.com/poll/102277/Gallup-Election-Review-October-2007.aspx.

Gillibrand, Kirsten, and Elizabeth Weil. *Off the Sidelines: Raise Your Voice, Change the World*. New York: Ballantine Books, 2014.

Jones, Robert P., and Daniel Cox. "How Race and Religion Shape Millennial Attitudes on Sexuality and Reproductive Health." Public Religion Research Institute, March 27, 2015. http://publicreligion.org/research/2015/03/survey-how-race-and-religion-shape-millennial-attitudes-on-sexuality-and-reproductive-health/.

Kennedy, Randall. *The Persistence of the Color Line: Racial Politics and the Obama Presidency*. New York: Pantheon, 2011.

Ko, Sei Jin, Melody S. Sadler, and Adam D. Galinsky. "The Sound of Power Conveying and Detecting Hierarchical Rank Through Voice." *Psychological Science* 26, no. 1 (January 1, 2015): 3–14.

Leibovich, Mark. *This Town: Two Parties and a Funeral—Plus, Plenty of Valet Parking!—in America's Gilded Capital*. New York: Blue Rider Press, 2013.

Mali, Meghashyam. "Bush drops 40 pounds on Paleo diet." *The Hill*, August 3, 2015. http://thehill.com/blogs/ blog-briefing-room/250077-bush-drops-40-pounds-on-paleo-diet.

Miller Center, University of Virginia. "American President—Miller Center." American President: A Reference Resource. Accessed September 4, 2015. http://millercenter.org/president.

Morris, Edmund. "The Unknowable." *New Yorker*, June 28, 2004.

Neffinger, John, and Matthew Kohut. *Compelling People: The Hidden Qualities That Make Us Influential*. New York: Hudson Street Press, 2013.

Oliphant, James. "On Hillary Clinton's Age, Republican Rivals Imply—But Never Say—She's Old." *Reuters*, May 1, 2015.

Osnos, Evan. "The Biden Agenda." *New Yorker*, July 28, 2014.

Raju, Manu. "Graham on Bachelorhood: I'm Not 'Defective.'" *Politico*, June 11, 2015. http://www.politico.com/story/2015/06/graham-on-bachelorhood -im-not-defective-118896.html.

Sides, John. "Social Science Confirms That Mitt Romney Is Really, Really Good-Looking." *The Monkey Cage*. http://themonkeycage.org/2012/08/ social-science-can-confirm-that-mitt-romney-is-really-really-good-looking/.

Sides, John, and Lynn Vavreck. *The Gamble: Choice and Chance in the 2012 Presidential Election*. Princeton, NJ: Princeton University Press, 2013.

Silverman, Stephen M. "PEOPLE's 50 Most Beautiful: Okay, Who?" *PEOPLE.com*, May 1, 2002. http://www.people.com/people/article /0,,623914,00.html.

Stolberg, Sheryl Gay. "Joni Ernst's Playbook, for Women to Win Men's Vote." *New York Times*, October 28, 2014.

Westen, Drew. *The Political Brain: The Role of Emotion in Deciding the Fate of the Nation*. New York: PublicAffairs, 2007.

White, Theodore H. *The Making of the President 1960*. Reissue edition. New York: Harper Perennial, 2009.

Chapter 5: HILLARY

INTERVIEWS BY AUTHOR:

Ambassador Melanne Verveer. March 3, 2015.

Celinda Lake. April 5, 2013, and September 9, 2014.

Eleanor Smeal. May 22, 2013.

Ilyse Hogue. September 10, 2014, and February 27, 2015.

Interviews at Hillary Clinton's book signing, Los Angeles. June 19, 2014.

Interviews at Hillary Clinton's Luskin Speech, UCLA, Los Angeles. March 5, 2014.

Liesl Gerntholtz. September 12, 2014.

Neera Tanden. January 16, 2015.

Senator Barbara Mikulski. September 8, 2014.

Stan Greenberg. July 23, 2014.

Stephanie Schriock. April 10, 2013, and February 6, 2015.

Wendy Greuel. July 8, 2015.

Wilma Goldstein. October 23, 2014, and other dates.

PUBLISHED SOURCES:

Allen, Jonathan, and Amie Parnes. *HRC: State Secrets and the Rebirth of Hillary Clinton.* New York: Crown, 2014.

Bernstein, Carl. *A Woman in Charge: The Life of Hillary Rodham Clinton.* Knopf, 2007.

Chozick, Amy, and Jess Bidgood. "Hillary Clinton Pushes to Expand Access to Pre-Kindergarten." *New York Times*, June 15, 2015. http://www.nytimes.com/politics/first-draft/2015/06/15/hillary-clinton-pushes-to-expand-access-to-pre-kindergarten/.

Cillizza, Chris. "Hillary Clinton Dominated the First Democratic Debate. Don't Be Surprised." *Washington Post*, October 14, 2015. https://www.washingtonpost.com/news/the-fix/wp/2015/10/14/why-no-one-should-be-surprised-that-hillary-clinton-dominated-the-1st-democratic-debate/.

"Clinton Brand: Centrism to Celebrity." *Politico.* http://www.politico.com/story/2014/10/hillary-clinton-bill-clinton-elections-111528.html.

Clinton, Hillary Rodham. *Hard Choices.* New York: Simon & Schuster, 2014.

————. *Living History*. New York: Simon & Schuster, 2003.

Cohen, Nancy L. *Delirium: The Politics of Sex in America*. Berkeley, CA: Counterpoint, 2012.

"Fusion's Massive Millennial Poll." *Fusion*, October 9, 2014. http://fusion .net/story/20367/fusions-massive-millennial-poll/.

Gold, Matea. "Why So Many Women Are Raising Money for Hillary Clinton." *Washington Post*, June 7, 2015. https://www.washington post.com/politics/clinton-bid-brings-wave-of-women-into-male-dominated-fundraising-world/2015/06/07/84c13570-0b8b-11e5-95fd-d580f1c5d44e_story.html.

Green, Joshua. "The Front-Runner's Fall." *Atlantic*, September 2008.

————. "The Hillary Clinton Memos." *Atlantic*, September 2008. http://www.theatlantic.com/magazine/archive/2008/09/ the-hillary-clinton-memos/306951/.

Harris, John F., and Maggie Haberman. "Clinton Brand: Centrism to Celebrity." *Politico*, October 2, 2014. http://www.politico.com/ story/2014/10/hillary-clinton-bill-clinton-elections-111528.html.

Healy, Patrick. "Early in 2016 Race, Clinton's Toughest Foe Appears to Be the News Media." *New York Times*, March 11, 2015. http:// www.nytimes.com/2015/03/12/us/politics/early-in-2016-race-clintons -toughest-foe-appears-to-be-the-news-media.html.

Karnie, Annie. "This Time Hillary Clinton Embraces the Gender Card." *Politico*, July 21, 2015.

Kornblut, Anne E. *Notes from the Cracked Ceiling: Hillary Clinton, Sarah Palin, and What It Will Take for a Woman to Win*. New York: Crown, 2009.

Milbank, Dana. "Hillary Clinton Towers Over Her Debate Rivals." *Washington Post*, October 13, 2015.

Norpoth, Helmut, and David F. Perkins. "War and Momentum: The 2008 Presidential Nominations." *PS: Political Science and Politics* 44, no. 3 (July 2011): 536–43.

Pew Research Center. "A Clinton Candidacy: Voters' Early Impressions." April 10, 2015. http://www.pewresearch.org/fact-tank/2015/04/10/ a-clinton-candidacy-voters-early-impressions/.

———. "Hillary Clinton's Strengths: Record at State, Toughness, Honesty." March 4, 2014. http://www.people-press.org/2014/03/04/hillary-clintons-strengths-record-at-state-toughness-honesty/.

Silver, Nate. "Hillary Clinton Is Stuck in a Poll-Deflating Feedback Loop." *FiveThirtyEight*, September 16, 2015. http://fivethirtyeight.com/features/hillary-clinton-is-in-a-self-reinforcing-funk/.

Thrush, Glenn, and Maggie Haberman. "How to Back Hillary into a Corner." *Politico Magazine*. Accessed October 16, 2015. http://www.politico.com/magazine/story/2014/10/how-to-back-hillary-into-a-corner-112175.html.

Traister, Rebecca. *Big Girls Don't Cry: The Election That Changed Everything for American Women*. New York: Free Press, 2010.

Verveer, Melanne, and Kim K. Azzarelli. *Fast Forward: How Women Can Achieve Power and Purpose*. Boston: Houghton Mifflin Harcourt, 2015.

Weissmann, Jordan. "Hillary Clinton Wants to Help More Women Go to Work. This Graph Shows Why That's So Crucial." *Slate*, July 13, 2015. http://www.slate.com/blogs/moneybox/2015/07/13/hillary_clinton_s_economic_plan_she_wants_to_put_more_women_to_work.html.

Zengerle, Jason. "Is Hillary Clinton Any Good at Running for President?" *New York Magazine*, April 5, 2015. http://nymag.com/daily/intelligencer/2015/04/hillary-clinton-2016-campaign.html.

Chapter 6: A BRIEF HISTORY OF WOMEN'S POLITICAL INEQUALITY

INTERVIEW BY AUTHOR:

Eric Foner. March 5, 2015.

PUBLISHED SOURCES:

Cohen, Nancy. *The Reconstruction of American Liberalism, 1865–1914*. Chapel Hill: University of North Carolina Press, 2002.

Cott, Nancy F. *The Bonds of Womanhood "Woman's Sphere" in New England, 1780–1835*. New Haven: Yale University Press, 1977.

———. *The Grounding of Modern Feminism*. New Haven: Yale University Press, 1987.

DuBois, Ellen Carol. *Feminism and Suffrage: The Emergence of an Independent Women's Movement in America, 1848–1869*. Ithaca: Cornell University Press, 1978.

Foner, Eric. *A Short History of Reconstruction: 1863–1877*. New York: Harper & Row, 1990.

———. *Reconstruction: America's Unfinished Revolution, 1863–1877*. New York: Harper & Row, 1988.

———. *The Story of American Freedom*. 1st ed. New York: W.W. Norton, 1998.

Ford, Lynne E. *Women and Politics: The Pursuit of Equality*. 3rd ed. Boston: Wadsworth, 2011.

Horowitz, Helen Lefkowitz. "Victoria Woodhull, Anthony Comstock, and Conflict over Sex in the United States in the 1870s." *Journal of American History* 87, no. 2 (September 1, 2000): 403–34.

Kann, Mark E. *The Gendering of American Politics: Founding Mothers, Founding Fathers, and Political Patriarchy*. Westport, CT: Praeger, 1999.

Keyssar, Alexander. *The Right to Vote: The Contested History of Democracy in the United States*. New York: Basic Books, 2000.

Miller Center, University of Virginia. "American President—Miller Center." American President: A Reference Resource. http://millercenter.org/president.

New York Herald. "The Courts: Woodhull—Beecher—Claflin—Tilton: Tennie C. Claflin and Victoria Woodhull Arrested." November 3, 1872.

Ornstein, Norman J., Thomas E. Mann, Michael J. Malbin, Andrew Rugg, and Raffaela Wakeman. "Vital Statistics on Congress." Brookings Institution and American Enterprise Institute, July 2013. http://www.brookings.edu/research/reports/2013/07/vital-statistics-congress-mann-ornstein.

Ryan, Mary P. *Mysteries of Sex: Tracing Women and Men Through American History*. Chapel Hill: University of North Carolina Press, 2006.

Rymph, Catherine E. *Republican Women: Feminism and Conservatism from Suffrage through the Rise of the New Right*. University of North Carolina Press, 2006.

Wilentz, Sean. *The Rise of American Democracy: Jefferson to Lincoln.* New York; London: W. W. Norton & Company, 2006.

Wood, Gordon S. *Empire of Liberty: A History of the Early Republic, 1789–1815.* Oxford; New York: Oxford University Press, 2009.

Zagarri, Rosemarie. *Revolutionary Backlash: Women and Politics in the Early American Republic.* Early American Studies. Philadelphia: University of Pennsylvania Press, 2007.

Chapter 7: THE REPUBLICAN DILEMMA

INTERVIEWS BY AUTHOR:

Candace L. Straight. November 21, 2014.

Chriss Winston. December 11, 2014.

Geoffrey Kabaservice. July 23, 2014.

Governor Christine Todd Whitman. December 11, 2014.

Katie Packer Gage. December 14, 2014.

Margaret Hoover. February 19, 2015.

Maria Cino. November 21, 2014.

Robert P. Jones. July 23, 2014.

Ronee Schreiber. October 24, 2014.

Senator Kay Bailey Hutchison. November 24, 2014.

Senator Olympia Snowe. February 3, 2015.

Senator Susan Collins. November 25, 2014.

Wilma Goldstein. October 23, 2014, and other dates.

PUBLISHED SOURCES:

Abramowitz, Alan I. "Ideological Realignment in the American Electorate: A Comparison of Northern and Southern White Voters in the Pre-Reagan, Reagan, and Post-Reagan Eras." *Politics and Policy* 34, no. 1 (March 2006): 94–108.

Anderson, Kristen Soltis. "Grand Old Party for a Brand New Generation." Washington, DC: College Republican National Committee, June 2014.

Baldez, Lisa. "Political Women in Comparative Democracies: A Primer for Americanists." In *Political Women and American Democracy*, edited by Christina Wolbrecht, Karen Beckwith, and Lisa Baldez. Cambridge: Cambridge University Press, 2008.

Ford, Lynne E. *Women and Politics: The Pursuit of Equality*. 3rd ed. Boston: Wadsworth, 2011.

Horowitz, Jason. "Hillary Clinton Aims to Capture the Cool." *New York Times*, May 22, 2015. http://www.nytimes.com/2015/05/24/fashion/hillary-clinton-aims-to-capture-the-cool.html.

New York Times. "Americans' Views on Income Inequality and Workers' Rights." June 3, 2015. http://www.nytimes.com/interactive/2015/06/03/business/income-inequality-workers-rights-international-trade-poll.html.

Ornstein, Norman J., et al. "Vital Statistics on Congress." Brookings Institution and American Enterprise Institute, July 2013. http://www.brookings.edu/research/reports/2013/07/vital-statistics-congress-mann-ornstein.

Pew Research Center. "A Deep Dive into Party Affiliation." http://www.people-press.org/2015/04/07/a-deep-dive-into-party-affiliation/.

———. "GOP's Favorability Rating Takes a Negative Turn." July 23, 2015. http://www.people-press.org/2015/07/23/gops-favorability-rating-takes-a-negative-turn/.

———. "Republican Party Favorability." Chart of 1992–2015 Trends. http://www.pewresearch.org/data-trend/political-attitudes/republican-party-favorability/.

———. "Women and Leadership." January 14, 2015. http://www.pewsocialtrends.org/2015/01/14/women-and-leadership/.

Poggione, Sarah. "Exploring Gender Differences in State Legislators' Policy Preferences." *Political Research Quarterly* 57, no. 2 (June 1, 2004): 305–14.

Republican National Committee. "Growth and Opportunity Project." March 2013.

Rymph, Catherine E. *Republican Women: Feminism and Conservatism from Suffrage through the Rise of the New Right*. University of North Carolina Press, 2006.

Stolberg, Sheryl Gay. "Joni Ernst's Playbook, for Women to Win Men's Vote." *New York Times*, October 28, 2014.

Thomsen, Danielle. "Why So Few (Republican) Women? Explaining the Partisan Imbalance of Women in the U.S. Congress." *Legislative Studies Quarterly*, forthcoming.

Chapter 8: THE POLITICS OF WOMEN'S BODIES

INTERVIEWS BY AUTHOR:

Candace L. Straight. November 21, 2014.

Cecile Richards. May 21, 2013.

Dawn Laguens. April 10, 2013.

Ilyse Hogue. September 10, 2014, and February 27, 2015.

Karen Finney. September 8, 2014.

Katie Packer Gage. December 14, 2014.

Lisa Grove. September 26, 2014.

Margaret Hoover. February 19, 2015.

Senator Olympia Snowe. February 3, 2015.

PUBLISHED SOURCES:

Abramowitz, Alan I. "It's Abortion, Stupid: Policy Voting in the 1992 Presidential Election." *Journal of Politics* 57, no. 1 (February 1995): 176–86.

Alvarez, R. Michael, and Jonathan Nagler. "Economics, Issues and the Perot Candidacy: Voter Choice in the 1992 Presidential Election." *American Journal of Political Science* 39, no. 3 (August 1995): 714–44.

Andy Kroll. "Scott Walker Wants to Totally Outlaw Abortion. In This Sneaky New Ad, He Pretends He Doesn't." *Mother Jones*. Accessed August 26, 2015. http://www.motherjones.com/mojo/2014/10/ scott-walker-wisconsin-governor-ban-abortion-rape-incest.

Cohen, Nancy L. *Delirium: The Politics of Sex in America*. Berkeley, CA: Counterpoint, 2012.

Dann, Carrie. "How the Public Views Planned Parenthood and the NRA." *NBC News*, August 3, 2015. http://www.nbcnews.com/meet-the-press/how-public-views-planned-parenthood-nra-n403451.

Deckman, Melissa, and John McTague. "Did the 'War on Women' Work? Women, Men, and the Birth Control Mandate in the 2012 Presidential Election." *American Politics Research*, July 9, 2014.

Editorial Board. "Fiorina's Falsehoods." *Washington Post*, September 26, 2015.

Gallup. "Abortion Edges up as Important Voting Issue for Americans." Gallup.com May 29, 2015. http://www.gallup.com/poll/183449/abortion-edges-important-voting-issue-americans.aspx.

———. "Americans Choose 'Pro-Choice' for First Time in Seven Years." Gallup.com. Accessed August 7, 2015. http://www.gallup.com/poll/183434/americans-choose-pro-choice-first-time-seven-years.aspx.

Goldin, Claudia, and Lawrence F. Katz. "The Power of the Pill: Oral Contraceptives and Women's Career and Marriage Decisions." *Journal of Political Economy* 110, no. 4 (2002): 730-770.

"GOP: Planned Parenthood Fight to Go On." *Politico*, August 3, 2015. http://www.politico.com/story/2015/08/planned-parenthood-defund-fight-government-shutdown-funding-bill-120951.html.

Greenhouse, Linda, and Reva B. Siegel. "Before *Roe V. Wade*: New Questions About Backlash." *Yale Law Journal* 120 no. 8 (2011): 2028-2087.

Guttmacher Institute. "Laws Affecting Reproductive Health and Rights: State Trends at Midyear, 2015," July 1, 2015. http://www.guttmacher.org/statecenter/updates/2015/statetrends22015.html.

———. "State Policy Trends: Abortion and Contraception in the Crosshairs." http://www.guttmacher.org/media/inthenews/2012/04/13/index.html.

———. "State Trends for 2014 on Abortion, Family Planning, Sex Education and Insurance." http://www.guttmacher.org/statecenter/updates/2015/statetrends22015.html.

Jones, Robert P., and Daniel Cox. "How Race and Religion Shape
    Millennial Attitudes on Sexuality and Reproductive Health." Public
    Religion Research Institute, March 27, 2015. http://publicreligion.org/
    research/2015/03/survey-how-race-and-religion-shape-millennial
    -attitudes-on-sexuality-and-reproductive-health/.

Kliff, Sarah. "Inside Planned Parenthood's Campaign Strategy."
    Washington Post, December 5, 2012. http://www.washingtonpost
    .com/news/wonkblog/wp/2012/12/05/inside-planned-parenthoods
    -campaign-strategy/.

———. "What Americans Think of Abortion." *Vox*, March 8, 2015. http://
    www.vox.com/a/abortion-decision-statistics-opinions.

Lee, Michelle Ye Hee. "Jeb Bush's False Claim that Planned Parenthood Is
    'Not Actually Doing Women's Health Issues.'" *Washington Post*, August
    26, 2015.

MacGillis, Alec. "Joni Ernst Is One of 2014's Most Extreme Candidates—
    But You Wouldn't Know It From Iowa's Press Coverage." *New Republic*,
    November 4, 2014. http://www.newrepublic.com/article/120118/
    joni-ernst-capitalized-broken-media-landscape-iowa.

Manza, Jeff, and Clem Brooks. "The Gender Gap in U.S. Presidential
    Elections: When? Why? Implications?" *American Journal of Sociology*
    103, no. 5 (March 1, 1998): 1235–66.

"Opposition to Allowing Small Businesses to Refuse Services on Religious
    Grounds, Continued Majority Support for Employer Contraception
    Mandate." Public Religion Research Institute, June 2014. http://public
    religion.org/research/2014/06/employer-contraception/.

Parker, Ashley. "Romney Attacks Obama on Birth Control Rule."
    New York Times, February 6, 2012. http://thecaucus.blogs.nytimes
    .com/2012/02/06/romney-attacks-obama-on-birth-control-rule/.

Pew Research Center. "GOP's Favorability Rating Takes a Negative
    Turn." July 23, 2015. http://www.people-press.org/2015/07/23/
    gops-favorability-rating-takes-a-negative-turn/.

———. "Majority Says Any Budget Deal Must Include Planned Parenthood
    Funding." September 28, 2015. http://www.people-press.org/2015/09/28/
    majority-says-any-budget-deal-must-include-planned-parenthood-funding/.

———. "Millennials in Adulthood." March 7, 2014.

————. "Republican Party Favorability." Chart of 1992–2015 Trends. http://www.pewresearch.org/data-trend/political-attitudes/republican-party-favorability/.

"Planned Parenthood to Forgo Payment for Fetal Tissue." *New York Times*, October 13, 2015. http://www.nytimes.com/2015/10/14/us/planned-parenthood-to-forgo-payment-for-fetal-tissue-programs.html.

S.1881, 114th Congress (2015–2016): A Bill to Prohibit Federal Funding of Planned Parenthood Federation of America." Legislation, July 30, 2015. https://www.congress.gov/bill/114th-congress/senate-bill/1881.

Seitz-Wald, Alex. "Romney: I Would 'Absolutely' Support State Constitutional Amendment to Define Life as Beginning at Conception." *Think Progress*, October 3, 2011. http://thinkprogress.org/justice/2011/10/03/334190/mitt-romeny-constitutional-amendment-abortioneption/.

Vox Media poll. March 2015. https://cdn2.vox-cdn.com/uploads/chorus_asset/file/3570070/Vox_Poll_Toplines__2_.0.pdf.

Williams, Vanessa. "Ben Carson Likens Abortion to Slavery, Wants to See *Roe v. Wade* Overturned." *Washington Post*, October 25, 2015.

Chapter 9: BREAKTHROUGH

INTERVIEWS BY AUTHOR:

Ambassador Melanne Verveer. March 3, 2015.

Celinda Lake. April 5, 2013, and September 9, 2014.

Danielle Mulein. November 20, 2014.

Eleanor Smeal. May 22, 2013.

Emma Gibbens. November 22, 2014.

Group interview of Women Get It Done members, San Francisco. October 6, 2014.

Interviews with Denai Joseph, Andrea Chu, Jordan Long, and Tiffany and Chloe Majdipour at Hillary Clinton's book signing, Los Angeles. June 19, 2014.

Interviews with Vanessa Perez, Crystal Boceta, Natalie Kirsten, Zach Rosa, William Gleason, Clarice Chan, Liliana Kroll, Asseret Frausteo, and others at Hillary Clinton's Luskin Speech, UCLA, Los Angeles. March 5, 2014.

Irene Natividad. February 5, 2015.

Kate Maeder. September 16, 2014, and October 6, 2014.

Katie Packer Gage. December 14, 2014.

Lisa Grove. September 26, 2014.

Margaret Hoover. February 19, 2015.

Representative Tulsi Gabbard. October 23, 2014.

Robert P. Jones. July 23, 2014.

Ronee Schreiber. October 24, 2014.

Senator Amy Klobuchar. December 10, 2014.

PUBLISHED SOURCES:

Baer, Denise, and Heidi Hartmann. "Building Women's Political Careers: Strengthening the Pipeline to Higher Office." Institute for Women's Policy Research, May 2014. http://www.iwpr.org/publications/pubs/building-women2019s-political-careers-strengthening-the-pipeline-to-higher-office.

Campbell, David E., and Christina Wolbrecht. "See Jane Run: Women Politicians as Role Models for Adolescents." *Journal of Politics* 68, no. 2 (May 2006): 233–47.

Ford, Lynne E. *Women and Politics: The Pursuit of Equality*. 3rd ed. Boston: Wadsworth, 2011.

"Fusion's Massive Millennial Poll." *Fusion*, October 9, 2014. http://fusion.net/story/20367/fusions-massive-millennial-poll/.

Horowitz, Jason. "Hillary Clinton Aims to Capture the Cool." *New York Times*, May 22, 2015. http://www.nytimes.com/2015/05/24/fashion/hillary-clinton-aims-to-capture-the-cool.html.

Langer, Gary. "Poll Finds Vast Gaps in Views on Gender, Race and Religion." *ABC News*, October 28, 2013. http://abcnews.go.com/blogs/politics/2013/10/polll-finds-vast-gaps-in-basic-views-on-gender-race-religion-and-politics/.

Lawless, Jennifer L. "Politics of Presence? Congresswomen and Symbolic Representation." *Political Research Quarterly* 57, no. 1 (March 1, 2004): 81–99.

Pew Research Center. "2014 Party Identification Detailed Tables." April 7, 2015. http://www.people-press.org/2015/04/07/2014-party -identification-detailed-tables/.

———. "A Clinton Candidacy: Voters' Early Impressions." April 10, 2015. http://www.pewresearch.org/ fact-tank/2015/04/10/a-clinton-candidacy-voters-early-impressions/.

———. "A Deep Dive into Party Affiliation." April 7, 2015. http://www .people-press.org/2015/04/07/a-deep-dive-into-party-affiliation/.

———. "A Different Look at Generations and Partisanship." April 30, 2015. http://www.people-press.org/2015/04/30/a-different-look-at -generations-and-partisanship/.

———. "Gender Gap in Intensity of Potential Democratic Support for Clinton." *Pew Research Center.* http://www.people-press.org/2015 /04/02/campaign-2016-modest-interest-high-stakes/gender-gap-in -intensity-of-potential-democratic-support-for-clinton/.

———. "GOP's Favorability Rating Takes a Negative Turn." July 23, 2015. http://www.people-press.org/2015/07/23/gops-favorability-rating-takes -a-negative-turn/.

———. "The Gender Gap: Three Decades Old, as Wide as Ever." March 29, 2012. http://www.people-press.org/2012/03/29/ the-gender-gap-three-decades-old-as-wide-as-ever/?src=prc-headline.

———. "Women and Leadership." January 14, 2015. http://www.pewsocial trends.org/2015/01/14/women-and-leadership/.

Schaffner, Brian F. "Priming Gender: Campaigning on Women's Issues in U.S. Senate Elections." *American Journal of Political Science* 49, no. 4 (October 1, 2005): 803–17.

Schaller, Thomas. "So Long, White Boy." Salon.com, September 17, 2007.

Wolbrecht, Christina, and David E. Campbell. "Leading by Example: Female Members of Parliament as Political Role Models." *American Journal of Political Science* 51, no. 4 (October 1, 2007): 921–39.

Chapter 10: WHY WOMEN'S LEADERSHIP MATTERS

INTERVIEWS BY AUTHOR:

Celinda Lake. April 5, 2013, and September 9, 2014.

Eleanor Smeal. May 22, 2013.

Gwynn Thomas. September 9, 2015.

Irene Natividad. February 5, 2015.

Jennifer Piscopo. July 17, 2014.

Karin Johanson. April 9, 2013.

Katie Packer Gage. December 14, 2014.

Liesl Gerntholtz. September 12, 2014.

Margaret Hoover. February 19, 2015.

Maria Cino. November 21, 2014.

Mary Hughes. June 21, 2013.

Neera Tanden. January 16, 2015.

Representative Tulsi Gabbard. October 23, 2014.

Ronee Schreiber. October 24, 2014.

Senator Amy Klobuchar. December 10, 2014.

Senator Barbara Mikulski. September 8, 2014.

Senator Benjamin Cardin. July 23, 2014.

Senator Olympia Snowe. February 3, 2015.

Senator Susan Collins. November 25, 2014.

Tara McGuinness. April 4, 2013.

Wilma Goldstein. October 23, 2014, and other dates.

PUBLISHED SOURCES:

Anzia, Sarah F., and Christopher R. Berry. "The Jackie (and Jill) Robinson Effect: Why Do Congresswomen Outperform Congressmen?" *American Journal of Political Science* 55, no. 3 (July 1, 2011): 478–93.

Atkeson, Lonna Rae, and Nancy Carillo. "More Is Better: The Influence of Collective Female Descriptive Representation on External Efficacy." *Politics & Gender* 3, no. 1 (2007): 79–101.

Ayata, Ayşe Güneş, and Fatma Tütüncü. "Critical Acts without a Critical Mass: The Substantive Representation of Women in the Turkish Parliament." *Parliamentary Affairs* 61, no. 3 (July 1, 2008): 461–75.

Baldez, Lisa. "Political Women in Comparative Democracies: A Primer for Americanists." In *Political Women and American Democracy*, edited by Christina Wolbrecht, Karen Beckwith, and Lisa Baldez. Cambridge: Cambridge University Press, 2008.

Barsh, Joanna, and Lareina Yee. "Unlocking the Full Potential of Women in the U.S. Economy." McKinsey & Company, 2011. http://www.mckinsey.com/client_service/organization/latest_thinking/unlocking_the_full_potential.

Bell, Linda A. "Women-Led Firms and the Gender Gap in Top Executive Jobs," IZA (Institute for Labor Studies) Bonn, Discussion Paper #1698, July 2005.

Bratton, Kathleen A. "Critical Mass Theory Revisited: The Behavior and Success of Token Women in State Legislatures." *Politics & Gender* (March 2005): 97–125.

Campbell, David E., and Christina Wolbrecht. "See Jane Run: Women Politicians as Role Models for Adolescents." *Journal of Politics* 68, no. 2 (May 2006): 233–47.

"Chilean President Speaks of Her Torture under Pinochet." *Yahoo News*. Accessed September 11, 2015. http://news.yahoo.com/chilean-president-speaks-her-torture-under-pinochet-192814454.html.

Devlin, Claire, and Robert Elgie. "The Effect of Increased Women's Representation in Parliament: The Case of Rwanda." *Parliamentary Affairs* 61, no. 2 (April 1, 2008): 237–54.

Dolan, Kathleen. "Is There a 'Gender Affinity Effect' in American Politics? Information, Affect, and Candidate Sex in U.S House Elections." *Political Research Quarterly* 61, no. 1 (March 2008): 79–89.

Dovi, Suzanne. "Theorizing Women's Representation in the United States." In *Political Women and American Democracy*, edited by Christina Wolbrecht, Karen Beckwith, and Lisa Baldez. Cambridge: Cambridge University Press, 2008.

Ford, Lynne E. *Women and Politics: The Pursuit of Equality*. 3rd ed. Boston: Wadsworth, 2011.

Franceschet, Susan, and Jennifer M. Piscopo. "Gender Quotas and Women's Substantive Representation: Lessons from Argentina." *Politics & Gender* 4, no. 03 (September 2008): 393–425.

Franceschet, Susan, Jennifer M. Piscopo, and Gwynn Thomas. "Supermadres, Maternal Legacies, and Women's Political Participation in Contemporary Latin America," *Journal of Latin American Studies,* 2015, doi: 10.1017/ S0022216X15000814.

Gerrity, Jessica C., Tracy Osborn, and Jeanette Morehouse Mendez. "Women and Representation: A Different View of the District?" *Politics & Gender*, no. 02 (June 2007): 179–200.

Gillibrand, Kirsten, and Elizabeth Weil. *Off the Sidelines: Raise Your Voice, Change the World.* New York: Ballantine Books, 2014.

Itkowitz, Colby. "In Male-Dominated Congress, It's Male-Dominated Committee Hearings." *Washington Post*, September 11, 2014. http://www.washingtonpost.com/blogs/in-the-loop/wp/2014/09/11/ in-male-dominated-congress-its-male-dominated-committee-hearings/.

Kathlene, Lyn. "Power and Influence in State Legislative Policymaking: The Interaction of Gender and Position in Committee Hearing Debates." *American Political Science Review* 88, no. 3 (September 1, 1994): 560–76.

Klein, Mariel. "Working Together and Across the Aisle, Female Senators Pass More Legislation Than Male Colleagues." *Quorum*, February 19, 2015. https://www.quorum.us/blog/ women-work-together-pass-more-legislation/.

Koch, Michael T., and Sarah A. Fulton. "In the Defense of Women: Gender, Office Holding, and National Security Policy in Established Democracies." *Journal of Politics* 73, no. 1 (January 1, 2011): 1–16.

Lawless, Jennifer L., and Richard L. Fox. "Girls Just Wanna Not Run: The Gender Gap in Young Americans' Political Ambition." Washington, DC: Women and Politics Institute, March 2013. (Appendix B.)

Lean In and McKinsey & Company. "2015 Women in the Workplace Study." http://womenintheworkplace.com.

"Michelle Bachelet Is Chile's Next President: The Country's New Leader Discusses Education, Protests, and Her Family History under Pinochet." March 7, 2014. http://www.slate.com/articles/news_and_politics /foreigners/2014/03/michelle_bachelet_is_chile_s_next_president _the_country_s_new_leader_discusses.html.

Mundy, Liza. "The Secret History of Women in the Senate." *Politico Magazine*, January 5, 2015. http://www.politico.com/magazine/story/2015/01/senate-women-secret-history-113908.html.

Newton-Small, Jay. "Women Are the Only Adults Left in Washington." *Time*. Accessed September 1, 2015. http://swampland.time .com/2013/10/16/women-are-the-only-adults-left-in-washington/.

Norton, Noelle H. "Uncovering the Dimensionality of Gender Voting in Congress." *Legislative Studies Quarterly* 24, no. 1 (February 1, 1999): 65–86.

Perlberg, Steven. "S&P: The Shutdown Took $24 Billion Out of the US Economy." *Business Insider*, October 16, 2013. http://www.business insider.com/sp-cuts-us-growth-view-2013-10.

Philpot, Tasha S., and Hanes Walton Jr. "One of Our Own: Black Female Candidates and the Voters Who Support Them." *American Journal of Political Science* 51, no. 1 (January 2007): 49–62.

Piscopo, Jennifer M. "Beyond Hearth and Home: Female Legislators, Feminist Policy Change and Substantive Representation in Mexico." *Revista Uruguaya de Ciencia Politica* 23, no. 2 (2014): 87–110.

———. "Rethinking Descriptive Representation: Rendering Women in Legislative Debates." *Parliamentary Affairs*, March 3, 2011.

Poggione, Sarah. "Exploring Gender Differences in State Legislators' Policy Preferences." *Political Research Quarterly* 57, no. 2 (June 1, 2004): 305–14.

Raaum, Nina C. "Gender Equality and Political Representation: A Nordic Comparison." *West European Politics* 28, no. 4 (September 1, 2005): 872–97.

Reingold, Beth. "Women as Officeholders: Linking Descriptive and Substantive Representation." In *Political Women and American Democracy*, edited by Christina Wolbrecht, Karen Beckwith, and Lisa Baldez. Cambridge: Cambridge University Press, 2008.

Reingold, Beth, and Jessica Harrell. "The Impact of Descriptive Representation on Women's Political Engagement: Does Party Matter?" *Political Research Quarterly* 63, no. 2 (June 2010): 280–94.

Rosin, Hanna. "The End of Men." *Atlantic*, June 8, 2010.

Sandberg, Sheryl. *Lean In: Women, Work, and the Will to Lead*. New York: Knopf, 2013.

Schwindt-Bayer, Leslie A., and William Mishler. "An Integrated Model of Women's Representation." *Journal of Politics* 67, no. 2 (May 2005): 407–28.

Swers, Michele. "Are Women More Likely to Vote for Women's Issue Bills Than Their Male Colleagues?" *Legislative Studies Quarterly* 23, no. 3 (August 1, 1998): 435–48. i:10.2307/440362.

———. "Connective Descriptive and Substantive Representation: An Analysis of Sex Differences in Cosponsorship Activity." *Legislative Studies Quarterly* 30, no. 3 (2005): 407–33.

———. *The Difference Women Make: The Policy Impact of Women in Congress*. 1st ed. Chicago; London: University of Chicago Press, 2002.

———. "Understanding the Policy Impact of Electing Women: Evidence from Research on Congress and State Legislatures." *PS: Political Science and Politics* 34, no. 2 (June 1, 2001): 217–20.

———. "Unpacking Women's Issues: Gender and Policymaking on Health Care, Education, and Women's Health in the U.W. Senate." In *Representation: The Case of Women*, edited by Maria C. Escobar-Lemmon and Michelle M. Taylor-Robinson. New York: Oxford University Press, 2014.

Tolbert, Caroline J., and Gertrude Steuernagel. "Women Lawmakers, State Mandates and Women's Health." *Women & Politics* 22, no. 1 (2001): 1–39.

Van Staveren, Irene. "The Lehman Sisters Hypothesis." *Cambridge Journal of Economics* 38, no. 5 (September 1, 2014): 995–1014.

Verveer, Melanne, and Kim K. Azzarelli. *Fast Forward: How Women Can Achieve Power and Purpose*. Boston: Houghton Mifflin Harcourt, 2015.

Weymouth, Lally. "'We Are Going to Reform the Whole System': An Interview with Chile's Incoming President, Michelle Bachelet." *Slate*, March 7, 2014.

Wolbrecht, Christina. *The Politics of Women's Rights: Parties, Positions, and Change*. Princeton, NJ: Princeton University Press, 2000.

Wolbrecht, Christina, Karen Beckwith, and Lisa Baldez. *Political Women and American Democracy*. Cambridge: Cambridge University Press, 2008.

Wolbrecht, Christina, and David E. Campbell. "Leading by Example: Female Members of Parliament as Political Role Models." *American Journal of Political Science* 51, no. 4 (October 1, 2007): 921–39.

World Economic Forum. "The Global Gender Gap Report 2015." Insight Report. Geneva, November 2015. http://www.weforum.org/reports/global-gender-gap-report-2015.

Zenger, Jack, and Joseph Folkman. "Are Women Better Leaders Than Men?" *Harvard Business Review*, March 2012. https://hbr.org/2012/03/a-study-in-leadership-women-do.

EPILOGUE

"Obama Says Republicans Trying to Scare Voters." *Associated Press*, July 31, 2008. http://www.nbcnews.com/id/25944141/ns/politics-decision_08/t/obama-says-republicans-trying-scare-voters/.

Wood, Gordon S. *Empire of Liberty: A History of the Early Republic, 1789–1815*. Oxford; New York: Oxford University Press, 2009.

INDEX